Against Us, But For Us

Against Us, But For Us

Martin Luther King, Jr.

and the State

Michael G. Long

Mercer
University
Press
MMII

ISBN 0-86554-768-8
MUP/H580

© 2002 Mercer University Press
6316 Peake Road
Macon, Georgia 31210-3960

First Edition.

∞The paper used in this publication meets the minimum requirements of American National Standard for Information Sciences—Permanence of Paper for Printed Library Materials, ANSI Z39.48-1992.

Library of Congress Cataloging-in-Publication Data

CIP data are available from the Library of Congress

CONTENTS

ABBREVIATIONS

MLKP, MBU   Martin Luther King, Jr., Papers, Boston
                University, Boston Massachusetts.

MLKJP, GAMK   Martin Luther King, Jr., Papers, King Library
                and Archives, Atlanta, Georgia.

Acknowledgments

This book grows out of my graduate work in ethics at Emory University, where a community of brilliant scholars assisted me in clarifying and expressing my ideas. A special word of thanks is immediately due to Theodore Weber, an expert in theological ethics and political thought, who offered the type of constructive criticism that makes him a scholar of scholars. My gratitude also extends to Noel Erskine, who encouraged me to explore the black preachers in King's life; Jon Gunnemann, whose analytical mind challenged my understanding of love, justice, and power; and Steven Tipton, whose creative ability to synthesize ideas is simply unmatched. Thanks, too, to J. Philip Wogaman, my first ethics professor, for introducing me to social ethics and the intellectual community at Emory.

In addition, I owe a debt of gratitude to Mercer University Press, especially Marc Jolley and Kevin Manus, for guiding the manuscript to publication. Andrew Manis, formerly of the press, first expressed interest in publishing my study, and an anonymous reviewer provided invaluable suggestions for strengthening the manuscript.

I express my heartfelt appreciation to the hardworking staff at the Martin Luther King, Jr., Center for Nonviolent Social Change and Boston University's Mugar Memorial Library. Another institution, Harris Street United Methodist Church, played a key role in my work when the members generously granted me a summer sabbatical for research and writing.

My entire family, especially Karin and Jack, deserve praise upon praise, and thanks upon thanks, for their quiet support during my late-night excursions through King's works. I am also deeply grateful to my dearest friend, Sharon Herr, whose gift in proofreading is exceptional.

All of the individuals and institutions cited above, as well as many others I have not listed, made for a beloved community while I pursued my passion for studying Martin Luther King, Jr.'s vision of the good state. I know exactly what King meant when he said that each of us is caught in an "inescapable network of mutuality."

INTRODUCTION

Curiously, King scholars have devoted little attention to Martin Luther King, Jr.'s understanding of the state. Ever since King's ministry in Montgomery, when he first attracted the public eye, writers of all kinds, popular and academic, have subjected much of his thought to intense study and criticism. Hundreds of studies about King have addressed a wide range of subjects, including his cultural and intellectual resources, his theory and practice of nonviolence, his personal life, his theology and its relationship to the black church, his understanding of education, his emphasis on "somebodyness," and more. Further, King studies have continued to increase, quantitatively and qualitatively, since his death, and the King Papers Project, under the direction of Clayborne Carson, has significantly contributed to the increase. But there has been no systematic study of King's interpretation of the state, although several authors have touched upon the topic.[1]

The absence of a systematic study is especially curious inasmuch as King spent his entire public life addressing the state. From the days of his leadership in the Montgomery boycott to his final moments in Memphis, King acknowledged the state's omnipresence within and power over people's lives, including his own, and so devoted his public life to

---

[1] See, for example, John J. Ansbro, *Martin Luther King, Jr.: The Making of a Mind* (Maryknoll: Orbis Books, 1982); Anthony E. Cook, *The Least of These: Race, Law, and Religion in American Culture* (New York: Routledge, 1997); Michael Eric Dyson, *I May Not Get There With You: The True Martin Luther, King, Jr.* (New York: The Free Press, 2000); John T. McCartney, *Black Power Ideologies: An Essay in African-American Political Thought* (Philadelphia: Temple University Press, 1992); and Preston Williams, "An Analysis of the Conception of Love and Its Influence on Justice in the Thought of Martin Luther King, Jr.," *The Journal of Religious Ethics* 18 (Fall 1990): 15–31.

encouraging (and forcing) the state to provide the conditions required by the beloved community he envisioned. Day after day after day, King actively assumed the role of the state's conscience. Given his continual interactions with the state, I contend that it is virtually impossible to grasp King's thought on so many of the topics already heavily studied, especially nonviolence, without dealing with his understanding of the state.

Nevertheless, the absence of a systematic study is not totally surprising, mainly because King himself never offered a theoretical account of the state. What is more, his public discourse is notable for the few times in which the word "state" actually appears. King simply was not inclined to offer political theory on any level. Still, it is possible to study, grasp, and evaluate King's interpretation of the state, primarily because he has left us with enough material—written, spoken, and enacted—for discovering his political views. Admittedly, however, it will be necessary, for the sake of clarity, to piece this material together in such a way as King himself never did.

The Study's Questions and a Matter of Definition

What was King's understanding of the state? Answering this question with some comprehensiveness has required my study to attend to base issues and elements in theories of the state, including beliefs about the origin, character, purpose, authority, and form of the state. With these issues in mind, I will explore the following questions: What was the substantive content of King's beliefs, if existent, about each of the base issues? Why did King adopt these beliefs? Which sources did he rely on when developing his thought? Did his interpretation of the state evolve throughout his lifetime and, if so, how did it evolve?

King developed a Christian theological understanding of the state. It is important to note here that there is not a definitive Christian interpretation of the state against which we can describe and evaluate an individual contribution to Christian political thought. Both historical and contemporary Christian interpretations of the state are far from monolithic. Theodore Weber has rightly argued that Christian thinkers have not even defined and used the term "state" in the same way. "It is used," Weber writes, "to refer to a particular territory, the administrative apparatus of the society, the government, the nation, the body politic, the nation state, the polis, or the organization and monopoly of power or violence in a given society."[2] In my study of King's works, I have had in mind a helpful definition offered by the French Catholic philosopher Jacques Maritain, whose works King relied on and adapted when developing his own political views.

For Maritain, "The state is only that part of the body politic especially concerned with the maintenance of law, the promotion of common welfare and public order, and the administration of public affairs. The state is a part which *specializes* in the interests of the *whole.*"[3] With this definition, Maritain distinguishes the state from the body politic, or political society, which he understood to be "the whole." Political society, for Maritain, is "the most perfect of temporal societies."[4] It is required by the sociality of human nature, achieved by reason, and comprised of not only the nation, which Maritain defines as "a self-network of common feelings and representations that human nature and instinct have caused to swarm around a number of physical, historical and social data,"[5] but also all other communities of the nation, including family units and voluntary associations. As the whole, political society also includes and gives life to the state, a specialized part of the body politic. But the state is not just any part but the superior and unique part of political society, endowed with authority to use power and coercion in the promotion of common welfare and public order. For Maritain, then, the state is a specialized instrument of and accountable to the body politic, including the national community.

Maritain's definition, the highlights of which I have only briefly summarized, is helpful, but not because King relied on the same definition. In fact, King's public rhetoric used the word "state" and "nation" interchangeably, and the term "body politic" does not even appear in his work. Nevertheless, Maritain's definition is helpful because its nuances add conceptual clarity to the subject at hand. Neither King's inter-

---

[2] Theodore R. Weber, "State," in *Dictionary of the Ecumenical Movement,* ed. Nicholas Lossky et al. (Geneva: WCC Publications; Grand Rapids: William B. Eerdmans Publishing Company, 1991) 953. I am indebted to Professor Weber's article for its identification of the significant elements, including definitional issues, in theologies of the state.

[3] Jacques Maritain, *Man and the State* (Chicago: University of Chicago Press, 1951) 12.

[4] Ibid., 10.

[5] Ibid., 6.

pretation of the nation or political society is the subject here, but rather the subject is his understanding of the state, the part of political society that is "especially concerned with the maintenance of law, the promotion of the common welfare and public order, and the administration of public affairs." With this definition in mind, I will show that, although King only occasionally used the word "state" in his public rhetoric, and then without precision, his life and works are filled with references to political institutions and roles that maintain law, promote common welfare and public order, and administer public affairs. Simply stated, there is no lack of references to the state in King's life and works. What is more, these references were most explicit when King directly commented on and confronted his primary target for developing the beloved community—the United States government in its federal, state, and local forms. Indeed, King seemed to use the words "state" and "government" interchangeably, and so this study will do the same.

The Argument

The thesis of my book is threefold.

The primary part of my argument claims that King adopted a theologically-based dialectical attitude towards the state. Theologians familiar with King may consider it of minor significance to argue that his understanding of the state was deeply theological, but it is important to note that not all students of King's political thought have addressed the foundational significance of his theology. For example, John McCartney, in his otherwise helpful book on Black Power ideologies, attempts to explicate King's theory of the state without ever discussing his doctrine of God.[6] In opposition to McCartney's, this study claims that King's theology is in, with, and under his dialectical attitude towards the state.

I argue that, on the one hand, King understood the state to be reflective of and involved in the creating, preserving, and reconciling work of God. Thus, I argue that it would be wholly insufficient to characterize King's state as merely an "order of creation," or merely an "order of preservation," or merely an "order of redemption." Traditional theological categories simply do not suffice when characterizing King's

---

[6] McCartney, *Black Power Ideologies*, 105–106.

political thought, and that is because King saw a role for the state in the whole work of God—in creation, preservation, and reconciliation.

On the other hand, King portrayed the state as deeply sinful. Although he affirmed the role of the state in the creating, preserving, and reconciling work of God, and believed it quite possible for the state to fulfill its proper role, King openly acknowledged that the state often fails in its purpose. King acknowledged such because of his experiences on the underside of political society, where the state was more an enemy to avoid than a friend to receive, and because of his theological belief that the state, like all of humanity, is a force for not only good but also evil.[7]

King's dialectical attitude towards the state shifted back and forth according to what he perceived to be the mandates of his particular context, and the standard of measure he relied on when evaluating the state was his vision of the beloved community. Indeed, this study suggests that King's christocentric vision of the beloved community is the foundation of and interpretive key to his understanding of the proper role of the state.

For King, the state is God's minister for the good when it reflects divine love and justice by creating and preserving the conditions required by the beloved community intended by God in Christ—a community where integration has replaced segregation, where economic justice has eliminated poverty, and where a just order has supplanted violent chaos. Conversely, for King, the state is sinful—deeply sinful—when it formulates and implements policies of division, injustice, and violence.

Regarding the form of the state, King embraced not a liberal democracy but a social democracy in his pursuit of the beloved community.[8] In fact, King came to believe that Sweden's democratic

---

[7] Dyson, *I May Not Get There With You*, hints at the dialectic when he writes: "Thanks to his religious beliefs, King refused to idolize the state…. And despite the charge that he subverted the social order, King was a tireless advocate of democracy" (4).

[8] Douglas Sturm offers an excellent description of the key differences between liberal democracy and social democracy.

> The former is individualistic and atomistic in its social ontology. It promotes a politics of self-interest. Its doctrine of rights is fundamentally negative: one's rights are to be left alone, to be free from imposition and encroachment by others. The latter, on the other hand, is solidaristic and relational in its basic social theory. It promotes a politics of participation. Its doctrine of rights is affirmative: one's rights are to be empowered or enabled to find fulfillment within an encompassing

socialism in particular was more adept at providing the conditions for the beloved community than were other forms of the state in existence during his life. I contend that King's vision of the good state was that of an actual state within history—Sweden's welfare state. By offering this argument, my study stands in opposition to the works of Vincent Harding, Hanes Walton, Greg Moses, and John McCartney, which claim that King did not offer an alternative model for his vision of the good state.[9]

It has been faulty to write of "King's understanding" without discrimination, for King's political thought evolved throughout his lifetime. Nevertheless, I agree with Clayborne Carson's claim that there is a general consistency in King's "basic religious and political convictions," including, I argue, those on the state.[10] The second part of my thesis maintains that King's theological understanding of the state remained relatively constant in most of its fundamental elements but developed in

---

community of fellow citizens. In their respective doctrine of rights, the former is primarily concerned with freedom of speech and association, whereas the latter is concerned, as well, with education, meaningful employment, and housing.

"Martin Luther King, Jr., as Democratic Socialist," *Journal of Religious Ethics* 18 (Fall 1990): 82–83. Sturm's characterization of liberal democracy is what King had in mind when he referred to "anemic democracy."

[9] Vincent Harding, *Martin Luther King: The Inconvenient Hero* (Maryknoll: Orbis Books, 1996) 50, argues that King "was not inclined" to suggest an alternative model for building a socialist state and society. "For him," Harding writes, "the answers, the models, the hopes, the new constructions were still in the hearts and minds of all those men and women who were being drawn away from the old and working their lives toward a new way." I disagree. King pointed very specifically to the democratic socialism of Sweden and extolled what he perceived to be its virtues on several occasions. Sweden, in King's mind, provided the model that could lead the United States to provide the conditions required by the beloved community. I also disagree with Hanes Walton, *The Political Philosophy of Martin Luther King, Jr.* (Westport: Greenwood Publishing, 1971) 39, and Greg Moses, *Revolution of Conscience: Martin Luther King, Jr. and the Philosophy of Nonviolence* (New York: The Guilford Press, 1997) 15–16, both of whom contend that King did not offer an alternative form of government. (It should be noted, too, that these authors do not tend to the texts in which King commented directly on Sweden's democratic socialism.) On a similar note, John T. McCartney, *Black Power Ideologies*, argues that King, unlike Marcus Garvey, provided no "vision of his ideal state" (105). Contrary to McCartney, I believe that King focused on Sweden when developing his vision of the ideal state.

[10] Clayborne Carson, "Martin Luther King, Jr., and the African-American Social Gospel," in *African-American Religion: Interpretive Essays in History and Culture*, ed. Timothy Fulop and Albert Raboteau (New York: Routledge, 1997) 349.

substantive content and expression throughout his life. My study therefore stands in some opposition to King scholarship that posits a radical transformation between the first decade and the last three years of King's public ministry—a transformation during which King, allegedly full of despair and rage, suddenly became focused less on piecemeal efforts to transform society and more on the need for structural change.[11]

Familiar with the radicalization thesis, I began with the expectation of finding a radical transformation in the political thought of his last three years, but the evidence simply did not meet the expectation. Although my study clearly suggests that King's political realism deepened throughout his life, that his plan to move the state towards the beloved community had different foci at different points in his life, and that his tactics in confronting the sinful state changed as he grew older, my study also refuses to claim that King's political thought suddenly became revolutionary in the last three years of his life. On the contrary, I argue that King's devotion to social democracy, and to its internal demands for structural changes, extends back to his high school and college years.

Two significant shifts in his political thought are identified, one of which occurred in the first part of his career. With a developing understanding of the mandates of cruciform love, and with a sense that the emergence of nuclear weapons could lead to total nuclear war, King moved away from his early acceptance of war as a work of love and began, in the first part of his public career, to call upon the state to assume a pacifist stance in its international relations. In addition, in the last third of his public life, King conceded that a temporary formation of some separate black institutions could better counter the oppressive powers of a white state than could integrated institutions. Even with these changes in mind, however, I choose to refrain from using the word "radicalization," especially in relation to the last three years of his life, and to emphasize instead that the root of King's political thought—the beloved community—remained generally consistent in substance throughout his life.

---

[11] See, for example, Frederick L. Downing, *To See the Promised Land: The Faith Pilgrimage of Martin Luther King, Jr.* (Macon GA: Mercer University Press, 1986); Adam Fairclough, *Martin Luther King, Jr.* (Athens: University of Georgia Press, 1990); Vincent Harding, *Martin Luther King;* and Kenneth Smith, "The Radicalization of Martin Luther King, Jr: The Last Three Years," *Journal of Ecumenical Studies* 26/2 (Spring 1989): 270–88.

The third part of my thesis argues that King's understanding of the state has its roots in the African-American tradition he experienced through his family, church, and Morehouse professors, as well as in European-American religious and republic traditions.[12] King's political thought was the result of a hardworking *bricoleur*.[13]

If there is one clearly identifiable area of controversy in King studies, it involves claims regarding the sources of King's thought. Clayborne Carson has rightly maintained that a marked trend in King studies is to emphasize the role played by African-American religious traditions in the formation of King's thought.[14] Although Carson understands the trend to

---

[12] I mean to refer to the civic republicanism identified by William M. Sullivan, *Reconstructing Public Philosophy* (Berkeley: University of California Press, 1982) 11–22; and by Robert Bellah and others, *Habits of the Heart: Individualism and Commitment in American Life* (New York: Harper & Row, 1985) 28–31. This tradition, represented in the early years of the United States by John Winthrop and Thomas Jefferson, among others, eschewed a despotism that "encouraged the untrammeled pursuit of greed and power" in favor of a democracy that supported a just order (Sullivan, 11). Wanting to avoid a society based on lawless self-interest, the American republicans spoke of the moral dignity of all citizens and "sought to promote civic virtue through an active public life built up through an egalitarian spirit of self-restraint and mutual aid" (Sullivan, 12). In the view of the American republicans, the goal of state action is not to free the individual to live a life based merely on self-interest, but to empower all citizens to work together towards the attainment of justice and the public good. In this sense, the American republicans held a substantive notion of freedom. The work of freedom is not a matter of removing restrictions so that citizens can do whatever they choose, but of providing the conditions under which the citizenry might pursue the public good. Thus, foreign to the thought of the republicans was the notion of a state that would simply establish procedures under which various interests would compete to survive (Bellah and others, 253). For the American republicans, the state should provide the conditions under which diverse segments of political society might work together in order to create a moral, inclusive, and just order.

[13] For more on the meaning of *bricoleur*, see Jeffrey Stout, *Ethics after Babel: The Languages of Morals and Their Discontents* (Boston: Beacon Press, 1988) 74–77. Stout views Aquinas, for example, as a *bricoleur*, "a strong moralist engaging in a kind of selective retrieval and reconfiguration of available moral languages for his own use" (76). On the general identification of King as *bricoleur*, I am indebted to Stanley Hauerwas, "Remembering Martin Luther King, Jr.," *Journal of Religious Ethics* 23/1 (Spring 1995): 139, 141. But I do not believe that Hauerwas is specific enough in his characterization of King. Moving beyond Hauerwas, I suggest that it is important to identify King as a black *bricoleur*.

[14] Clayborne Carson, "Martin Luther King, Jr., and the African-American Social Gospel," 343. In his own footnote on those who emphasize the African-American

be a necessary corrective to earlier King studies that focused almost exclusively on European-American sources,[15] he also maintains that it may "understate the extent to which King's African-American intellectual roots were intertwined with the European-American intellectual influences of his college years."[16]

I agree with Carson. I suggest that the question of whether King's roots are in either African-American or European-American traditions presents nothing if not a false dilemma. The roots of King's African-American heritage intertwined not only with the influences of his college years but also those of his seminary and graduate school years. Throughout this book, then, I tend to the interrelations between, for example, Daddy King's realism and Reinhold Neibuhr's, Benjamin Mays's vision of social democracy and Walter Rauschenbusch's, and more.

Nevertheless, I argue that it is not sufficient to speak merely of interrelations. King, I argue, was not just any *bricoleur*, he was a black

---

religious tradition, Carson cites James H. Cone, "Martin Luther King, Jr.: Black Theology—Black Church," *Theology Today* 40 (January 1984): 409–12; and Lewis Baldwin, *There Is a Balm in Gilead: The Cultural Roots of Martin Luther King, Jr.* (Minneapolis: Fortress Press, 1991). Other King scholars who have tended, though not exclusively, to the African-American roots of King's thought include: Garth Baker-Fletcher, *Somebodyness: Martin Luther King, Jr., and the Theory of Dignity* (Minneapolis: Fortress Press, 1993); Downing, *To See the Promised Land*; Luther Ivory, *Toward a Theology of Radical Involvement: The Theological Legacy of Martin Luther King, Jr.* (Nashville: Abingdon, 1997); Richard Lischer, *The Preacher King: Martin Luther King, Jr. and the Word That Moved America* (New York: Oxford University Press, 1995); Thomas Mikelson, "The Negro's God in the Theology of Martin Luther King, Jr.: Social Community and Theological Discourse" (Th.D. diss., Harvard University, 1988); and Keith D. Miller, *Voice of Deliverance: The Language of Martin Luther King, Jr. and Its Sources* (New York: The Free Press, 1992).

[15] See, for example, Ira Zepp, *The Social Vision of Martin Luther King, Jr.* (Brooklyn: Carlson Publishing, 1989). This book—a published version of Zepp, "The Intellectual Sources of the Ethical Thought of Martin Luther King, Jr., as Traced in His Writings with Special Reference to the Beloved Community" (Ph.D. diss., St. Mary's Seminary and University, 1971)—provides a strong analysis of the many (and varied) intellectual sources behind King's words and deeds. Its problem, as Carson notes, is that it fails to address the African-American cultural roots of King's thought. Zepp agrees with the critique. In his preface to the 1989 edition of his dissertation, Zepp fully acknowledges that it is impossible to understand King without dealing with his African-American cultural roots.

[16] Carson, "Martin Luther King, Jr. and the African-American Social Gospel," 343. For a similar argument on this same point, see Lischer, *The Preacher King*, 38–71.

bricoleur whose thought was ultimately rooted in his African-American experiences. King initially learned about the state not by reading Thomas Jefferson, Walter Rauschenbusch, Jacques Maritain, Karl Marx, or even Reinhold Niebuhr, but through his personal encounters with his Christian family, especially Daddy King, and with his Morehouse professors, especially the clergy-scholar Benjamin E. Mays. The ultimate root of King's understanding of the state, then, is not in civic republicanism, theological liberalism, Marxism, Niebuhrian realism, or in any other such school, but in the religious tradition he experienced at home and at college.[17]

Primary Sources and Method

I offer a thick explication and analysis of his published articles, sermons, addresses, essays, interviews, and books regarding King's political thought—even though I am quite aware that King employed ghost writers and that he borrowed heavily from other written material (many times without acknowledgment) when publishing under his name. Like some students of King,[18] however, I assume that all material published under his name reflects his view—partly because he gave his approval for publication, partly because he never disavowed material published under his name, and partly because King scholars have yet to discover significant themes in ghostwritten or borrowed passages that are not consistent with the major themes of King's own work. My study also relies on material that King did not intend for publication but that has been published as part of the Martin Luther King, Jr., Papers Project, as well as on unpublished material available at Boston University and at the Martin Luther King, Jr., Center for Nonviolent Social Change.

Though it does not even begin to offer a description of the civil rights movement, I also explore King's life—for example, his actions while leading the Montgomery Improvement Association and the Southern Christian Leadership Conference—for information regarding his

---

[17] For use of the phrase "ultimate root," I am indebted to Sturm, "Martin Luther King, Jr., as Democratic Socialist," 84. One of Sturm's theses is that "the ultimate root of King's democratic socialist orientation derives from the black religious tradition that formed the deepest fundament of his emotional and intellectual life."

[18] See, for example, Baldwin, *There Is a Balm in Gilead,* 11–14; Ivory, *Toward a Theology of Radical Involvement,* 19; and Sturm, "Martin Luther King, Jr., as Democratic Socialist," 82.

interpretation of the state. I recognize that ideas largely emerge as reactions not only to other ideas but also to events within history, and so I have sought to place King's political thought within its historical setting. Tracing King's thought as it manifested itself in the various nonviolent, direct action movements has been especially helpful for tracking the evolution of his political thought.

I hope that this book will not only clarify King's theological interpretation of the state but also assist the reader in his or her attempts to develop an adequate understanding of the state, especially one in dialogue with King's. To this end, I offer in the conclusion a critical analysis of King's political thought, highlighting some of its strengths and weaknesses.

1

BLACK CHURCH, WHITE STATE

1929–1944

"Black America still wears chains," Martin Luther King, Jr., stated in an oratorical contest held during his junior year at Atlanta's Booker T. Washington High School.[1] The year was 1944, and the black America that King knew most intimately was anything but free from white domination. Jim Crow had already come to roost in Atlanta, dividing the city according to race, and placing various types of chains on blacks, in order to establish a "purity" that the mixing of the races did not permit. Postbellum Atlanta had not always sanctioned the chaining of its black residents, but with the coming of Jim Crow, many of Atlanta's white residents championed the chains as proper restraints in a world gone astray from sacrosanct customs and traditions. But young King knew that in the minds of Atlanta's blacks the chains clinked ominously, recalling the period of slavery and all of its horrors.

---

[1] Martin Luther King, Jr., "The Negro and the Constitution," *Called to Serve, January 1929–June 1951*, vol. 1 of *The Papers of Martin Luther King, Jr.*, ed. Clayborne Carson, Ralph E. Luker, and Penny A. Russell (Berkeley: University of California Press, 1992) 361. The editorial practice of the King Papers Project is to refrain from changing some of the grammatical and spelling errors in King's writing. Some of the quotations I draw from the King Papers Project, then, include writing errors.

Though inextricably linked together, the chains differed in the sense that some were largely social, others largely economic, and still others largely political in nature. The social chains institutionalized racial segregation, either *de jure* or *de facto*, in residential zones, restaurants, bars, elevators, parks, libraries, and even restrooms and jail cells. Equally restrictive, the economic chains prevented blacks from applying for all the jobs for which they were qualified, earning the type of pay white workers received, establishing businesses in Atlanta's business core, and enjoying many of the privileges offered to white customers. Interestingly, racial segregation in the economic world contributed to the development of Atlanta's "Sweet Auburn," a once-flourishing black business district along Auburn Avenue, as well as the growth of black businesses near the Atlanta University area, where black consumers could feel as if they were valued customers. Still, the existence of the economic chains brought financial distress to many blacks, causing Atlanta's black economy to pale in comparison to its white counterpart. Just as painful as the social and economic chains, the political chains prevented heavy and consistent black participation in matters political. Slapped with a poll tax, denied the right to vote in primaries, and subjected to a race-baiting that worked effectively in many political campaigns, Atlanta's blacks were made to play second fiddle on the electoral stage, although they were able to exercise some influence in general, open, and special elections.[2]

Of course, the black America beyond King's immediate environment also wore chains in 1944. Jim Crow ruled throughout the South, and though he did not officially enter other sections of the United States, blacks across America were nothing less than second-class citizens, unable to experience the social privileges, economic security, and political status enjoyed by many white Americans.[3] Even the blacks who had

---

[2] See, for example, Christopher Silver and John V. Moeser, *The Separate City: Black Communities in the Urban South, 1940–1968* (Lexington: University Press of Kentucky, 1995); Robert J. Alexander, "Negro Business in Atlanta," *Southern Economic Business Journal* 17 (1951): 454–55; Clarence A. Bacote, "The Negro in Atlanta Politics," *Phylon* 16 (1955): 333–50; and John Ditmer, *Black Georgia in the Progressive Era* (Urbana: University of Illinois Press, 1977).

[3] See Joel Williamson, *The Crucible of Race: Black-White Relations in the American South Since Emancipation* (New York: Oxford University Press, 1984); David Garfield, *Black, White, and Southern: Race Relations and Southern Culture, 1940 to the Present* (Baton Rouge: Louisiana State University Press, 1990); and C. Vann Woodward, *The Strange Career of Jim Crow* (New York: Oxford University Press, 1955).

achieved national (and international) reputations by excelling in their fields, let alone the many common black laborers, did not have access to the same opportunities open to white persons.

Constitutional Democracy

The issue of equal opportunity and access hit young King especially hard. "The finest Negro," he said in his oration, "is at the mercy of the meanest white man."[4] King had in mind Marian Anderson, the black contralto who became the subject of a heated controversy after the Daughters of the American Revolution had barred her from singing in Constitution Hall. The Anderson case was especially fitting for the speech's theme, "The Negro and the Constitution," and for illustrating King's claim that there is an unjustifiable discrepancy between constitutional values and racist actions.[5] In King's mind, it was sadly ironic that "the professional daughters of the very men who founded this nation for liberty and equality" had denied Anderson the opportunity of performing in, of all places, Constitution Hall.[6]

But King also noted that, though the Daughters of the American Revolution had barred Anderson from singing at Constitution Hall, she went on to a bigger and better event—an Easter Sunday performance on the steps of the Lincoln Memorial. When she sang "America" and "Nobody Knows De Trouble I Seen," King remarked, "there was a hush on the sea of uplifted faces, black and white, and a new baptism of liberty, equality and fraternity."[7] A hopeful King noted, too, that presidential cabinet members and a Supreme Court justice were present for the performance.

Nevertheless, after remarking on Anderson's warm reception, King added: "That was a fitting tribute, but Miss Anderson may not as yet spend the night in any good hotel in America." Further, in his conclusion

---

[4] King, Jr., "The Negro and the Constitution," *Papers*, 1:110.

[5] King continued a well-established black tradition by appealing to the Constitution as a moral source in the fight for freedom. See Donald G. Nieman, *Promises to Keep: African-Americans and the Constitutional Order, 1776 to the Present* (New York: Oxford University Press, 1991).

[6] King, Jr., "The Negro and the Constitution," *Papers*, 1:110.

[7] Ibid.

to the Anderson case, King portrayed white Americans as racist, sadistic schizophrenics. "So with their right hand, they raise to high places the great who have dark skins, and with their left, they slap us down to keep us in 'our places.'"[8]

The high school student appealed to republican principles when criticizing this schizophrenia. "Slavery has been a strange paradox in a nation founded on the principles that all men are created free and equal."[9] The treatment of Anderson was no less a strange paradox, given the historical events of 1865, which gave rise to a "new order...backed by amendments to the national constitution making it the fundamental law that thenceforth there should be no discrimination in the 'land of the free' on account of race, color or previous condition of servitude."[10] King concluded that democracy, as intended by the US Constitution, was far from present.

> We cannot have an enlightened democracy with one group living in ignorance. We cannot have a healthy nation with one-tenth of the people ill-nourished, sick, harboring germs of disease which recognize no color line—obey no Jim Crow laws. We cannot have a nation orderly and sound with one group so ground down and thwarted that it is almost forced into unsocial attitudes and crime. We cannot be truly Christian people so long as we flaunt the central teachings of Jesus: brotherly love and the Golden Rule. We cannot come to full prosperity with one great group so ill-delayed that it cannot buy goods.[11]

These words reflect not only King's sense of the interconnectedness of humanity, a theme he would stress throughout his life, but also his developing understanding of the state. On the one hand, King's speech criticized the state, though not by name, for sponsoring undemocratic policies that denied blacks access to education, health care, and the market, among other things. At this early stage, then, King was already expressing political realism. He understood the state to be racist, self-interested, and negligent of its own constitutional principles.

---

[8] Ibid.
[9] Ibid., 1:109–10.
[10] Ibid., 1:110.
[11] Ibid.

On the other hand, the speech also included an invitation to the state. Though he found the state to be racist, he did not wholly reject it. King thus concluded the above indictment with a direct invitation: "So as we gird ourselves to defend democracy at home, let us see to it that increasingly at home we give fair play and free opportunity for all people."[12] For King, "fair play" and "free opportunity" called for the state to grant all people access to the basic material goods they need for flourishing in a democracy. Indeed, King affirmed a social democracy that understands liberty to be not freedom from the state but freedom for economic empowerment and material and emotional well being. Democratic freedom, he believed, would not exist as long as blacks remained uneducated, physically deprived, subject to Jim Crow laws, inclined towards social disorder, and alienated from the market.[13] King thus called upon the state not to be a "night watchman" in its domestic politics, but to assume an active role in safeguarding and serving the physical well being of all its citizenry.[14]

King believed that a wholly democratic state would also eliminate the disfranchisement of blacks. Appealing to the state's self-interest, he even claimed that, if the state enfranchises blacks, "they will be vigilant and defend even with their arms, the ark of federal liberty from treason and destruction by her enemies."[15] These words point to King's future efforts with voter registration, but they also reveal his belief that the state should defend itself, even with forcible means, for the cause of freedom

---

[12] King, Jr., "The Negro and the Constitution," *Papers*, 1:110.

[13] Thus, Robert Michael Franklin, "An Ethic of Hope: The Moral Thought of Martin Luther King, Jr.," *Union Seminary Quarterly Review* 40 (January 1986), is partly wrong when he argues that in the last years of his life, King "revised his vision of the just society from a mere participatory political democracy to a democratic socialist society in which America's highest values could be realized" (43). What makes this argument partly wrong is its assumption that King once embraced a "mere participatory political democracy." Even in high school, as my study shows, King embraced a social democracy, the type favored by his father and grandfather.

[14] The image of the "night watchman" is grounded in Adam Smith's minimalist approach to the state. In Smith's view, "Little else is requisite to carry a state to the highest degree of opulence from the lowest barbarism, but peace, easy taxes, and a tolerable administration of justice; all the rest being brought about by the natural course of things." D. Stewart, "Account of the Life and Writings of Adam Smith, LL.D.," in Adam Smith, *Essays in Philosophical Studies* (Oxford: Oxford University Press, 1980) 322.

[15] King, Jr., "The Negro and the Constitution," *Papers*, 1:110.

for all.[16] As a high school student, then, King was neither a pacifist nor an anarchist. He fully accepted, though without emphasizing, that one of the responsibilities of the state is to keep order at home and abroad.[17] Still, King's emphasis was on encouraging the state to educate the uneducated, feed the hungry, provide care for the sick, eliminate segregation, and open the market to all.

Behind this emphasis was King's theology. Even at this early stage, King grounded his political ethics in Jesus Christ, "who promised mercy to the merciful, who lifted the lowly, strengthened the weak, ate with publicans, and made captives free."[18] In fact, King expressed fondness for Lincoln exactly because he believed that Lincoln's political leadership exemplified Jesus' teachings about freedom for all of humanity. Merging biblical and republican traditions, King pointed to the examples of both Jesus and Lincoln, implying that, because they embraced a freedom of opportunity that included care for the weak and lowly, the state should do no less.

King also recognized, even at this early age, that the state was not a monolithic entity. His appeal to Lincoln, as well as his observation that presidential cabinet members and a Supreme Court justice were present at Anderson's concert, reveal King's belief that, in the United States, the executive and judicial branches were more sympathetic to black concerns than was the legislative branch, let alone local government in the South. But King also acknowledged that the state as a whole was far from translating the Constitution "from writing on the printed page to an actuality."[19] Nevertheless, King concluded his oration with hopeful

---

[16] I flag the point that the young King, writing in the context of World War II, expressed no pacifist inclinations in this speech. This is a critical point for tracing King's understanding of the state's use of forcible means, a topic I will pursue throughout my study.

[17] King's high school comments on the domestic and international role of the United States push back Baldwin's good argument, made against William Watley's claim that King did not transcend Southern particularism until after the Selma campaign, that "King's vision had national and international implications as early as the Montgomery Bus Boycott in 1965, and that that vision expanded and found its fullest maturity between 1963 and the time around King's death in 1968." Baldwin, *To Make the Wounded Whole: The Cultural Legacy of Martin Luther King, Jr.* (Minneapolis: Fortress Press, 1992) 247. Baldwin is right about the expansion of King's vision in the latter part of his life, but King's vision included national and international topics even in high school.

[18] King, Jr., "The Negro and the Constitution," *Papers*, 1:111.

[19] Ibid.

comments on the realization of "perfect freedom" in America. "Already," he observed, "closer understanding links Saxon and Freedman in mutual sympathy." There is "a new birth of freedom," a new incarnation of the spirit of America's "martyred chief," and a renewed devotion to the work Jesus left undone. "My heart," King said, "throbs anew in the hope that inspired by the example of Lincoln, imbued with the spirit of Christ, [Saxon and Freedman] will cast down the last barrier to perfect freedom."[20]

Far from arising in a vacuum, King's dialectical response to the state was the product of a variety of forces in his life. In particular, his response initially emerged out of the black church, especially the preachers in his own family. King initially learned about the state not by reading Abraham Lincoln, Reinhold Niebuhr, Jacques Maritain, or Karl Marx, but by hearing the words, and seeing the deeds, of such figures as Reverends A. D. Williams, Daddy King, and William Holmes Borders. These black church ministers—not Niebuhrian realism, nor Boston personalism, nor any other theoretical school—built the ultimate foundations of King's political thought.

Reverend Martin Luther King, Sr.

One need not wonder why King, Jr., identified the state as racist. It was a lesson deeply imbedded in his father's life. Martin Luther King, Sr., known to his family and friends as "Daddy King," was a forceful presence in the lives of his children.[21] But there was at least one time in Daddy King's life when no one seemed to care much about his presence—when he was witness to a lynching as a youngster in Stockbridge, Georgia, where he lived with his sharecropping family. Interestingly, Daddy King traced part of the cause of this lynching to Southern white politicians. "The politicians," he wrote, "had been stumping through the area for

---

[20] Ibid. It is not clear what type of empirical evidence King had in mind when referring to the "new birth of freedom." Perhaps, however, he was thinking of his own family's involvement with such organizations as the NAACP and of its work with the local white power structure. See sections within the text on King's father and grandfather.

[21] The forcefulness of Daddy King is unmistakable to those who have read Martin Luther King, Sr., with Clayton Riley, *Daddy King: An Autobiography* (New York: William Morrow, 1980). See also Taylor Branch's account of Daddy King throughout Branch, *Parting the Waters: America in the King Years, 1954–1963* (New York: Simon & Schuster, 1988).

several weeks before this, and it was a basic tactic of these officeholders...to stir up the passions of all potential voters by appealing to their sense of insecurity." At the time of the lynching, according to King, Stockbridge's economy, like other local economies, was suffering heavily, primarily because the price of cotton was low and because a harsh winter had damaged all of the other crops. Angered by a failing economy, voters, in typical fashion, blamed the politicians for not re-sponding adequately to their economic discontent. "And the politicians," wrote King, "would come back: 'Hell, neighbors, it's not our fault. If it wasn't for all these damn niggers, the whole world would be a lot better off.'"[22] In King's recollection, shortly after the politicians traveled through Stockbridge, scapegoating "niggers" for the economic woes of the region, the white workers lynched their black coworker.

Young King learned very early in his life that the state he experienced most directly, in the form of racist Southern politicians, was not a friend that blacks could rely on for support. "Southern politicians," he believed, "built up whole careers with a single issue: Niggers. Not people. Niggers. Not life. Niggers."[23] The state that Michael King knew was an enemy to avoid.

King carried this understanding of the state with him as he moved from Stockbridge to Atlanta, the city of his dreams of freedom, where he hoped to become a successful minister. Once in Atlanta, he began to upgrade his formal education, an act that required him, as a young man in his late teens, to begin at the fifth-grade level. At Atlanta's Bryant School, King met Charles Clayton, a black attorney and teacher, who introduced King and other students to America's electoral process and to its unjust exclusion of blacks. "This I'd never thought much about," King wrote. "White folks handled all that, I told myself. Who needs to vote? What's there to vote for except one white man or another, both of them trying to keep you back?"[24]

Clayton taught King a lesson that would reappear in King, Jr.'s speech—not all state powers are equally resistant. King learned that federal law actually prohibited denying blacks the right to vote in national elections and, with Clayton's prodding, came to believe that participating in the electoral process could make a difference for black

---

[22] Ibid.

[23] Ibid., 75.

[24] Ibid., 64.

life. So King decided to register to vote. Once at city hall, however, he realized that, though federal law may occasionally be on his side, the state of Georgia was certainly resistant to implementing federal mandates regarding race matters.

Directed by a city hall employee, King headed for the "colored" elevator that was supposed to take him to the "colored" registrar's window. But he quickly discovered that the elevator marked "colored" was broken, and that the only available staircase was marked for "whites only." Undeterred, King tried again for several days, observing that the whites-only elevator, just steps away from the colored one, always worked well. "And I'd stand there," King recalled, "feeling a rage build up in me as I watched white schoolteachers herding their young white pupils onto their elevator so they could tour Atlanta City Hall and see just how democracy worked."[25]

Equally resistant, King fought back, refusing to accept the political forces as final authorities. In the case of his own registration as a voter, King defied city hall by riding the whites-only elevator to the registrar's office. In 1935, four years after assuming the pastorate at Atlanta's Ebenezer Baptist Church, King led a public protest against the segregation of elevators at the Fulton County Courthouse, and even helped the Atlanta branch of the NAACP in directing a voter registration drive to protest a bond issue that would not funnel sufficient funds into black schools. Three years later, in 1938, the Atlanta Civic and Political League elected King to its executive board, which led voter registration drives, criticized the city's lack of support for black schools, and led the effort to defeat another bond issue that failed to provide for black schools.[26]

Also active as the leader of Atlanta's Baptist Ministers Union, King organized a voter registration march in 1939, which, according to him, met resistance in Atlanta's black community, especially among black ministers, with some remarking that "there was no need for anybody in the black community to vote as long as those who knew what government was really about exercised that right wisely for themselves and for those folks who attended church."[27] Some ministers, Daddy King stated, trusted in government-by-favors, a system by which black ministers would meet with city politicians, pass on the officials' messages to the

---

[25] Ibid., 65.
[26] "Chronology," in *Papers*, 1:77–80.
[27] Martin Luther King, Sr., with Clayton Riley, *Daddy King*, 99.

black community, and then receive personal favors from satisfied white politicians. Repulsed by this method of governance, King wanted to ensure that the inalienable rights embraced in America's founding documents would be sustained and protected for all blacks, and believed that voting power was the right button to push for transforming favors for the few into inalienable rights for all.

Daddy King showed King, Jr., the importance of not only resisting the state but also developing a theological understanding of politics. King understood his political action as part and parcel of his ministerial identity and beliefs. In a 17 October 1940 speech that addressed "the true mission of the church," he argued that the church must become involved in politics. In Jesus' life, King stated, "we find we are to do something about the broken-hearted, poor, unemployed, the captive, the blind, and the bruised...God hasten the day when every minister will become a registered voter and a part of every movement for the betterment of our people."[28]

King clearly believed that the practice of politics, reflecting Jesus' concern for the downtrodden, should be about providing adequate jobs, food, shelter, health care, and clothing for those in need. But King recognized that the state would need prodding to assume its proper role in caring for the marginalized. Hence, he appealed to ministers to become politically active, ensuring that politics leads to substantive freedom, especially for society's marginalized, just as Christ intended.

Daddy King continued to take his own advice. In 1942, while attending the National Baptist Convention, he assisted in the drafting of a resolution that implored President Roosevelt to end racist actions toward black passengers. On the local level, and one year later, he led a protest against unequal pay for Atlanta's black teachers, a protest that occurred in "a time when city governments in the South kept themselves so far away from Negro concerns that City Hall could have as easily been located on the moon."[29] And less than a year before King, Jr., delivered "The Negro and the Constitution," Daddy King's ministerial union (ABMU) condemned the use of forced black labor in cotton fields near Athens, Georgia.[30]

---

[28] "Introduction," in *Papers*, 1:34. The manuscript of the address is part of the Christine King Farris Collection (in private hands).

[29] King, Sr., and Riley, *Daddy King*, 106.

[30] "Introduction," in *Papers*, 1:83–84.

Of course, King constantly met political pressure, especially when his challenges affected the economics of the local community power structure. In his perspective, Atlanta's political powers "consistently favored the interests of businessmen," which meant that any challenge to state-sponsored business practices would meet serious political resistance. "Politicians," he wrote, "were traditionally the friends of the corporate mind here, and Atlanta's ties to the people often came after businesses had tied *their* knots with elected officials."[31] King never went so far as to say that politicians were merely tools of the bourgeoisie, but his experience certainly taught him that Atlanta's political powers were comforts to business owners, rather than their challengers.

Reverend A. D. Williams and the NBC, USA, Incorporated

A. D. Williams, Daddy King's father-in-law and predecessor at Ebenezer Baptist, was a major impetus behind Daddy King's involvement in politics. "It was through [Williams]," wrote King, "that I came to understand the larger implications involved in any churchman's responsibility to the community he served." Williams's strong conviction, which he passed on to Daddy King, was that the ways of God are not always the ways of the state, and that it is proper to use knowledge of God as a critical tool for judging a sinful state.

Throughout his own life, Williams refused to accept the state uncritically, as if it were God. In 1906, the year of the Atlanta race riot, he joined the Georgia Equal Rights League, a black organization devoted to eliminating a variety of injustices: the white primary, lynching, the convict lease system, and the exclusion of black men from juries and the militia, among other things.[32] In 1917, he helped organize the Atlanta branch of the National Association for the Advancement of Colored People, through which he and others protested a decision by Atlanta's Board of Education to eliminate seventh-grade classes in black schools so that there would be adequate funds for building a new junior high school for whites. Using God as a critical tool for judging the school board's actions, the protesters argued: "You, with fifty schools, most of them ample, efficient and comfortable, for the education of your children, can

---

[31] King, Sr., and Riley, *Daddy King,* 146.
[32] "Introduction" in *Papers,* 1:10.

square neither your conscience in God nor your conduct with your oaths, and behold Negro children in fourteen, unsanitary, dilapidated, unventilated school rooms...”[33] Williams's judgment of the political powers continued in other ways, too. As head of the NAACP during two different points in his life, he organized voter registration, boycotts of buildings where blacks were prohibited from using the elevators, and bloc voting on issues critical to the black community.

One example of bloc voting stands out as especially helpful for interpreting Williams's understanding of political authority. In the 1920s, Williams noted the possibility of a referendum on a municipal bond issue that would not provide sufficient funds for black schools. Discouraged by the board of education's failure to meet the educational needs of Atlanta's black population, Williams led a voter registration rally for blacks, who, though excluded from voting in primaries, were permitted to vote in general, open, and special elections. His efforts in registering voters effectively killed any chance for a successful passage of the referendum. Stopping this particular municipal bond issue, Williams's leadership eventually engineered the successful passage of a bond issue that provided millions of dollars to the construction of eighteen new black schools, including Booker T. Washington High School, where young Martin delivered “The Negro and the Constitution.”[34]

On the one hand, then, Williams refused to recognize the state, in the form of the board of education, as an ultimate source to be accepted uncritically. On the other hand, however, he accepted its role as a major player in the educational advancement of the black community. Moreover, his actions regarding the bond issue reveal his conviction that, although the state has the right to demand what is necessary (money for education, for example), the state is never right to demand more than what is due it, especially when it demands something that contradicts the ways of God (money earmarked for racist policies, for example). Williams's understanding of political authority is clear: Give Caesar what is his, but when Caesar overextends his boundaries, obey God rather than Caesar.

Interestingly, Williams saw no contradiction between God and a state that protects the lives of its citizens by using weapons. Williams was no pacifist. Though the primary issue was race, Williams's participation

---

[33]Ibid., 15.
[34] See ibid., 17; and King, Sr., and Riley, *Daddy King,* 100–101.

in the Georgia Equal Rights League's fight against the exclusion of blacks from the militia suggests that he fully supported the state's preserving role, even if the act of preservation and protection required the use of weapons.

Williams's activism in matters political, especially through the NAACP and the Georgia Equal Rights League, reflected the evolving political views of his and his family's church denomination—the National Baptist Convention, USA, Incorporated. Lincoln and Mamiya, sociologists of the black church, report that even though the central concern of the NBC at its founding was global missions, the convention always involved itself in the political arena. At the beginning of the century, the NBC "spoke out against racial violence and waged campaigns against segregation in public accommodations and discrimination in the armed service, education, and employment." Underpinning these views at the time was "the ideological framework of self-help," popularized by Booker T. Washington and his followers.[35]

The NBC's support of Washington was never absolute, however, because an "undercurrent of dissent," as Paul Harvey puts it, ran through the denominational ministers' public discussions on Washington's policy of "industrial education."[36] In fact, the NBC eventually moved beyond Washington's self-help ideology to support the political practices of the NAACP—a move forcefully encouraged by Nannie Burroughs, who planned and organized in 1900 the formation of the Woman's Convention, an auxiliary to the NBC, and whose social gospel advocated viewing men and women as equal in the divine creation, a revolutionary idea within the NBC. According to Harvey, Burroughs "urged black Baptists to cooperate with the NAACP, the Southern Sociological Congress, and other groups working for progress in race relations."[37]

The NBC took Burroughs's (and other's) advice and eventually became an active supporter of the NAACP, so much so that the NBC joined the NAACP in becoming a vocal critic of the state on such matters as black disfranchisement and black participation on juries.[38] Jim Crow

---

[35] C. Eric Lincoln and Lawrence H. Mamiya, *The Black Church in the African American Experiment* (Durham: Duke University Press, 1990) 30.

[36] Paul Harvey, *Redeeming the South: Religious Cultures and Racial Identities among Southern Baptists, 1865–1925* (Chapel Hill: University of North Carolina Press, 1997) 236.

[37] Ibid., 241.

[38] Lincoln and Mamiya, *The Black Church in the African American Experiment*, 30.

laws, in particular, raised the official ire of the NBC. Fighting against Jim
Crow, National Baptists on the local level eventually created voter registration drives and called upon NBC pastors to encourage their con-
gregants to pay the poll tax and register to vote.[39]

But the NBC was much more than a critic of the state. In fact, Elias
Camp Morris, who assumed the presidency of the NBC at its founding in
1895 and held onto office for twenty-five years, was a Republican stalwart
who, having been elected a delegate to the Republican National Nomi-
nation Convention in 1884, sought to ensure, not always successfully,
that the NBC backed certain policies of the Theodore Roosevelt administration.[40] On a related note, the NBC vigorously supported the world
wars as wars for the freedom of humanity.

Interestingly, the white counterpart of the NBC, the Southern
Baptist Convention, easily matched the dialectical attitude towards the
state expressed by the NBC. Like the NBC, the SBC regularly praised and
critiqued state policy. For example, at the time of A. D. Williams's
ministry, the SBC praised the policies, domestic and international, of one
of the South's own sons, the Presbyterian Woodrow Wilson.[41] But,
during the time of Daddy King's ministry, the SBC criticized President
Truman's policy of enlisting the Catholic Church in the fight against
communnism, as well as his decision to appoint an official ambassador to
the Vatican in 1951.[42] The SBC was about as anti-communist as possible,
understanding communism to be godless and inherently anti-Christ. But
the SBC, Manis observes, was as equally anti-Catholic as it was anti-
communist, viewing Catholicism as a threat to the Baptist tradition of
church-state separation and to its freedom to believe without priestly
mediation.[43]

The difference between the NBC and the SBC, according to Andrew
Manis, was not the extent to which they praised or criticized the state, but
the content of their criticisms and praises.[44] National Baptists, with their

---

[39] Andrew Michael Manis, *Southern Civil Religions in Conflict: Black and White
Baptists and Civil Rights, 1947–1957* (Athens: University of Georgia Press, 1987) 23.

[40] Harvey, *Redeeming the South*, 235.

[41] Ibid., 29.

[42] Ibid., 47.

[43] Ibid., 47–48.

[44] Manis, *Southern Civil Religions in Conflict*, argues that both the NBC and the
SBC, equally political in focus, embraced a civil religion but that the content of this
religion differed significantly, especially on the issues of communism, Catholicism, and

own tradition of religious freedom and church-state separation, joined ranks with the SBC in criticizing Truman's pro-Catholic policies. But the National Baptist perspective, Manis observes, was never as anti-Catholic, nor as anti-communist, as the "near-hysteria" view of the Southern Baptists.[45] For National Baptists at this time, the primary problem with state policy was not the degree to which it was anti-Catholic or anti-communist but its failure to support domestic policies that would lead to the end of segregation as well as discrimination in all economic and political areas. "National Baptists, hence, carried an image of an America intimidated more by its internal dilemma than by external enemies."[46]

Unsurprisingly, then, A. D. Williams, a faithful member of the NBC, focused his dialectical attitude towards the state on the domestic problems of segregation, political disfranchisement, and economic injustices. Given Williams's activism in matters political, it is also no surprise that Daddy King, who held Williams in high esteem, became active in Atlanta politics. And, given the influence of Daddy King over young Martin, as well as the apostolic connection between Williams and Daddy King, it is no surprise that Martin would make such strong political statements while a junior at Booker T. Washington High School. It is quite clear then that Williams's dialectical response to the state—a "no" to the state that degrades blacks, and a "yes" to the state that orders and assists the lives of its citizens, especially blacks in need of freedom and justice—runs through Daddy King's words and deeds and into the speech Martin delivered in the high school his grandfather helped establish. Even though A. D. Williams died when Martin was only one-year old, he nevertheless played a formative role in Martin's understanding of the state.

Reverend William Holmes Borders: The Politics of Local Productivity

Daddy King and A. D. Williams were not the only ministers in young King's neighborhood. Just a block away was William Holmes Borders, pastor of Wheat Street Baptist, a church that enjoyed wide influence and

---

civil rights. Regarding the last issue, the NBC and the SBC engaged in a "holy war of civil rights" (9).

[45] Ibid., 53.

[46] Ibid., 54.

prestige in the Auburn Avenue area, so much so that a bitter rivalry of sorts developed between Daddy King and Borders. The rivalry, however, did not keep young King away from Wheat Street. King visited the church, especially when he was considering ministry, to discover the identity of his father's rival, as well as the reason why he was attracting so many people. But just the large presence of Wheat Street and Borders in the Auburn area is enough to suggest that young King could not have walked through his neighborhood without breathing the successful ministry and politics of the rival up the street.

King, Jr., would have seen Borders as a political preacher. There were significant differences between Borders and Daddy King, but both believed that ministry is much more than saving souls for a God in heaven. Like King, Borders held that ministry necessarily involves the pastor in worldly politics. "So much of our life today is political," he observed, "that the preacher is involved in politics by necessity, if not by choice." Basic needs such as jobs and streetlights are political, and because the church's role includes addressing basic needs, the church must get its hands dirty in the field of politics. "The church simply cannot escape politics, nor should it."[47]

King, Jr., would have noted, too, that, like Daddy King and A. D. Williams, Borders chose to avoid seeing the state as an impenetrable fortress that held within it just a few privileged white men. Borders believed that, with the right number of registered voters, he could storm the fortress and begin to make a change in the political process. Like King and Williams, then, Borders took up the cause of voter registration drives, one of which he led, shortly before World War II, with the purpose of pressuring local government in Atlanta to hire a black police officer. Borders fulfilled his purpose when, with a list of 20,000 black

---

[47] James W. English, *Handyman of the Lord: The Life and Ministry of the Rev. William Holmes Borders* (New York: Meredith Press, 1967) 160. Borders took his politics so seriously that he even became a candidate for political office in 1965, thus revealing his conviction that the state is not merely an enemy to avoid but also a potential ally in the fight for justice. Separating himself from the masses of blacks aligning themselves with the Democrats, Borders ran as a Republican for the Georgia State House of Representatives. Daddy King, a Democrat by that time, must have been delighted when Borders was defeated by 10,000 votes—not a small defeat at all in a state house race. But the more significant point here is that Borders saw his political candidacy as a natural evolution from his many years as a community minister, extending back to the early days when he led voter registration efforts (159).

voters in hand, he took his request to the mayor, who reportedly then asked exactly how many black police officers Borders desired.

Borders continued to resist the state even during the war, when patriotism ran high. Like other blacks, Borders criticized the state for pursuing democracy abroad but not at home. This criticism permeated the community one day when, as the new pastor at Wheat Street, he found himself in the middle of a mob intent on killing a streetcar driver. The driver had pinned a black soldier, and threatened him with a gun to his chest, after the soldier had tried to leave the streetcar by the front door—an illegal act under Georgia's segregationist policies. Having made his way through the angry mob, Borders entered the streetcar and appealed to the self-interest of both men, telling the young man he was too young to die and the streetcar driver that the mob would kill him instantly if he dared to kill the soldier. After Borders defused the volatile situation, he then rode the streetcar to an area just beyond the mob and exited—out the front door.[48] Young King's neighborhood soon buzzed with the news about the pastor who had fought, and won, a battle with segregation. In Borders, then, young King saw an example of a successful activist pastor who protested, with heart and hands, the injustice of segregation.

In Borders, King also encountered a firm believer in social democracy. Borders favored storming the political fortress of racism, but he did not seek to burn it down. Like Daddy King and Williams, Borders was a die-hard reformist who believed in and loved democracy, especially as expressed in the US Constitution. Borders publicized his embrace of democracy on a radio program he began during the early part of World War II. In one of the inaugural programs, he addressed the question of whether blacks should leave the South and travel to northern cities, where life seemed to hold greater promise. "I cast my vote," Borders stated, "with those who feel called upon to dig in, grapple with the problem, knowing that the future is mortgaged to God, democracy, and Christianity."[49] This statement clearly shows not only Border's general appreciation for democracy but also his theological conviction that full democracy is located within the divine will. God, according to Borders, is a democrat.

---

[48] Ibid., 44–47.
[49] Ibid., 57.

Borders's reformist love for democracy extended to the political sentiments he expressed about US involvement in World War II. Criticizing blacks who deemed the war to be just "a white man's war," Borders called upon his followers to help defeat the forces of totalitarianism. But his primary interest was in expanding democracy at home, and he often called upon the government to institute medical care for all of the poor, black and white, to create common recreational areas for all city residents, and to equalize salaries for black teachers.[50] His radio listeners also heard him draw a causal connection between the increase in crime in Atlanta and the social and economic disadvantages of blacks, a connection that young King also drew in his high school speech. For Borders, the cause of the rise in crime was nothing less than low wages, inadequate housing, the absence of job training and recreational areas, and the failure of local government to enforce its laws of protection.[51] Only a social democracy—one that would provide the black community with a sound economic and social base—would begin to eliminate the "law and order" problems within the city of Atlanta.

Though he called for the expansion of democracy, Borders was not idealistic enough to believe that the state would act anytime soon to further the cause for which it had fought in Europe and Japan. Rather than trusting in city government to find jobs for the black community, Borders set up his own employment agency, and through his church office he connected neighborhood folks, skilled and unskilled, to employers across the city. Borders's church also ran self-help classes that addressed such issues as personal grooming and the virtues required for successful employment.[52] He later backed his employment ministry with yet another faith-based initiative—the Wheat Street Baptist Credit Union, which provided financial counseling, loaned money at low rates, provided dividends on members' deposits, and kept money within the black community.[53]

Although he called upon government to expand democracy, then, Borders's own politics reflected a deep and abiding realism about the intransigence of the white political powers. To be sure, Borders hoped that the state would create a more constitutional democracy, but his own

---

[50] Ibid., 15.
[51] Ibid., 57.
[52] Ibid., 60.
[53] Ibid., 85.

politics focused less on embracing large government programs and more on developing self-sufficiency within the black community. Borders's localism was always evident, but became even more visible after the late 1950s, when the interstate highway program displaced many blacks in the Atlanta metropolitan area. Shortly after that displacement, when homeless men and women traveled to Wheat Street Baptist, Borders learned of a major government program, proposed by the Atlanta Housing Authority, to clear slums within his own neighborhood. James English reports that Borders, still stinging from the highway program, sharply doubted the ability of government, in and of itself, to better the quality of housing for the black community.[54] So Borders created, in the 1960s, still another faith-based initiative—the Wheat Street Garden Homes, a non-profit organization that would build low-income housing within the Wheat Street Baptist neighborhood.

Both during and after the years when young King walked the streets of Auburn Avenue, Borders's politics were local, grounded in his neighborhood and designed to improve the productivity of his neighborhood community. Borders recognized his localism, even during the nationally staged civil rights movement led by the son of the rival down the street:

> Yes, I am for the sit-ins, the marching. There is a time when the good they perform cannot be accomplished by other means. But I do not believe that civil rights goals are attained only through marching, sit-ins, wade-ins, and kneel-ins. God bless the marchers...
>
> However, I sincerely believe that there must also be a local productivity. By productivity I mean constructive action which clearly demonstrates the Negro can and will take his share of responsibility.[55]

Borders's emphasis on local productivity did not mean that he envisioned the state as an enemy to avoid at all costs. On the contrary, Borders affirmed the state in the role it provided in helping his local initiatives to succeed, and he pursued all advantages made possible through political offices, especially those of Atlanta's mayor. Beyond that, Borders believed that his politics of local productivity served, rather than

---

[54] Ibid., 113.
[55] Ibid., 155.

undermined, the expansion of the democratic state. Like Daddy King, Borders never wholly rejected the state, even while looking upon it with deep suspicion. But Borders, even more than Daddy King, did not count on the state to provide what he deemed necessary for the black community, and so he turned his efforts to faith-based initiatives that focused on local productivity within his own black neighborhood. In this sense, Borders provided King with his first taste of Black Power.

Summary

The young King's dialectical response to the state was the product of the black church he experienced through A. D. Williams, Daddy King, and William Holmes Borders. Through these black church preachers, young King learned that the state is not a divine fortress, unassailable and impenetrable. King came to realize what he would later read in the works of Christian realists—the state is a human institution, with human faults, weaknesses, even sins. Likely, King even heard family members portray the state as an enemy to avoid, not a friend to love. King also learned that, in its sinful moments, the state does not escape the stern judgment of God, but exists in, with, and under the divine will. Further, the black church preachers taught him that Christians do well to refuse the state as a final institution, subject to none. Caesar is not God, and thus is not an object of ultimate loyalty for Christians.

On the other hand, the black church preachers taught him that rather than wholly rejecting the state, he should accept the state when its ways coincide with the ways of God. Caesar may not be God, but, on occasion, Caesar may be God's minister for good. More particularly, the state's ways are God's ways when they both order human life and recognize, support, and enhance the freedom and equality of its citizens, especially blacks in need of freedom and justice. Only occasionally—when the school board, at Williams's urging, funded the construction of black schools, for example—did the experiences of the King family confirm the New Testament view that the state can be God's minister for the good.

King, then, learned at an early age that a member of the black church should neither accept the state uncritically nor deny it unreservedly, but should critique it, especially its racist ways, recognize that its practice of politics is necessary for setting the captive free, and push it to effect freedom for all, just as Christ intended. More particularly, King also learned, especially from Daddy King and William Holmes Borders, about the other views expressed in "The Negro and the Constitution"—that freedom is connected with economic empowerment and material and physical well-being; that the state, more than a "night watchman," should assume an active role serving the well-being of its citizens; that all citizens are equal and of one body; that the practice of democracy as expressed in the US Constitution is a good to be affirmed; that the practice of democratic politics often dismisses the interests of the underclass; and that it is right for the state to prepare for (and sometimes to resort to) war. But Borders's emphasis on local productivity also informed King that the state is not to be wholly relied on when seeking the good for the black community. On the contrary, Borders, like the Black Power activists who would come later, taught that blacks would do well to establish their own institutions rather than rely on the state to plan a rescue through massive programs. King would join Borders in proclaiming the virtue of local productivity, but he would never stop pushing for massive state-sponsored programs that would bring about the physical conditions required by the beloved community.

2

Morehouse and More Democracy

1944–1948

One of the many domestic side effects of black participation in World War II was the draining of many young males from historically black colleges, including Morehouse College in Atlanta. Faced with a wartime enrollment dwindling to less than 500, Morehouse's president, Benjamin E. Mays, a theologian with an expertise in black religion, decided to open the college doors to high school juniors who evidenced a capacity for college work. Among the applicants to this early-admissions program was Martin Luther King, Jr., whose father and grandfather had attended Morehouse. The college accepted his application, and in September 1944, eight months after the US military had introduced blacks into combat, King began his Morehouse studies at the age of fifteen.[1] The extant writings of King from his college years do not provide enough material for carefully tracing the development of his understanding of the state while a Morehouse student. But it would be unwise to pass over his college years as if they did not matter, for Morehouse professors introduced King to more theoretically developed ideas than those he experienced in his family—ideas about democracy, realism, communism, and the politics of resistance.

---

[1] See Taylor Branch, *Parting the Waters: America in the King Years, 1954–1963* (New York: Simon & Schuster, 1988) 59–60.

Mays on Social Democracy

One of the more vocal critics of the state was Benjamin Mays, who, according to King's own account, was "one of the great influences in my life."[2] A Baptist minister, theologian, and social activist, Mays gained the respect of many Morehouse students in part by delivering his Tuesday morning chapel talks, which sometimes prompted King to follow Mays back to his office for further discussion. According to Mays, the chapel lectures often focused on what he perceived as the need for blacks to express their God-given freedom. Mays believed that he was "born to rebel" against systems that degraded his freedom, and he frequently encouraged his students to join him in the rebellion, claiming that "the only way they could be free in a rigidly segregated society was by consistent refusal ever to accept subservience and segregation in their own minds."[3]

Part of Mays's own rebellion was his ongoing, critical commentary on the strengths and weaknesses of the US government. Before and during King's stay at Morehouse, Mays published articles that commented very directly on the state, and it is more than likely that, even if the articles themselves escaped the scholarly attention of his students, King and others often heard their content in Mays's chapel talks. The articles reveal that Mays's interpretation of the state reinforced, and built upon, King's earlier instruction. In particular, the articles advance a theological interpretation of the state, as well as a theoretically developed argument that supports a social democracy.

Mays began his political thought with the theological conviction that God the Creator made the human person to be free and equal, of inestimable worth and significance, and in unity with all other humans. Mays communicated this conviction explicitly in the language of the social gospel, speaking frequently of the "brotherhood of man," the "fatherhood of God," and the "ethical laws" of the universe, language that would find its way into King's own sermons and writings. A social gospeler at heart, Mays argued in a 1939 article that the fundamental Christian beliefs are simply "that God is father and all men are brothers

---

[2] Martin Luther King, Jr., *Stride Toward Freedom: The Montgomery Story* (New York: Harper & Row, 1958) 145.

[3] Benjamin E. Mays, *Born to Rebel* (New York: Charles Scribner's Sons, 1971) 196.

and that there is neither Greek nor Jew, bond nor free, male nor female, scythian nor barbarian; for we are all one in Christ Jesus."[4]

Mays also held that the judgment of God would visit anything that would deny these fundamental Christian beliefs, including the state. In a 1940 article that offered advice on educating black students, he encouraged religious leaders to communicate a faith that knows that individuals "cannot build systems of government nor systems of economics as they please." When individuals and their governments ignore justice and the sacredness of the human personality, God's judgment will appear.[5] Mays's belief in a God who judges individuals and their governments resonated deeply with King, Jr., whose first public speech during the Montgomery struggle would express the conviction that God disciplines wayward nations.

King's thought also would include Mays's dialectical attitude towards US democracy. Mays remained faithful to his black roots by focusing on the problems of discrimination and segregation and even by taking the US government to task for its failures to rectify the problems faced by blacks. In continuity with King's earlier teachers, Mays understood the state as a racist force that ignored the cries for freedom arising from the black community. In a 1945 article that addressed the state's responsibilities to black soldiers returning home from World War II, Mays excoriated the state for making the world safe for democracy in World War I, while refusing to make democracy perform more effectively at home. The state, he claimed, led blacks to believe that after World War I, justice in the courts would increase, lynching would cease, the ballot would be given to all, and jobs would be distributed more equitably—in short, that democracy would become a reality in the lives of blacks. But

---

[4] Benjamin E. Mays, "The American Negro and the Christian Religion," *Journal of Negro Education* 8 (July 1939): 533.

[5] Benjamin E. Mays, "The Religious Life and Needs of Negro Students," *Journal of Negro Education* 9 (July 1940): 342–43. For more on this theme, see Benjamin E. Mays, *Seeking to Be Christian in Race Relations* (New York: Friendship Press, 1957) 4–7. In this book, Mays reiterated his belief that humanity cannot build the world, including the state, as it pleases. "Many have tried it—the Pharaohs, Cyrus the Great, Nebuchadnezzar, Alexander the Great, the Caesars, Napolean, Kaisar Wilhelm, Hitler, Mussolini, and many others—but to no avail" (4). For Mays, God's laws of justice and peace will always prevail over a sinful humanity.

the state's promises, Mays held, were empty, with the effect that undemocratic conditions still pervaded black life.[6]

But, again like King's earlier teachers, Mays did not merely critique the state; he also positively encouraged it to correct its abuses and faults. More particularly, he called upon governors and mayors to ensure "that which is guaranteed to every American in the Federal Constitution and the Bill of Rights and vouchsafed to all in the Christian religion."[7] For Mays, this meant that political leaders should provide black veterans with jobs that fit their abilities, fair treatment by the police and the court system, decent housing, proper hospital care, the ballot, and equalized educational opportunities. Mays also meant immediate political action. His suggested actions may not be politically expedient, he conceded, but "man does not live by political office alone." Politicians should begin to attend to what is right and just, not merely to what is politically expedient. In words that King would adopt throughout his life, Mays argued: "The time is always ripe to do that which is right and just.... There is a sense of urgency in justice."[8] Like King's earlier nurturers, then, Mays did more than condemn the state; he also encouraged it to become an active player in immediately establishing the material conditions that would allow blacks to become full participants in democracy.

What is more, Mays affirmed partial democracy. Even though he was sharply critical of the US government, nowhere did Mays suggest that returning black soldiers should reject the state outright. On the contrary, he stressed that returning soldiers should exercise "poise and restraint," virtues that could best be expressed by employing existing democratic processes. The returning soldier "should be encouraged to use the machinery set forth in our democratic framework for achieving the rights accorded him in the Federal Constitution."[9] Like Borders, Mays was far from being a rabid revolutionary committed to hating, rejecting, and overthrowing the state.

On the one hand, then, Mays castigated the state for its undemocratic ways and for its stalling tactics. But, on the other hand, he affirmed its partial democracy, as well as its potential for becoming truly

---

[6] Benjamin E. Mays, "Veterans: It Need Not Happen Again," *Phylon* 6/3 (1945): 205–206.

[7] Ibid., 207.

[8] Ibid., 209.

[9] Ibid., 210.

democratic. This double response, consistent with what King had learned as a youngster, also appeared in a commencement address that Mays delivered at Howard University, at the end of King's first year at Morehouse. Revealing his inclinations for the social gospel, as well as his embrace of a social democracy, the address was an attempt to defend and explain the thesis that "the United States of America can be democratized and christianized within this generation."[10] The following themes of the address, which show that Mays had a more substantive understanding of what the state should do than had King's earlier nurturers, would reappear repeatedly in King's later works.

Christianization, Mays told the Howard seniors, calls for the church to enact its stated convictions: that its ultimate allegiance is owed to God alone; that all individuals are united as sisters and brothers because they all have a common origin in God; and that all human life is sacred, possessing intrinsic worth and value.[11] The church, he lamented, has not carried out this responsibility but has chosen to be subservient to the state, which does not recognize its dependence upon God and thus does not affirm the sociality or the sacredness of human life. Rather than standing in awe of the state, passively accepting its degradation of the human, the church must begin to set the standard for it—to show the state that its allegiance is owed to God, that each person is worthy, and that all persons are united together.

As the church has the responsibility to christianize the United States, Mays argued, the state has the responsibility to democratize it. Frustrated with state and local governments, however, Mays this time stated that the federal government in particular should be the key player in democratizing the United States.[12]

Mays's notion of democratization is key to his understanding of what the state should do if it is to enact the principles of America's founding documents, to recognize its dependence on God, and to base its actions upon divine law. As he understood it, democratization requires the state to become fully committed to ensuring that "every able-bodied man is entitled to an opportunity to work and to advance on the job." Mays actually had in mind a five- or ten-year plan that would allow for a

---

[10] Benjamin E. Mays, "Democratizing and Christianizing America in this Generation," *Journal of Negro Education* 14/4 (Fall 1945): 528.

[11] Ibid., 528.

[12] Ibid.

smooth transition into full employment. Reflecting distaste for both state socialism and unfettered capitalism, he believed that the federal government should initiate the plan but also that industry and university leaders should participate in its development and implementation: "The question of full employment after the war should not be left wholly in the hands of the Government and it should not be left wholly in the hands of private capital." In Mays's view, the problem of full employment is the most pressing one for the state to tackle, primarily because work, and the resources earned, would permit society to repair the tears of the social fabric. If full employment were to be met, he argued, friction between the races would diminish, health would improve, and educational facilities would be enhanced. "And it is the responsibility of the Federal Government to see that these things are done."[13]

Second, democratization calls for the federal government to solve America's educational problems, particularly the deficiencies in the education of blacks. Mays's policy recommendation was the establishment of "a minimum annual per capita expenditure and a minimum classroom expenditure below which no American child would fall."[14]

Third, democratization means that the federal government must become an active player in clearing slums across the United States. Positively stated, democratization requires decent housing for every American. "Here again," Mays stated, "the Federal Government could work out a program with private industry and within a period of twenty years, every American could have a decent house in which to live."[15] Again, wanting to separate himself from radical state socialists and laissez-faire capitalists, Mays suggested that the federal government should be a key player in the area of housing, but that it should supplement, not supplant, private housing.

Fourth, democratization requires the federal government to ensure "proper hospital care for every citizen—those who are able to pay and those who are not able to pay."[16] And fifth, democratization means that the federal government must seek to abolish segregation and discrimination in any area where federal money is used. The federal government should "see to it that where federal money is spent, no

---

[13] Ibid., 530.
[14] Ibid.
[15] Ibid.
[16] Ibid.

discrimination of any kind would exist because of class, religion, or race."[17]

The different elements of Mays's notion of democratization, each of which would appear in King's own political thought, clearly show that Mays had no thin understanding of democracy. The democracy that Mays embraced was not a thin democracy that gives individuals the ballot and minimal protection, and then leaves them to exist as they would choose, largely unhampered by the state. Rather, Mays embraced a social democracy that seeks to bind all individuals together as participants in society by ensuring full employment, equalized education, decent housing, proper health care, and the opportunity to exist without being subject to discrimination. Mays's goal was to open the full benefits of American citizenship to blacks, and he believed that a social democracy, rather than any other type of democracy, would accomplish this goal.

Underlying this embrace of social democracy was a relational and solidaristic view of human nature. Contrary to those who understood the human individualistically and atomistically, Mays viewed humanity as "tied together with an inescapable destiny," a phrase that King would adapt time and again when speaking of "the inescapable network of mutuality." As Mays put it: "What affects one, affects all. What affects the sharecropper in Mississippi, affects the millionaire on Park Avenue. What hurts the poor Negro hurts the poor whites."[18]

Correlatively, Mays did not have a thin understanding of the state's proper role. Mays believed that if the federal government is to establish democracy, it must not leave individuals alone to fend for themselves in providing for their own welfare. Positively stated, he held that the federal government must become actively involved in providing the material resources required for full citizenship. But Mays was no proponent of state socialism; he never suggested that there should be a centralized state bureaucracy that controls productive and distributive processes. Rather, Mays encouraged the state to act cooperatively with private industries in order to establish a truly democratic society. As the key to unlocking Mays's normative vision of the state, then, his notion of democratization suggests that he wanted the state to be much more than a passive entity that leaves individuals alone.

---

[17] Ibid., 531.
[18] Ibid., 533.

The Realism of Walter Chivers

King's later works included not only the sweeping themes of Mays's vision of social democracy, but also the concrete realism of sociologist Walter Chivers, from whom King took seven courses. Unlike Mays and others influenced by the social gospel, Chivers was deeply pessimistic about the onward progress of humanity, especially regarding the issue of race relations. In a 1944 article in which he traced trends of race relations in the South during World War II, Chivers even sharply ridiculed those who claimed, as had metropolitan newspapers and "professional inter-racialists," that racial tensions had become relaxed during the war years. Chivers was especially hard on the black "talented tenth," who "are too solidly insulated by religious ethics, emotionalized intellects and the theories of the sacredness of human personalities to admit to themselves that filthy ways of race prejudice are so deeply rooted in human history as to form a Maginot Line strong enough to defy the war machines of democracy and the preachments of Christian ministry."[19] The "masses of Negroes," in Chivers's view, knew better than the "talented tenth" that race relations had not improved and that a "war" raged in the United States, run largely by Southern white politicians, whose symbol of democracy in action was nothing less than the all-white primary.[20]

Interestingly, Chivers's objects of ridicule included, by implication though not by name, Benjamin Mays, Chivers's own boss, who had helped co-found the Southern Regional Council, an interracial group committed to improving race relations in the South. Chivers claimed that the council was nothing less than "a project in 'gradualism,'" a charge that Mays would most certainly have denied. But if anything met Chivers's wrath, it was gradualism. "Gradualism itself is like fascism in being a restrictive formula which will eventually explode under pressure from within. It is the core of race riots."[21] Racism was too deeply engrained in the United States, in Chivers's estimation, for state-sponsored racism to be conquered by the gradualist approach of the "talented tenth." Rejecting the political practices of the black intelligentsia, Chivers put his hopes for a more fully democratic state in the "masses of

---

[19] Walter Chivers, "Current Trends and Events of National Importance in Negro Education: Trends of Race Relations in the South During War Times," *The Journal of Negro Education* 13/1 (Winter 1944): 107.

[20] Ibid., 108.

[21] Ibid., 109.

Negroes," especially economically-dispossessed youth, whom he saw as increasingly active in the struggle for full democracy.

It was not Black Power, then, that first introduced King to the problems of gradualism within black leadership itself, and it was not the Student Non-Violent Coordinating Committee that first introduced King to the practical wisdom of including dispossessed youth in the civil rights movement. The political realism of Walter Chivers entered King's thought long before Black Power and SNCC even existed.

George Kelsey's Love Ethics

Like Walter Chivers, George Kelsey, whose biblical course King took in his junior year, was sharply critical of liberal Protestantism, even while embracing it. In an article published in 1947, King's junior year, Kelsey took liberal Protestantism to task for adjusting itself too easily to society. "While Protestant orthodoxy has often maintained a rigid orthodoxy between God and the world, liberal Protestantism is monistic."[22] Kelsey argued that Protestantism should always and everywhere stand in judgment of historic persons, groups, and values: "The Protestant ethic must ever condemn all social values, patterns and relationships in light of the absolute demands of the Kingdom."[23] By implication, Kelsey, like Mays, firmly believed that rather than existing unto itself, as if it were somehow isolated from the divine will, the state exists under the moral laws of God.

For Kelsey, the standard by which to measure the state is love, the substantive content of the Protestant ethic. This is the key point that King would include in his own political thought. Kelsey held that the doctrine of Christian love "contains radically transforming power for intergroup relations."[24] Adopting the themes of the Christian realist Reinhold Niebuhr, Kelsey claimed that groups are inner-focused, impelled only by the will-to-power, and thus cooperate only on the grounds of self-interest. But separating himself from Niebuhr, as King would do, Kelsey also insisted on applying the doctrine of Christian love to groups. "The

---

[22] George Kelsey, "Protestantism and Democratic Intergroup Living," *Phylon* 8/1 (1947): 81.

[23] Ibid., 80.

[24] Ibid.

Absolute reference of Protestantism [love] is not confined to the relations of persons, but extends to all historic standards, patterns, values and goals."[25]

Kelsey believed that the Protestant ethic could permeate group life, break down the barriers of groups, and establish interpersonal relations across group lines. At its best, the doctrine of Christian love "destroys intergroup relations and establishes interpersonal relations."[26] Interpersonal relations are not nationalistic, racial, or classist, but are wholly democratic, based on the notion that all individuals are equally worthy in the mind of God. Indeed, Kelsey maintained that the Protestant ethic, with its doctrine of love, properly results in a democracy with a radical equalitarianism.

But Kelsey also counseled realism. Separating himself again from liberal Protestantism, Kelsey drew from Niebuhr's work on sin to warn Protestants that the application of the doctrine of Christian love to intergroup relations faces the obstacle of human sinfulness. As Kelsey put it, "Man is a sinful creature. His vision is only partially clear; and his will is only partially directed."[27] Just so, individuals resist the democracy that the Protestant ethic issues, choosing instead to see themselves or their group as uniquely special in the mind of God. Kelsey's example of human sinfulness was the group of Puritans who, believing themselves to be elect, "developed the stake-in-society theory of government, which is that those who own the most property have a right to be the rulers of society and the determiners of social policy."[28]

Still, Kelsey did not counsel defeatism in the face of sinfulness. As it is theologically shallow to believe that democratic intergroup living can be established with relative ease, he argued, so too is it mistaken to hold that society is "so involved in the sins of the earth that it is incapable of moral salvation."[29] Kelsey was a hopeful democrat who viewed the state not only as an actual sinner but also as a potential force for good.

---

[25] Ibid., 80.
[26] Ibid., 78–79.
[27] Ibid., 80.
[28] Ibid.
[29] Ibid., 81.

Samuel Williams on Communism

A realistic appraisal of the state's resistance to improving the lot of blacks was also forthcoming from Morehouse's Samuel Williams, who taught an introductory philosophy course in which King enrolled during his last year at Morehouse. Like Kelsey and Mays, Williams was an ordained Baptist minister with a strong social conscience. And, especially like Chivers's, Williams's social conscience was quick to go on the offensive regarding what he perceived to be the absence of democracy. In an article published the year after he had King in class, Williams wrote: "Georgia has not yet learned the elementary lesson about democracy—the fact that it is a thing done; it is acted or otherwise it does not exist."[30] Unlike Mays, who wanted to speak of a partial democracy, Williams believed that democracy was nonexistent in Georgia and throughout the South. As he put it, "Georgia, like the rest of the South, has only one effective political party—the Democratic Party. It is the party of segregation, discrimination, disfranchisement and vested interests."[31] Williams also characterized Georgia as a lawless state that permitted lynching to go unpunished and hate groups to exist with impunity. Unhappy with the intransigence of the political powers, Williams even became a leader in the People's Progressive Party of Georgia, a small and politically ineffective party that threw its meager support to the presidential campaign of Henry A. Wallace. Like Chivers, then, Williams spoke of the deep resistance of the state, of the undemocratic character of the state, and of the need to operate out of the political mainstream when attempting to transform state practices—themes that King would express throughout his public life.

Williams was somewhat politically radical, but he was never radical enough that he would embrace communism, the arch nemesis of most Americans in the 1940s and 1950s. In 1949, the year after King left Morehouse, Williams published a Christian critique of communism, in which he noted communism's "moral strength" but evaluated it as unchristian.[32] This point, along with the following themes of Williams's critique, would reappear in King's own critique in later years.

---

[30] Samuel W. Williams, "The People's Progressive Party of Georgia," *Phylon* 10/3 (1949): 227.

[31] Ibid., 226.

[32] Samuel W. Williams, "Communism: A Christian Critique," *The Journal of Religious Thought* 6/2 (1949): 122.

Drawing from Jacques Maritain, a Catholic intellectual on whom King would write a paper while a Crozer student, Williams argued that the "moral strength" of communism grows out of its promise to assist the working class and its efforts to correct the failings of Christianity to liberate humanity. He even suggested that both Christianity and communism have the same goal—the liberation of humanity from oppressive conditions.[33] Further, he claimed that both agree that history is meaningful, that the future can hold bright possibilities for the oppressed, that a class is the bearer of historical destiny, that theory and practice are properly united, and that individuals are to be deeply valued.[34] But Williams also argued that communism faltered in its own mission to liberate the oppressed and that there are serious divergences between communism and Christianity. He especially warned that Christians should steer away from communism's relativism, from its capacity for tyranny and oppression, and from its utopian inclinations, particularly those regarding the emergence of the classless society and the withering away of the state.[35]

Regarding the state, Williams noted that communism views the state as an "evil thing," "an instrument used by the class in power," "the police power of the ruling class," and "the product of the antagonisms which now exist in society."[36] Moreover, he highlighted communnnism's beliefs that once the proletarian achieves power and the instruments of common production become common property, the state will no longer be necessary; its work of asserting the interests of the ruling class will be finished, and thus it will wither away. Williams then critiqued this view of the state, but not by questioning its description of the state as an evil police power of the ruling class. Rather, he questioned whether changes in production would eventually necessitate the withering away of the state. Christianity, he stated, "teaches that even when these changes will have been accomplished, there will yet exist in men the tendency to vanity, pride, love of power for its own sake, selfishness, etc., which will express themselves in other forms and must be eradicated."[37] Williams's point here, which King would adopt, is that the state must continue to

---

[33] Ibid., 131.
[34] Ibid., 132–33.
[35] Ibid., 133–34.
[36] Ibid., 130.
[37] Ibid., 134.

exist in history so that it can check the sinful tendencies of humanity, but his implied point elsewhere is that the state is necessary to secure and serve the economic interests of its citizens.

Williams was also critical of dictators who had transformed the idealism of communnnism into justification of the oppression of dissenters. This is problematic from a Christian perspective because "Christianity explicitly teaches that the only way to treat an opponent is to love him. He is not to be liquidated, exterminated, or annihilated, but loved!" Communism uses a good end (the liberation of humanity) to justify bad means (the oppression of dissenters), but Christianity holds that a "moral end must control the means, that is, must keep the means moral."[38]

Thoreau on Resisting the State

Morehouse is significant for tracing King's understanding of the state not only because of the political views of the professors themselves but also because of an important political essay King read while a Morehouse student, namely, Henry David Thoreau's "Resistance to Civil Government." The essay "moved" King, as he stated in his reflections on Montgomery, and acted as an interpretive tool for analyzing the Montgomery boycott as well as other resistance movements. In accord with Thoreau's work, King wrote: "We were simply saying to the white community, 'We can no longer lend our cooperation to an evil system.'"[39]

Indeed, Thoreau's essay portrays US government (in its state and federal forms) as an evil system, guilty of sanctioning slavery, an unjust war with Mexico, ill treatment of Native Americans, a collapse of church-state separation, unjust imprisonment, and the use of only force and power in its dealings with the citizenry. Thoreau understood government to be the "mode which the people have chosen to execute their will," but also believed that it is "liable to be abused and perverted before the people can act through it," and that legislators, intent on executing their own will, are the very ones who abuse and pervert government of the

---

[38] Ibid., 135.
[39] King, Jr., *Stride Toward Freedom*, 51.

people, by the people, and for the people.[40] Moreover, government, in Thoreau's view, is incompetent and bumbling. In and of itself, government has never furthered the people's business, "but by the alacrity with which it got out of its way."[41]

Thoreau's understanding of the government as evil and incompetent is behind his famous words: "I heartily accept the motto—'That government is best which governs least.'" Thoreau moved beyond this, too, when he stated "That government is best which governs not at all."[42] Thoreau's negative view of government, then, led to his insistence that government, if it is to exist, must be as minimalist in function as possible.

King would never really embrace Thoreau's argument regarding the minimalist state, but he certainly would adapt Thoreau's advice on resisting the state according to the dictates of individual conscience. Indeed, the primary intent of Thoreau's essay is to encourage his neighbors to resist the civil government of the state of Massachusetts, especially on matters related to slavery. Thoreau's advice to abolitionists is that they "should at once effectively withdraw their support, both in person and property, from the government of Massachusetts" and not wait until they gain a majority of dissent. "I think that it is enough if they have God on their side, without waiting for that other one."[43]

In Thoreau's view, the state exists not unto itself but in, with, and under a higher law—a law known through individual conscience. And when the law of the state conflicts with the moral law known in the individual conscience, the individual must follow the dictates of his or her conscience. "The only obligation which I have a right to assume is to at any time what I think right."[44] An individual's sense of right, then, trumps the law of the state. But individuals, Thoreau believed, should not actively resist the state in all cases in which their conscience is in discord with state-sanctioned injustices. "If the injustice is part of the necessary friction of the machine of government let it go, let it go: perchance it will wear smooth—certainly the machinery will wear out." But if the injustice

---

[40] Henry David Thoreau, "Resistance to Civil Government," in *Henry David Thoreau: Reform Papers*, ed. Wendell Glick (Princeton: Princeton University Press, 1973) 63.

[41] Ibid., 64.

[42] Ibid., 63.

[43] Ibid., 74.

[44] Ibid., 65.

"requires you to be the agent of injustice to another, then, I say, break the law."[45] Thus, Thoreau believed that the authority of the state is not absolute but "impure." The state "must have the sanction and consent of the governed. It can have no pure right over my person and property but what I consent to it."[46]

Nevertheless, Thoreau did not present a wholly negative view of government.[47] If one does not submit all government behavior to detailed analysis, he observed, one can conclude that "even this State and this American government are, in many respects, very admirable and rare things, to be thankful for, such as a great many have described them."[48] Thoreau also granted a role for government to play, albeit a minimal one, when he stated: "For government is an expedient by which men would fain succeed in letting one another alone." Far from an anarchist, Thoreau wrote: "I ask for, not at once no government, but *at once* a better government,"[49] one that would allow individual conscience, not majorities, to decide what is right and wrong.[50]

Summary

King's Morehouse experience continued and built upon the understanding of the state that he learned from the three ministers of his childhood and youth. On the one hand, the professors and Thoreau reinforced King's early sense that the state can be a force for evil. Mays

---

[45] Ibid., 73.

[46] Ibid., 89.

[47] I agree with Len Gougeon's argument that Thoreau's understanding of the state was much more than negative and that it certainly was not anarchical. "Thoreau and Reform," in *The Cambridge Companion to Henry David Thoreau*, ed. Joel Myerson (Cambridge: Cambridge University Press, 1995) 202–203. For a contrary view, see John J. Ansbro, *Martin Luther King, Jr.: The Making of a Mind* (Maryknoll: Orbis Books, 1982) 113, who unqualifiedly portrays Thoreau as a "philosophical anarchist." Ansbro fails to note that, in Thoreau's earlier work, he even argued that one of the state's proper functions is to "provide for the education of children who would otherwise be brought up, or rather grow up, in ignorance." Henry David Thoreau, "Whether the Government Ought to Educate," in *Henry David Thoreau: Early Essays and Miscellanies*, ed. Joseph J. Moldenhauer, Edwin Moser, and Alexander Kern (Princeton: Princeton University Press, 1975) 60.

[48] Ibid., 86.

[49] Ibid., 64.

[50] Ibid., 65.

reinforced this view by excoriating the US government for failing to make democracy a reality for blacks in the post-World War I era. Chivers, who was much less optimistic than Mays, reinforced it by highlighting the futility of gradualism in the face of a state resistant to the betterment of black lives. Kelsey reinforced it by noting that the Puritanical theory of government, a "stake-in-society" theory, is not to be unexpected, given a realistic appraisal of the sinful human tendency to resist democracy. Williams reinforced it by noting that Georgia, governed by the Democratic Party, was a state of vested interests—interests inimical to blacks. And Thoreau reinforced it by portraying the Massachusetts and United States governments as evil systems because of their support for slavery and the Mexican War, among other things, and by calling for resistance to the evil governing authorities.

On the other hand, King's Morehouse professors refused an unqualified ethic of resistance by teaching that rather than wholly rejecting the state, King should accept its good elements and encourage it to become a better state than before. Mays affirmed the "partial democracy" of the American state, and proposed the exercise of "poise and restraint" in using the democratic machine to build a more democratic state and society. With a nuanced view of US government, Mays also affirmed the federal government over racist (and undemocratic) state and local governments. Chivers, though more radical than Mays, also never counseled the rejection of the state, but suggested that "the masses" fight for full democracy. Kelsey, too, embraced the democratic state and hoped for its full realization. Williams, the most radical of the Morehouse group, never hoped for the withering away of the state, but affirmed its role in checking the sinful tendencies of humanity. Even Thoreau, who personally desired to "withdraw and stand aloof" from the state and encouraged his neighbors to resist the state as it was, refused anarchy in favor of a state that would serve individual conscience as the highest good. From his Morehouse professors, and even a little from Thoreau, King learned that the state can be not only a force for evil but also a force for the good of humanity.

But the professors and Thoreau did more than simply reinforce what King had learned from his family; they also added to the different dimensions—theological, philosophical, and sociological—of King's developing interpretation of the state. Mays introduced King to the social gospel's notion of "democratization," the act of building a social democracy. For Mays, the state must assume an active role in seeking to bind all individuals together as participants in society by ensuring full employment, equalized education, decent housing, proper health care, and the opportunity to exist without being subject to discrimination. Mays's vision of an activist state thus sharply conflicted with Thoreau's vision of a minimalist state. Chivers also set forth a similar vision of social democracy, but used sociology, rather than theology or philosophy, to advance his view. With a realist's appreciation for the obstinacy and selfishness of the state, Chivers's work also counseled King to be realistic about his expectations of the state—in particular, more realistic than Mays. Chivers even suggested that the "masses of Negroes" might have to explode for the state to become a full democracy. The theologian Kelsey also counseled realism, but, more significantly, introduced King to the idea that Christian love should be the critical measure of any Christian assessment of the state. Williams taught the Marxist belief that "the class in power," not just the white race, uses the state to accomplish its purposes—a lesson that King, Sr., had taught, though not with the theoretical tools of Marxism. And Thoreau laid out a philosophical case for resisting the state, appealing to individual conscience as a higher law than the law of the state.

While at home, King encountered social democracy, realism, and a class-conscious perspective on the state. Morehouse added to this experiential encounter by introducing King to the intellectual arguments, and the theoretical language and history, of theological liberalism, realism, and Marxism. Morehouse taught King to think systematically about his interpretation of the state.

Morehouse, then, prepared King to continue the double attitude towards the state that he learned from his family and church. But it also built upon this attitude by exposing him to, and providing him with, new categories—theological, sociological, and philosophical—in which to think about, and act in response to, the state.

3

AN EMERGING THEOLOGY OF THE STATE,

1948–1951

In the fall following the beginning of the Berlin blockade and the convening of the First General Assembly of the World Council of Churches, Martin Luther King, Jr., began his studies at Crozer Theological Seminary in Chester, Pennsylvania. Although Crozer was a white, northern seminary, there were convergences between Morehouse and Crozer.[1] Like Mays and Kelsey, some Crozer professors were Christian liberals who believed that the practice of politics necessarily followed from the Christian gospel. Crozer professors thus encouraged their students, King among them, to attend to the political implications of their own religious beliefs. The seminarian did exactly that, especially in his senior year, when he took courses in what is now known as Christian ethics. In particular, there are four extant writings from King's Crozer years that offer clues about his developing interpretation of the state.

---

[1] See Taylor Branch, *Parting the Waters: America in the King Years, 1954–1963* (New York: Simon & Schuster, 1988) 70–71.

The Seminarian on the State

One of the earliest papers that King wrote at Crozer addressed, albeit very briefly, the political implications of religion (and the religious implications of the state). In a Hebrew Bible course taught by James Bennett Pritchard, King wrote a paper entitled "The Significant Contributions of Jeremiah to Religious Thought," in which he praised Jeremiah as "a shining example of the truth that religion should never sanction the status quo."[2] Christians, King argued, should follow Jeremiah's prophetic lead and recognize the inappropriateness of supporting the status quo. "How often has religion gone down," King wrote, "chained to a status quo it aligned itself with."[3] Continuing the sociological insight he learned at Morehouse, King also registered a specific complaint with religions that are mere reflections of the will of the state and thus fail to advance the spiritual life of humanity. Borrowing almost verbatim from a book on Jeremiah, King wrote: "Durkheim and other sociologists rejoice to find in each religion simply the reflection of the State's opinion of itself foisted upon the divine, and along this they agree that no advancement can be looked for in spiritual affairs."[4]

In this early Crozer paper, King advanced two related (and undeveloped) points about religious beliefs and the state. First, he noted that, if given the opportunity, the state would attempt to deify its character and functions. For King, this was not good. The state was not God, and when it pretended to be so, it precluded real advancement in spiritual affairs. Second, King highlighted his belief that faithful and good religion challenges the state-sponsored status quo in order to advance the will of God for humanity. Religious beliefs are not for protecting the state in religious cloaks but for challenging it so that the spiritual affairs of humanity may advance as necessary.

Beyond Pritchard's course, King continued to articulate the political implications of his religious beliefs, especially in classes taught by

---

[2] Martin Luther King, Jr., "The Significant Contributions of Jeremiah to Religious Thought," *Called to Serve, January 1929–June 1951*, vol. 1 of *The Papers of Martin Luther King, Jr.*, ed. Clayborne Carson, Ralph E. Luker, and Penny A. Russell (Berkeley: University of California Press, 1992) 194.

[3] Ibid.

[4] Ibid. The book, as reported by the papers project, is T. Crouther Gordon, *The Rebel Prophet: Studies in the Personality of Jeremiah* (New York: Harper & Brothers, 1932) 193.

Kenneth Smith, from whom he took two courses in his senior year. One of the more significant papers of this period is "War and Pacifism," which King wrote in Smith's course on Christianity and society. The focus of this paper is not on the state itself but, as the title indicates, the ethics of war and peace. Nevertheless, King's comments on the topic reveal, often implicitly, his emerging theological thought about the character and purpose of the state.

Declaring that he "cannot accept an absolute pacifist position,"[5] King argued: "A position of absolute pacifism allows no grounds for maintaining even a police force, since there is no real difference in kind between war and police action. Their position logically results in anarchy." In King's view, anarchy is wholly unacceptable: the state must exist, and it has a fundamental obligation to maintain a police force and thereby keep order within its territory. This point was partly an anthropological issue for King. He believed that people are in need of a coercive state just because they are so deeply sinful. Indeed, King argued that a fundamental problem with absolute pacifists is "that they fail to recognize the sinfulness of man."[6] For King, the continuous presence of human sin requires the continuous presence of a coercive state so that anarchy does not break out in society.

King noted an additional political implication of his view of human nature: As a group of sinful people, the state, too, is in need of coercion. King applied this point to his thought on war, allowing for war as a coercive check on the sinful practices of an oppressive state. But he did not view the issue quite so simply, for his budding views understood people and their institutions as not only sinful but also good. Thus, King held, implicitly in the text, that the state is also at least partly good and worthy of affirmation. This meant that war between states, though sometimes justifiable, is never between an entirely good state and an entirely evil state. It also meant that the proper end of war should include reconciliation among the warring states. As King put all this,

It seems to me that we must recognize the presence of sin in man and that it can be done without seeing that there is also good. Since man is so often sinful there must be some coercion to keep one man from injuring his fellows. This is just as true between nations as

---

[5] Martin Luther King, Jr., "War and Pacifism," *Papers*, 1:434.
[6] Ibid., 435.

it is between individuals. If one nation oppresses another a Christian nation must, in order to express love of neighbor, help protect the oppressed. This does not relieve us of our obligation to the enemy nation. We are obligated to threat them in such a way as to reclaim them to a useful place in the world community after they have been prevented from oppressing another. We must not seek revenge.[7]

Given the topic of the paper, King clearly stressed the sinfulness rather than the goodness of the state and its citizens. This emphasis was consistent with the realist perspective to which Smith had introduced King through required readings of the works of Paul Ramsey and Reinhold Niebuhr. Though King cited neither Ramsey nor Niebuhr in this paper, it is doubtless that their realism, with its conviction that humanity is deeply sinful and that the state must respond to this sinfulness by establishing internal and external order, acted as a driving force behind King's own expressed realism.

Nevertheless, the paper reflects King's synthesis of liberal and neo-orthodox views of human nature. King explained this synthesis in "How Modern Christians Should Think of Man," an earlier theological essay. The essay is so important because it is simply impossible to understand King's developing views of the state without exploring his theological understanding of human nature.

In the paper's introduction, King wrote that his "thinking about man is going through a state of transition." Sometimes he leaned towards a "mild neo-orthodox view of man," and other times he leaned towards "a liberal view of man." He traced the former to "certain experiences that I had in the south with a vicious race problem," ones that made it difficult for him "to believe in the essential goodness of man." He traced the latter to the positive experiences he had in the South. "In noticing the gradual improvements of this same race problem, I came to see noble possibilities in nature." He also traced his liberal inclinations to his contact with liberal theologians and his "ever present desire to be optimistic about human nature." With these two leanings—one towards neo-orthodoxy and the other towards liberalism—King decided "to synthesize the best" of both schools of thought, leaving behind neo-orthodoxy's

---

[7] Ibid.

"one-sided generalizations" about the sinfulness of humanity as well as liberalism's failure to recognize the pervasiveness of sin.[8]

The resulting synthesis that King offered included the following very brief arguments about humanity. First, the human person "is neither good nor bad by nature, but has potentialities for either."[9] Second, people are limited insofar as they are constrained by the "laws of nature."[10] Third, people are rational beings, "able to think abstractly." Fourth, the human person is a "free and responsible human being."[11] Fifth, each human person is a sinner. Neo-orthodox theologians, King argued, are right to observe that "many of the ills in the world are due to plain sin." And sixth, the human person is "a being in need of continuous repentance."[12]

This undeveloped synthesis of liberal and neo-orthodox theologies, then, constitutes part of the underpinning of King's understanding of the state in "War and Pacifism." For King, the state is a combination of good and evil, and its role is to recognize and respond to both the goodness and evil present within and beyond its borders. On the one hand, the state must be aware of the pervasiveness of evil and the need to restrain it through police keeping and even war. On the other hand, the state must also recognize that the potential for goodness abounds and that all people and institutions are capable of redemption within the world community.

But it was more than his theological view of human nature that formed his political beliefs in "War and Pacifism." King's doctrine of Christian love played a significant role, too. In the passage cited above, King highlighted the importance of love especially within the life of a Christian nation. He did not clearly express his understanding of "a Christian nation," and so he left unanswered key issues about the role of the state in confessing a particular religion. But he clearly had a sense that a Christian nation (and its state) must, by virtue of its confession to be Christian, allow neighbor-love to inform and give shape to its international politics. For King, to express love of neighbor, the Christian state must assist oppressed states in conducting war against their oppressors. Christian love does not require the state to "turn the other cheek" when

---

[8] Martin Luther King, Jr., "How Christians Should Think of Man," *Papers*, 1:274.
[9] Ibid.
[10] Ibid., 1:276.
[11] Ibid., 1:277.
[12] Ibid., 1:278.

dealing with oppressive states but to coerce them, even through the practice of war.[13] Thus, King believed that Christian love, coupled with an understanding of humanity as sinners, requires the state to include war among its basic responsibilities. Interestingly, King's understanding of the role of love in the life of the state would change significantly in the years to come.

The emerging theological dimension of King's developing views of the state was buttressed by another subject King wrote on under the direction of Kenneth Smith—the political thought of Jacques Maritain. In Smith's course on social philosophy, King wrote a two-page summary of an oral report he delivered on the French Catholic philosopher. The paper itself, though very brief and undeveloped, offers a few more clues about King's developing views. Especially interesting and revelatory are the topics from Maritain's work that King chose to highlight.[14]

The first topic King addressed was Maritain's "analysis of the present situation," his diagnosis that modernity, separated from Christian theological beliefs, is diseased, and that agnosticism, naturalism, and individualism are symptoms of modernity's diseased nature.[15] The implication here, which Maritain explicated in the works that King cited in his bibliography, is that the modern state has no foundations apart from God. The state is not God, but it is a minister of God, a steward entrusted with managing society's goods to benefit the will of God.[16] For Maritain, the authority of the state has its source not in sheer power but in God, who alone is the ultimate source of state authority.[17]

Perhaps King highlighted Maritain's analysis of modernity because its political implications were so consistent with what he had learned at home and at college. Like Maritain, King's earlier teachers had refused to separate the state from what they perceived to be its foundations in God, although King's teachers would not have presented a markedly Catholic

---

[13] See Paul Ramsey, *The Just War: Force and Political Responsibility* (New York: Charles Scribner's Sons, 1968) 150. "Jesus did not teach that his disciples should lift up the face of another oppressed man to be struck again on the other cheek." Ramsey argued that "neighbor-regarding love" allows for war under certain circumstances.

[14] This paper is a report rather than a critical review, and so King's opinions of Maritain's works are largely absent, or, at least, hidden between the lines.

[15] Martin Luther King, Jr., "Jacques Maritain," *Papers*, 1:437.

[16] Jacques Maritain, *Christianity and Democracy* (London: Centenary Press, 1945) 29.

[17] Ibid., 33.

analysis of the separation of state from religion. Further, perhaps King highlighted this view because he liked it and agreed with it—which surely he did, given the connection he drew in "War and Pacifism" between his Christian beliefs and his understanding of the state. Though he did not say so directly in his report on Maritain, King, like Maritain, refused to posit a state separate from God the Creator.

The second topic King highlighted was Maritain's views on communnism. Doing so, King followed the example of his Morehouse professor, Samuel Williams, whose writings on communnnism were clearly inspired by Maritain. In his paper, King briefly summarized Maritain's belief that communnnism itself is symptomatic of both a diseased modernity and a diseased Christianity. On the one hand, King noted Maritain's belief that communnnism is "logically bound up with atheism." The problem with communnnism is not its economic proposal (after all, early Christian communities were economically communistic) but its "absolute rejection of divine transcendence."[18] On the other hand, King summarized Maritain's belief that communnism "originated chiefly through the fault of a Christian world unfaithful to its own principles,"[19] a point that Williams also offered in his Christian critique of communnnism.

Though King did not offer a critical analysis of Maritain's views on communnism, the topic is significant because it reappears in King's later works. Like Maritain (and Williams), King would criticize communnism on specifically theological grounds, taking specific issue with communnism's materialism. But, like Maritain, King would also use his theological beliefs to affirm parts of communnism, and though he would never explicitly affirm communist states, he would point to a democratic-socialist state as exemplary for all of humanity.

Maritain's view on democracy was the third topic that King addressed. First, King tended to Maritain's positive reading of democracy. "When Maritain comes to a discussion of democracy he quite readily speaks of it as the most ideal political system created by the mind of man. Its virtue lies in the fact that it grew out of Christian inspiration. Says Maritain, 'the democratic impulse burst forth in history as a temporal manifestation of the inspiration of the gospel.'"[20] King was

---

[18] Maritain, *Christianity and Democracy*, 54.

[19] King, Jr., "Jacques Maritain," *Papers*, 1:438.

[20] Ibid.

right: Maritain loved democracy, especially if it assumed form in republican states.[21] Maritain also believed that democracy "springs in its essentials from the inspiration of the Gospel and cannot subsist without it."[22] For Maritain, Christianity affirms the unity of the human race, the natural equality of humanity, the inalienable dignity of every human, the dignity of labor and the poor, the importance of God's justice, and the submission of the state to the work of God.[23] And taking its cue from Christianity, he argued, the political philosophy of democracy celebrates inalienable rights of the individual, human equality, political rights of the governed, the state as vicar of the people, the primacy of justice and law in society, and human community.[24] Thus, for Maritain, the essential teachings of Christianity and those of democracy are largely the same, and this similarity gives reason for Christians to embrace democratic states. To be sure, Maritain firmly held that Christianity should not be identified with any one political system or "be enslaved to any temporal regime,"[25] but he clearly favored democracy and democratic states, especially activist ones that seek to secure justice, over any other political system or form of the state.

But Maritain recognized that the existing democratic states of his era were not the best ones possible, and King, who had mentioned this very point in "The Negro and the Constitution," was quick to note Maritain's work on the vices of democracy. Summarizing Maritain on the "tragedy of the democracies," King wrote: "But if democracy has its virtues it also has its concomitant vices, and its vices are found in the fact that it has failed to remain true to its virtues."[26] Maritain's point was nothing less than internal criticism: democratic states failed because they did not follow their own democratic creeds. As Maritain put it, "The tragedy of modern democracies is that they have not yet succeeded in realizing democracy."[27] King found a soul mate in Maritain, for this was King's exact criticism of the state in "The Negro and the Constitution": the state failed because it was not true to the democratic principles espoused in its

---

[21] Maritain, *Christianity and Democracy*, 46.

[22] Ibid., 18.

[23] Ibid., 29.

[24] Ibid., 45.

[25] Jacques Maritain, *Scholasticism and Politics* (London: Centenary Press, 1940) 68. King listed this book, too, in his bibliography.

[26] King, Jr. "Jacques Maritain," *Papers*, 1:438.

[27] Maritain, *Christianity and Democracy*, 17.

founding documents. Maritain's criticism went further, too, for he believed that modern democratic states would not succeed until they remembered their dependence on God.[28] The tragedy of modern democracies, then, was a deeply spiritual one: the democratic state had forgotten that it was not God.

King also noted Maritain's conviction that, for believers, Christianity is a tool with which to criticize the state, even the democratic state. Again, summarizing Maritain, King wrote: "For him, Christianity transcends all political systems, and it can never be made subservient to democracy as a philosophy of human and political life nor to any political form whatsoever." On a related note, Maritain's conception of the proper relationship between church and state is the fourth topic that King briefly highlighted in his summary paper. Noting that Maritain is "far from Catholic in many of his views," King stated that Maritain "has no desire to see the medieval supremacy of Church over state restored." But Maritain, he observed, does have a keen interest in having the church play the role of critic of the state. Indeed, "[h]e deplores the social inertia and reaction which beset so many Catholics."[29] Unlike them, Maritain himself felt free to criticize the state as it assumed form under, for example, General Franco—a criticism for which Maritain incurred a good amount of criticism from his fellow Catholics.[30]

Again, King did not offer a critical analysis of Maritain's call for the church to be a critic of the state in certain circumstances. But this is, in fact, a point with which King was already familiar. At home and college, King had witnessed many a cleric, Borders among them, offer harsh criticisms of the state. More, it is also a point King would adopt the rest of his life. As he would state in his later years, the church should be "the conscience of the state."

At the heart of Maritain's political thought is his conviction that the purpose of the state is to serve the human person in community. As he would put it in later writings, "But man is by no means for the State. The

---

[28] Ibid., 18.

[29] King, Jr. "Jacques Maritain," *Papers*, 1:438.

[30] Ibid., 439. The papers project reports that King borrowed this point, without citation, from William Marshall Horton, *Contemporary Continental Theology: An Interpretation for Anglo-Saxons* (New York: Harper & Brothers, 1938) 50.

State is for man."[31] Maritain believed that the state originated in human sociality—in the human desire to come together to meet the material and spiritual needs required for full human development. Individuals could not achieve their potential without the state, and so they formed the state to help provide and regulate the conditions for full human development. Humanity is not for the state, then; the state is for the common good of humanity. Unsurprisingly, King would directly adapt this Maritainian line in his own later writings on the state.

There is one more extant writing from King's Crozer years that is important for tracing his interpretation of the state. In the same course for which he wrote "War and Pacifism," King also took some crucial notes that reveal his view of the US government and its relationship to capitalism. In particular, King wrote of his conviction that "capitalism has seen its best days in America, and not only in America, but the entire world." Capitalism, he wrote, "has outlived its usefulness" and "has failed to meet the needs of the masses." His evidence for the failure of capitalism consisted of the labor strikes and the demand for "socialized medicine." Further, King predicted that the state would become socialist as soon as labor is "able to place a president in the White House." When this happens, the state will nationalize industry even more and "[t]hat will be the end of capitalism."[32]

These notes reveal King's belief that the state is not only a political entity but also an economic one, tied to a particular economic system as well as an economic class. The state, in his mind, is not a neutral arbiter among various class interests or economic systems. It is an interested entity that supports a particular economic system class. At the time he took these notes, King felt that the US government sponsored capitalism and the capitalists who benefited most in that economic era. But he also felt that the government would, with the interests of labor as a driving force, eventually offer wholehearted support to socialism and to the working class. For King, this transformation to state-sponsored socialism would be a good thing, for state-sponsored capitalism had failed to meet the material needs of the masses.

---

[31] Jacques Maritain, *Man and the State* (Chicago: University of Chicago Press, 1951) 13.

[32] Martin Luther King, Jr., "Notes on American Capitalism," *Papers*, 1:436.

Political Thought at Crozer

King's observation that the state is not only a political entity but an economic one was in accord with the beliefs of his professor, Kenneth Smith, who taught his students that the state is not an institution separate from the market. For Smith, the state and the market "cannot be separated. For government must look to taxes and revenue for its support, and the economic system must look to the government for its legalities and procedures."[33] Smith believed that, given the real interrelation between the state and the market, real social change occurs when both institutions are affected.

In his paper on war, King adapted another lesson emphasized by Smith—that the purpose of the state is to restrain human sinfulness, even through coercive practices. Smith believed that humanity created the state in order to control, limit, and liberate human desires,[34] but he clearly focused on the state's role in acting as a dike against corrupt human nature. Following Paul Ramsey, whose book he used in class, Smith argued that "all social institutions are proof of man's sin."[35] "Government itself," Smith taught, "is the greatest plight of human nature. If men were angels there would be no need for government or the state."[36] For Smith, this meant that the state is required primarily because of the need to restrain human sinfulness. Though King followed Smith in calling upon the state to restrain sin—in fact, his paper on war and pacifism did exactly that—he would never suggest that the primary role of the state is to coerce the citizenry. That point would prove to be much too negative to support his call upon the state to support the beloved community.

Nor would King uncritically adopt the relatively thin understanding of democracy and freedom that Smith espoused in the classroom. Smith taught his class that democracy "places the individual above the state,"[37] and "is that political order which has justice for every human being as its

---

[33] Martin Luther King, Jr., "Class Notes on Christianity and Society," box 112, folder XV 16, 30–31, MLKP, MBU.

[34] Ibid., 27.

[35] Ibid., 25. Paul Ramsey focused on this same issue in chapter 9 of *Basic Christian Ethics* (New York, Charles Scribner's Sons, 1950) 326–66.

[36] Smith took this point most directly from Ramsey, *Basic Christian Ethics*, 327, who drew from James Madison's point about angels and the state.

[37] King, Jr., "Class Notes," MLKP, MBU, 40.

aim."[38] The opposite of the democratic state is the totalitarian state, which institutionalizes a "strong, centralized government under one omnipotent ruler" and encourages statism, the belief system which holds that the state "is not a means to an end but an end within itself," that "the state is higher + greater than individuals," and that individual interests should be subjected to those of the state.[39] Smith claimed that democracy, unlike totalitarianism, respects the people, and the individual person, by embracing two essential beliefs: (1) that ultimate political control should rest with the majority, and (2) that every individual has a right to control his or her own actions as long as they do not seriously impinge upon the freedom of others. Political implications of the latter belief include freedom of speech, freedom of the press, and freedom of assembly. "Theoretically speaking," Smith noted, "the minority should have a right to express itself."[40]

Interestingly, Smith's embrace of democracy, at least as it is listed here, did not include the larger social vision that Mays and Maritain included in their writings. The freedom expressed by Smith was largely freedom from encroachment by the state, rather than freedom for a life of spiritual and material well being. King had already diverged from Smith on this point, choosing instead to follow Mays and Maritain in envisioning democracy as a guarantor of freedom for material well being. But King, who would come to like Maritain's phrase that "the state is for man," would have appreciated Smith's observation about democracy's role in serving humanity (rather than being served by humanity). Further, King would have made special note of Smith's claim about the rights of minorities within democracies. In fact, King would echo Smith in his first speech to the Montgomery crowds, when he would proudly claim that democracy is all about the right to protest.

There is one other key teaching from Smith's class that King would actively embrace throughout his life. Like the black church preachers and the Morehouse professors, Smith taught that Christians have a responsibility to obey the state when it follows the will of God and to disobey it when it runs counter to the divine will. Christians must recognize that ultimate authority belongs to God alone and that the authority of God may trump the authority of the state. On the relation

---

[38] Ibid., 42.
[39] King, Jr., "Class Notes," MLKP, MBU, 38.
[40] Ibid., 40.

between Christians and the state, King noted the following lesson from Smith: "The true Christian has an obligation higher than any other state. When conflict between state and God comes the Christian must obey God rather than man. The Christian has a loyalty to a God beyond the state, to humanity beyond the nation, and to the kingdom of God beyond any social order."[41] King would repeat these biblical phrases hundreds of times as his public life took shape against the powers that be. As noted above, he had already begun to express their theme in his paper for the Pritchard course.

George W. Davis was another professor who proved influential during King's years at Crozer. It was not until his first term of the second year that King first enrolled in a course taught by Davis, but this did not preclude him from taking 34 of his 110 course hours from Davis. King was attracted to Davis in part because he continued the liberal tradition that King had first experienced at Morehouse. Though King would never write about Davis's political views, it is doubtless that some of them found a home in his emerging understanding of the state.

Like Davis, who expressed themes found within Mays's writings, King would speak of the state in relation to the "moral foundations" (or, as Mays put it, "ethical laws") of the world—divine rules and regulations that guarantee the sanctity of individual human life as well as the importance of the common good. For Davis, Christian liberalism holds that all of reality has "moral foundations"[42] which reveal a divine power that "exists to guarantee the sanctity and dignity of human life, the inalienable right of the *individual* to life, liberty, and the pursuit of happiness."[43] As Davis understood them, the moral foundations of reality embrace an absolutism that protects the individual, as well as punishes self-seeking behavior and neglect of the common good.[44]

King would follow Davis not only in adopting this characterization of moral foundations but also in criticizing the state for ignoring its foundations. Davis believed that political powers ignored their foundations, and he found evidence of this in the anti-Semitism of Hitler, in the liquidation programs of Soviet communnism, and in Mussolini's

---

[41] Ibid., 42.

[42] George W. Davis, "Liberalism and a Theology of Depth," *Crozer Quarterly* 28/ 3 (July 1951): 198.

[43] Ibid., 199–200.

[44] Ibid., 200.

argument that the state alone is absolute. Davis condemned all forms of totalitarianism, which, in his view, destroy individuality, ignore God, and embrace a relativistic ethic that seeks the good for only a certain group of men and women. Davis's critical diagnosis was that totalitarianism, ripped away from "universal moorings," would meet disaster.[45] "Moral defects in nations," he wrote, "do lead to national and world disasters."[46]

On a more positive note, King would reflect Davis in arguing that the God of history moves the state to act in accord with the divine will to establish freedom for all—not a freedom from encroachment by others but a freedom for spiritual and material well-being. Davis's liberalism held that God is immanent, active within history, pushing and pulling human society towards a social democracy that would recognize the essential worth and dignity of every human personality. According to Davis, if the state is to roll with the tides of history created by God, it should be actively involved in providing for the social welfare of all the people, especially those on society's margins (children, women, the elderly, and the poor, for example).[47] Providing for the social welfare would allow the state to carry out its essential task—to help create free human personalities. Like King's earlier teachers, then, Davis rejected a minimalist state in favor of a state intensely active in creating a social democracy in which all of the citizenry could enjoy the full benefits, material and social, of their God-given freedom.

The divine will, in Davis's view, is for human life to leave individualism behind and to achieve solidarity. Because the state can unite people in common efforts and goals, the existence of the state itself is testimony to God's desire for human solidarity, especially if the state commits itself to countering the rank individualism evident in public policies that give favorable treatment because of one's lineage, natural abilities, intellect, nationality, race, or financial status. Davis cited numerous examples of such rank individualism throughout history, and included among them "the rugged individualists of our capitalist economy."[48] Like King's earlier teachers, Davis had little tolerance for a capitalism that runs roughshod over human lives, especially those of the

---

[45] Ibid.

[46] Ibid., 203.

[47] George W. Davis, "God and History," *Crozer Quarterly* 20 (January 1943): 24–26.

[48] Ibid., 28.

dispossessed, but great appreciation for social democracies committed to creating equality. On Davis's theological spectrum, though, a world community such as the League of Nations is an even greater expression of the divine will than is an individual state that institutionalizes social democracy.[49] The more social the political community, the more faithful it is to the divine push towards human solidarity. King would eventually express the same point, arguing for a move towards global social democracy.

Davis did more than provide King with substantive depth regarding the relationship between the state and the moral laws of God. He also required King to read Rauschenbusch's *Christianity and the Social Crisis*, a book that deeply influenced King's thought. There are no extant writings from King's Crozer years in which he commented directly on Rauschenbusch's view of the state, but if *Christianity and the Social Crisis* was as important to King as he said it was, then he was certainly familiar with Rauschenbusch's political thought.[50] King's own political thought would converge with and diverge from Rauschenbusch's in a number of areas.

Given his early political lessons, King would have enjoyed Rauschenbusch's point that Jesus and the early church liberated themselves from subjection to the political powers of their day. "Christians," Rauschenbusch wrote, "were citizens of a higher kingdom. The Empire was not their highest good."[51] So it was "neither strange nor reprehensible" that "the spirit of Christianity did not spread only sweet peace and tender charity, but the leaven of social unrest."[52] With this argument in mind, one can begin to understand why King claimed to have been deeply influenced by Rauschenbusch: the latter provided theological leaven for the unrest to come in the civil rights movement.

Rauschenbusch believed that the church must be in "perpetual but friendly" conflict with the state. The church must be in perpetual conflict because the state, in historical reality, always falls short of its purpose of maintaining justice for all. But the church must also be in friendly

---

[49] Ibid., 27–30.

[50] See Martin Luther King, Jr., *Stride Toward Freedom: The Montgomery Story* (New York: Harper & Row, 1958) 91.

[51] Walter Rauschenbusch, *Christianity and the Social Crisis* (New York: Macmillan Company, 1907) 136.

[52] Ibid., 139.

conflict because the state can be an instrument of justice.[53] What Rauschenbusch affirmed, and what King would hope for throughout the civil rights movement, was a church that both critiqued and affirmed the state according to the dictates of the situation.

Rauschenbusch held a relatively high view of the potential within the state. "If men conceive of political duties as a high religious service to man and God," he wrote, "the State can be a powerful agent in the bettering of human life."[54] The high purpose of the state (and the church) is nothing less than "to transform humanity into the kingdom of God,"[55] a "fellowship of justice, equality, and love," a place where violence is foreign and the sharing of social goods among all is familiar.[56] Again, it is easily believable that Rauschenbusch's book left an indelible mark on King's thought. Rauschenbusch's high view of the positive work of the state is nothing less than a foretaste of King's later claim that the purpose of the state is to provide the material conditions required by the beloved community.

On a related note, Rauschenbusch's understanding of the limits of the state also would be reflected in King's comments regarding the limited role of the state in establishing the beloved community. For Rauschenbusch, the state is properly concerned with legislation, but the "influences which really make and mar human happiness and greatness are beyond the reach of the law." Though it can require good behavior, state-sponsored law cannot require a good attitude and spirit in the citizenry. The state cannot make citizens truly moral, that is, good in behavior and attitude.[57] King would say the same about the role of church and state in creating the beloved community.

But King would never travel as far down the road of optimism as had Rauschenbusch. According to the latter, the "primitive attitude of fear and distrust toward the State has passed away. We do not regard the existing civilization and its governments as hostile to Christianity."[58] Clearly, King had already diverged from this point, so much so that he considered his own government to be inimical to the interests of the

---

[53] Ibid., 186–87.
[54] Ibid., 183.
[55] Ibid., 380.
[56] Ibid., 77.
[57] Ibid., 373.
[58] Ibid., 203.

black community. King's church and college, as well as his own experiences on the underside of political history, had instilled within him a clear sense of racism institutionalized within the white corridors of political power. But Rauschenbusch missed the point. Nowhere in *Christianity and the Social Crisis* did he portray the state as a racist entity largely unconcerned with the freedom of minorities.

This is not to say that Rauschenbusch envisioned the state as an angelic being. Though he did not criticize the state for being racist, he did sharply attack its classism. "Politics," he wrote, "is embroidered with patriotic sentiment and phrases, but at bottom, consciously or unconsciously, the economic interests dominate it always." Thus, "political power is simply a tool for the interests of the dominant class."[59] This economic lesson, which King would embrace, also came to King through Karl Marx, whose works he claimed to have studied in late 1949. According to Marx, the modern state has been "purchased gradually by the owners of property by means of taxation, has fallen entirely into their hands through the national debt, and its existence has become wholly dependent on the commercial credit which the owners of property, the bourgeois, extend to it, as reflected in the rise and fall of State funds on the stock exchange."[60] The state, Marx argued, had become separated from the whole of civil society and is now wholly tied to the dominant class. The state "is nothing more than the form of organization which the bourgeois necessarily adopt…for the mutual guarantee of their property and interests." It is "the form in which the individuals of a ruling class assert their common interests." Rauschenbusch and Marx, then, built upon the same lesson taught by Chivers, Williams, Smith, and Daddy King—the power of the state is the power of the dominant class exerting itself politically.

On a related note, Rauschenbusch's embrace of social democracy also would find a home in King's political thought. Like King's tradition, Rauschenbusch wholly embraced democracy as the best form of the state possible, believing that both biblical history and the life of Jesus supported it.[61] More particularly, Rauschenbusch claimed that democracy best reflected the Christian belief in the freedom and equality of

---

[59] Ibid., 254.

[60] Karl Marx, "The German Ideology," in *The Marx-Engels Reader*, ed. Robert C. Tucker (New York: W. W. Norton, 1972) 187.

[61] Rauschenbusch, *Christianity and the Social Crisis*, 2.

humanity. Democracy, with its institutionalization of approximate political equality, allowed people to be good members of their communities, whereas other forms of state divided people falsely, preventing them from acting as a community.

But not just any democracy would do. Rauschenbusch's ideal form of state is a democracy that assures both political and economic equality. Democracy, he held, does not exist when one class can exclude others from political power. "In short," he wrote, "we cannot join economic inequality and political equality."[62] To counter this problem, Rauschenbusch favored a "communistic" state, arguing that the state is already "communistic in its very nature," in the sense that it is "the organization by which people administer their common property and attend to their common interests."[63] This is a good thing; what is troubling is that the state is not wholly communistic. "The unrest and dissatisfaction is all at those points where the State is not communistic."[64] To count the unrest and dissatisfaction, Rauschenbusch highly favored a movement toward a more communistic state, but he also felt that absolute communnism would never be realized and that the best possible state is a democratic-socialist state.[65] Rauschenbusch's embrace of social democracy as the best form of state possible would echo through King years later as he accepted the Nobel Peace Prize, affirming Sweden's government as the model for his own.

But there was one other enduring issue from which King would diverge from (and then converge with) Rauschenbusch—the issue of love and the state. Like Kelsey, the liberal Rauschenbusch believed it proper to criticize the state, as well as other institutions, in light of the love ethic of Jesus. Rauschenbusch did not explicate in great detail what he meant by love, but he did provide a few indicators. "Love," he wrote, "creates fellowship."[66] It creates societies and holds them together without coercion.[67] Love is about offering forgiveness and the opportunity of reconciliation to those from whom we are estranged. Further, love creates the kingdom of God, where humanity recognizes and responds

---

[62] Ibid., 254.

[63] Ibid., 391.

[64] Ibid., 392.

[65] Ibid., 396.

[66] Ibid., 67.

[67] Ibid., 67–68.

appropriately to God as Creator and one another as sisters and brothers. This kingdom of God, a society of love, is the standard against which all institutions, including the state, must be measured. As Rauschenbusch put it: "This would be Christ's test for any custom, law, or institution; does it draw men together or divide them?"[68]

Following Kelsey and Rauschenbusch, King would apply the measure of love when critiquing the state and when encouraging it to reach its potential in creating the beloved community. But, while a Crozer student, King diverged from the ways in which Rauschenbusch had applied love, especially to the problem of war. The liberal Rauschenbusch, unlike the seminarian King, opposed the coercive ways of war and dreamed of a time when war would be no more.[69] King, as noted above, did not express the same dream in "War and Pacifism," but all that would change in the years to come.

King's insistence on granting the justifiability of a police force and even war is especially interesting, given the fact that he had already read the works of Mahatma Gandhi by the time he wrote "War and Pacifism." According to King's own recollections, he delved into Gandhi's life and works during his second year at Crozer, after having heard a lecture on Gandhi by Mordecai Johnson, president of Howard University.[70] Then, in the fall of 1950, King returned to Gandhi's works in a psychology of religion course taught by his favorite professor, George Davis.

King was not an uncritical disciple of Gandhi. Rather, as his seminary works show, King converged with but also diverged from Gandhi's position on the state and state coercion.

Gandhi did not like the state. Commenting on "the duty of disloyalty," Gandhi characterized his own state as "corrupt," "inhuman," and incapable of evoking loyalty.[71] But Gandhi held the same view of all states, finding all of them to be full not only of corruption but also violence and deception. The essence of the state, he held, was "brute force."[72] The state exists by coercing its citizens and others to bend to its

---

[68] Ibid., 71.

[69] Ibid., 350.

[70] King, Jr., *Stride Toward Freedom*, 96.

[71] Mahatma Gandhi, *The Moral and Political Writings of Mahatma Gandhi*, 3 vols., ed. Raghavan Iyer (Oxford: Clarendon Press, 1987) 3:110.

[72] Ibid., 3:127.

will. "It perishes, if it does not."[73] Sometimes the force is wholly visible to the people, but most times the state masks it through civil and criminal courts.[74]

The state—corrupt, violent, and deceptive—is about as far from God and truth as anything could ever be. The state is not God, Gandhi held, and so it is not truth.[75] What is more, as Raghavan Iyer has observed, Gandhi believed the state to be "soulless and unguided by conscience."[76] Indeed, no state, including Western democratic states, escaped Gandhi's scathing critiques. "Western democracy as it functions today," he wrote, "is diluted Nazism or Fascism. At best it is merely a cloak to hide the Nazi and the Fascist tendencies of imperialism."[77]

For Gandhi, the evil character of the state means that individuals should never treat the state as if it were divine or infallible. Individuals have a duty to be disloyal to the evil state, especially because the state crushes individual freedom.[78] Faced with an evil state—a state that knows neither love nor justice—the individual has an obligation to be nonviolently disloyal. But, what is more, the evil character of the state means that the ideal situation would actually exclude the existence of the state. Gandhi's ideal political world is "enlightened anarchy," where everyone is his or her own ruler. "In the ideal state therefore there is no political power because there is no State."[79] For Gandhi, only a stateless society would be the ultimately free society where individuals could exercise their consciences freely.

But Gandhi realized that "the ideal is never fully realized in life," especially given the existence of the imperfections of humanity.[80] So he favored what he thought was the best possible option: a decentralized, nonviolent, and democratic state. Rather than favoring a centralized state, which he believed took precious freedom away from the individual, Gandhi favored a loose federation of self-governing villages whose structure would resemble "an oceanic circle whose circle will be the

---

[73] Ibid., 3:99.

[74] Ibid., 3:127.

[75] Ibid., 3:29.

[76] Ibid., 3:6.

[77] Quoted in *Gandhian Concept of State*, ed. Biman Bihari Majumdar (Calcutta: M. C. Sarkar & Sons, 1957) ii.

[78] *The Moral and Political Writings of Mahatma Gandhi*, 3:96.

[79] *The Moral and Political Writings of Mahatma Gandhi*, 1:399.

[80] Ibid., 1:400.

individual always ready to perish for the village, and the latter to perish for the circle of villages, till the whole becomes one life composed of individual."[81] In these self-governing villages, the individual would be, as J. P. Suda puts it, "almost his own ruler."[82] Further, the governance of the villages would be nonviolent. There would more than likely be a police force, but its ranks would be "composed of believers in non-violence. They will be servants, not masters, of the people.... The police force will have some kind of arms, but they will be rarely used, if at all."[83] Decentralized and nonviolent, the best possible state would also be democratic in the sense that each person, even the untouchables, would be his or her own ruler, not in the sense that the majority wins.[84]

The extant writings from Crozer do not at all demonstrate that King was Gandhian in any substantive sense on the issue of the state and state coercion. To be sure, King's political thought converged with Gandhi's in the sense that both recognized that corruption occupied a significant place within the character of the state. But the seminarian (and later) King never subscribed to Gandhi's sense that corruption totally pervaded the state. For Gandhi, the state was all sin. But for King, the state, like all people, was both a force for good and a force for evil. On a related note, King, unlike Gandhi, never saw virtue in the notion of a stateless society. In King's view, the state is a necessary (and potentially positive) player in establishing a just and free society.[85] Indeed, the state's coercive role is especially necessary given the existence of sinful people. Whereas Gandhi hoped for a nonviolent state, King never granted validity to the notion; a nonviolent state would have been a fanciful notion to the realist seminarian. Finally, while King respected Gandhi's emphasis on human

---

[81]Quoted in J. P. Suda, "The Gandhian Concept of Democracy and Freedom," in *Gandhian Concept of State*, 112. Gandhi also liked to draw from David Thoreau's "On Civil Disobedience," which King had read at Morehouse, when discussing his preference for a minimalist state. In particular, Gandhi liked to extract Jefferson's and Thoreau's statement that the best government is the one that governs least. See *The Moral and Political Writings of Mahatma Gandhi*, 3:18.

[82] J. P. Suda, "The Gandhian Concept of Democracy and Freedom," 112.

[83] *The Moral and Political Writings of Mahatma Gandhi*, 2:436.

[84] See Bodh Raj Sharma, "The State in Gandhian Philosophy," in *Gandhian Concept of State*, 123–24.

[85] I am in full agreement with Ansbro, *The Making of a Mind*, 142. "In contrast to Gandhi," Ansbro writes, "King arrived at the conviction that the federal government could and should do more for blacks than they could do for themselves."

freedom, he refused to set forth the Gandhian view that the freedom of the individual is the highest moral good without qualification. Nevertheless, as is well known, the thought of King would deeply converge with Gandhi on the issue of nonviolent disobedience.

Summary

King's own statements on the state while a student at Crozer reveal continuity with those he had made earlier in "The Negro and the Constitution." As a seminarian, King expressed the dialectical attitude towards the state that he had first embraced in the high school speech. But the writings of the seminarian also show a marked evolution, especially in their theological depth. As a budding theologian, King carefully connected his thoughts about the character and function of the state to his theological understanding of people and God. This is not to say that King did not do so at all in high school, but only that, as a seminarian, he deepened the connection and made it more explicit and systematic than before. Indeed, it is impossible to understand King's interpretations of the character and function of the state without attending to his theological anthropology and his doctrine of God.

King's interpretation of the character of the state was deeply theological. In his view, the character of the state, like the character of the human person, is good and evil. Like all people, the state is neither an all-good entity that citizens must accept without qualification nor an all-evil entity that they must reject wholeheartedly. Moreover, King recognized that sometimes the character of a particular state weighed more heavily in favor of either good or evil. Indeed, in "War and Pacifism," King sounded much more like a Christian realist than a Christian liberal in his assumptions, implicit and explicit, about the pervasiveness of evil in humanity and in the character of the state.

As a seminarian, King also held that the character of the state is human, not divine. Hence, King implicitly registered, in the paper on Jeremiah, his dissatisfaction with the state that tries to deify itself and its beliefs so as to establish order in society. King's doctrine of God informed him that God alone is Creator and that all things human, including the state, must recognize their subservience to God.

King also relied heavily on his theology to explicate part of his understanding of the proper functions of the state. The seminarian's theology led him to argue that the sinfulness present in humanity requires the presence of a state that will keep internal and external order. In his realist view, a proper function of the state is to prevent sinful people from causing sinful anarchy within the state and in the world community. Unlike a hardcore realist, however, King did not believe that this function is the state's primary one. But King did not grant the validity of war in particular just because of his theological view of human nature; he also believed that to express love of neighbor, a Christian state must prevent external predation and terror.

That is the negative side of the seminarian's understanding of the proper function of the state. Positively, King also held, in his notes on capitalism, that the good state will meet the economic needs of the masses. Unfortunately, King did not unpack this point while at Crozer, either with or without the assistance of theology. But it is doubtless that his theology, informed in part by the theological traditions of both Morehouse and Crozer, provided the underpinning of this understanding of the state's proper functions. To be sure, behind this statement are the works of such theologians as Benjamin Mays, George Kelsey, Samuel Williams, George Davis, and Walter Rauschenbusch—all of them believers in a social democracy.

Also underlying King's understanding of the proper functions of the state, of course, is the theological conviction that King learned at home, at Morehouse, and at Crozer—that under God all persons are free and equal. For King, then, keeping order was important because it safeguarded God-given freedom, and meeting the needs of the masses was important because it established the equality humans already enjoyed in the eyes of God.

The deeply theological dimension of King's understanding of the state is not the only mark of evolution to note. King's seminary writings also reveal a Marxist interpretation of the state that King did not fully express as a student in high school. In his notes on capitalism, there is clearly a new recognition that the state supports a particular economic system as well as a particular economic class. As a student in high school, King had known that the state was racist, and, as a seminarian, King began to express his belief that the state was also classist. This evolution was the result of King's years at Crozer, where he read the works of Marx and Rauschenbusch, at Morehouse, where Williams taught the Marxist belief that the class in power uses the state to accomplish its purposes, and at home, where Daddy King believed that city government always protected the interests of Atlanta's business class. King also began to express a satisfaction with the passing of state-sponsored capitalism and the concomitant rise of state-sponsored socialism.

Finally, King himself experienced an evolution just in terms of exposure to additional arguments about the state. The writings of Jacques Maritain, for example, exposed King not only to a discussion on the relationship between church and state but also to the argument that the origins of the state lie in the sociality of the created human person—an argument that would reappear in King's graduate years. Smith taught King about theological realism and about the interrelations between the state and the market. The liberal theologian Walter Rauschenbusch and Mahatma Gandhi and others exposed King to the argument that war is not a proper function of the state—another argument that would reappear at Boston. The democratic socialist Rauschenbusch also further exposed King to the thought of Marx and to a developed argument for democratic socialism.[86] A variety of authors offered additional theoretical and theological support for King's acceptance of democracy as the best form of the state; Kelsey, in particular, claimed democracy to be the direct result of a God active in history. Kelsey also pushed the liberal notion that the state is not an atomized entity but an integral part of the world community. King would eventually comment on all of these additional arguments.

---

[86] See Adam Fairclough, "Was Martin Luther King a Marxist?" *History Workshop Journal* 15 (Spring 1983): 117–25. Fairclough argues that King's "hostility to excessive materialism, and his concern for the poor and the oppressed, owed more to the Social Gospel than to Marxist ideology" (122). Unfortunately, Fairclough's argument does not attend to King's understanding of the state as classist—an understanding he derived from Daddy King, Rauschenbusch, the early Niebuhr, and Marx. Was King a Marxist? If by Marxist one means the insistence on viewing the state as classist, then King, my study will show, certainly expressed Marxist inclinations.

4

ENCOUNTERING REALISM, COUNTERING REALISM

1951–1955

During his last year at Crozer, King chose Boston University as the place where he would pursue his doctorate. The choice was not especially surprising, primarily because Boston was home to Edgar S. Brightman, a theological personalist whose liberal writings had captured the favored attention of Crozer's professors, especially George Davis, King's mentor and adviser.[1] Unfortunately, there are few extant writings from King's years at Boston that shed light on his emerging theological understanding of the state. Still, the writings are important, and this chapter will explore them, as well as the various interpretations of the state that King encountered while a graduate student, particularly the Christian realism of Reinhold Niebuhr and the theological personalism of King's professors at Boston University.[2]

---

[1] See Taylor Branch, *Parting the Waters: America in the King Years, 1954–1963* (New York: Simon & Schuster, 1988) 90–91; "Introduction," in *Rediscovering Precious Values, July 1951–November 1955,* vol. 2 of *The Papers of Martin Luther King, Jr.,* ed. Ralph E. Luker, Penny A. Russell, and Peter Holloran (Berkeley: University of California Press, 1994) 4–5.

[2] For more on Christian realism, see Robin Lovin, *Reinhold Niebuhr and Christian Realism* (Cambridge: Cambridge University Press, 1995). For more on Boston

Encountering the Realism of Reinhold Niebuhr

In his second semester at Boston University, King wrote a paper on Reinhold Niebuhr for a systematic theology course taught by L. Harold DeWolf. The paper, "Reinhold Niebuhr's Ethical Dualism," is more of a report than a review, but it is nevertheless helpful for tracing King's views.

After referring to Niebuhr as "the brilliant and influential theologian," King began his paper with a summary of the pro-socialist sentiment that Niebuhr expressed in *The Contribution of Religion to Social Work.* In particular, King highlighted Niebuhr's belief that modern industrial civilization confronts "appalling" economic injustices; that economic power has "'become the source of more injustice than any other, because the private ownership of the productive processes and the increased centralization of the resultant power in the hands of a few, make inevitably for irresponsibility'"; that private enterprise alone cannot provide adequate housing for the poor; that, given the failures of reason and sentimental religion, the problem of economic injustice can be solved "'only by setting the power of the exploited against the exploiters'"; and that the future of industrial civilization belongs to the modern proletarian.[3]

After highlighting Niebuhr's view of the injustices of modern civilization, King then attended to Niebuhr's well-known distinction between "moral man and immoral society."[4] "He observed," King wrote, "a great distinction between the relatively decent, good behavior of man as an individual and man as society." Summarizing an important passage from *Moral Man and Immoral Society,* King noted Niebuhr's emphasis on the

> fact of the morality of man the individual, and the immorality of man the collective. Man the individual is natively equipped with certain unselfish impulses. He also has a conscience which is his sense of obligation to what he judges to be good. And yet, when men engage in collective activity they are overwhelmed by moral inability.

---

personalism, see *The Boston Personalist Tradition in Philosophy, Social Ethics, and Theology,* ed. Paul Deats and Carol Robb (Macon GA: Mercer University Press, 1986).
    [3] King, Jr., "Reinhold Niebuhr's Ethical Dualism," *Papers,* 2:142.
    [4] Ibid.

The goodness of the individual man in his immediate relationships disappears when he acts as a member of a group.[5]

The implication here, which King did not draw out but would have noted in his reading, is that Reinhold Niebuhr put great emphasis on the pathology of the state, a collective entity. Niebuhr's emphasis is especially visible in a chapter he wrote for *Moral Man and Immoral Society* on the morality of nations.[6] He began his analysis with a very simple sentence: "The selfishness of nations is proverbial."[7] Niebuhr then went on to describe in great detail the extraordinary immorality of the state. The state, he argued, is not wont to sacrifice its own interests, either short-term or long-term, for the benefit of other states. Without knowing the other's needs directly, a state relies more on its own self-interest as a guide and norm for state action. But even with an increase in communication, Niebuhr held, states would still be far from moral. The state simply lacks a reasonable restraint with sufficient power to criticize and fully check its selfish impulses.[8] What is more, the state's use of force to hold society together, the selfish use of state power by groups who wield the weapons of coercion, and the "unqualified character" of individual patriotism all add to the selfishness of the state.[9] The state is not merely selfish, though; it is also deceptive, hypocritical, and classist.[10] The state is so classist that "economic warlords"[11] control not only the market but also the state's instruments of coercion,[12] with the result being that "political power has been made more responsible to economic power."[13]

Niebuhr offered a stinging critique of the state in his other major works as well. In volume one of *The Nature and Destiny of Man*, a book

---

[5] Ibid., 2:143.

[6] In the beginning of the chapter, Niebuhr drew a proper distinction between "nation" and "state." But he decided, for the purposes of the chapter, to use the terms interchangeably.

[7] Reinhold Niebuhr, *Moral Man and Immoral Society* (New York: Charles Scribner's Sons, 1932) 84.

[8] Ibid., 85.

[9] Ibid., 89–95.

[10] Ibid., 96.

[11] Ibid., 5.

[12] Ibid., 129–30.

[13] Ibid., 15.

in King's bibliography, Niebuhr set forth perhaps his clearest expression of the pathology of groups, including the state. "The group," he wrote, "is more arrogant, hypocritical, self-centered, and more ruthless in the pursuit of its ends than the individual."[14] And the egotism of groups, he claimed, is most visible in the state's efforts to seize absolute authority within society.[15] The state is full of sinful pride and idolatrous pretension, and not just because of its desire to survive, either. Niebuhr believed that the egotism of states "is a characteristic of the spiritual life," the evidence of which is its pride, contempt, hypocrisy, lust for power, and its claim of moral autonomy.[16]

Nevertheless, it would be far too simplistic to argue that Niebuhr saw the state as only a sinner. Indeed, King rightly noted in his paper, in a section entitled "The Inevitability of Government," that the realist Niebuhr viewed the state as necessary. For Niebuhr, King wrote,

> government is very necessary, for men inevitably corrupt their potentialities of love through a lust for self-security which outruns natural needs. Men must be restrained by force, else they will swallow up their neighbors in a desperate effort to make themselves secure. In this sense government is approved of God. 'Government is divinely ordained and morally justified because a sinful world would, without the restraints of the state, be reduced to anarchy by its evil lusts.' The force of sinfulness is so stubborn a characteristic of human nature that it can only be restrained when the social unit is armed with both moral and physical might.[17]

As King rightly acknowledged, Niebuhr grounded his belief in the inevitability of the state in his theological belief in the inevitability of human sin: the state is necessary just because sin is so pervasive. Following Luther and Hobbes, who followed the Apostle Paul and others, the realist Niebuhr understood the state partly as a dike against sin. Niebuhr even referred to the state as a "principle of order" whose use of

---

[14]Reinhold Niebuhr, *Human* Nature, vol. 1 of *The Nature and Destiny of Man* (New York: Charles Scribner's Sins, 1941) 208.

[15] Ibid., 1:209.

[16] Ibid., 1:211.

[17] King, Jr., "Reinhold Niebuhr's Ethical Dualism," *Papers*, 2:147.

power and coercion rightly prevents internal and external anarchy.[18] Faced with the inevitability of social conflict, as well as the historical failure of reason and religion to counter the brutal character of humans in society, the state must depend upon power and coercion if it is to prevent anarchy from emerging. "While no state can maintain its unity purely by coercion," he wrote, "neither can it preserve itself without coercion."[19]

It is important to emphasize that Niebuhr insisted on viewing the state not as either immoral or necessary but as both immoral and necessary. Both views of the state, he believed, must be held in tension. King noted this tension in another summary statement:

> Niebuhr makes it quite clear that government, although holy as an instrument for restraining the sinful, must never be looked upon as divine. The individual's reverence for government extends only as far as the purpose for which that unit was created. When the government pretends to be divine, the Christian serves God rather than man. The Christian must maintain a 'dialectical' attitude toward government while the collective ego remains within its bounds, while being critical whenever these bounds are overpassed.[20]

King was right to highlight the double attitude. On the one hand, Niebuhr understood the state as an ordinance of God. Insofar as it uses its God-given power to prevent anarchy, the state is the proper object of respect and devotion. On the other hand, Niebuhr emphatically claimed that the state is not God and that its power is far from divine. In this sense, the state is not the proper object of ultimate allegiance and devotion. The state that recognizes its human qualities and its limited functions deserves qualified human allegiance, but the state that pretends to be God by absolutizing its own nature and functions deserves condemnation and even rebellion.[21]

---

[18]Reinhold Niebuhr, *Human Destiny*, vol. 2 of *The Nature and Destiny of Man* (New York: Charles Scribner's Sons, 1943) 267.

[19]Niebuhr, *Moral Man and Immoral Society*, 3.

[20] King, Jr., "Reinhold Niebuhr's Ethical Dualism," *Papers*, 2:147.

[21] For more on Niebuhr's dialectical approach, see Niebuhr, *The Nature and Destiny of Man*, 2:269.

After attending to Niebuhr's dialectical response to the state, King then noticed a nuance in Niebuhr's thought. As King put it: "While Niebuhr contends that the ambiguity of government is deeply embedded in every conceivable political form, he makes it clear that some political cohesions expose a greater surface of self-criticism than others. Critical insight reveals, he affirms, that the most desirable cohesion is democracy, even as the least desirable is totalitarianism."[22]

King was correct to observe that, for Niebuhr, democracies are the best possible states in existence. In *The Children of Light and the Children of Darkness*, a book King drew from in his very brief discussion of Niebuhr's view of democracy, Niebuhr offered his classic defense of democracy, which has both positive and negative dimensions. Positively, Niebuhr believed that, with its provision of conditions for freedom and order, democracy is the best possible political structure for recognizing and affirming the human as free and ordered in social relations. Negatively, Niebuhr stressed the need to check the power of the state itself. In Niebuhr's view, "one perennial justification for democracy is that it arms the individual with political and constitutional power to resist the inordinate ambition of rulers, and to check the tendency of the community to achieve order at the price of liberty."[23]

King cited this exact argument in his section on Niebuhr's understanding of democracy, and then explicated it further with a lengthy quotation from volume 2 of *The Nature and Destiny of Man*, in which Niebuhr praised democratic societies for embodying "the principle of resistance to government within the principle of government itself."[24] In other words, King highlighted Niebuhr's perception of the need to arm individuals with the power of resistance to the rules of the state. Summarizing Niebuhr, King wrote: "If society is not empowered with rights to free expression, it will explode from internal combustion."[25]

Though he affirmed democracy, Niebuhr fully recognized that historical democracies were not the ideal. This did not escape King's attention. "Niebuhr," King wrote, "makes it clear that a perfect democracy is just as impossible to reach as either a perfect society or a perfect

---

[22] King, Jr., "Reinhold Niebuhr's Ethical Dualism," *Papers*, 2:147.

[23] Ibid., 46–47.

[24] Niebuhr, *The Nature and Destiny of Man*, 2:268.

[25] King, Jr., "Reinhold Niebuhr's Ethical Dualism," *Papers*, 2:148.

individual."[26] Indeed, in *Moral Man and Immoral Society*, Niebuhr emphasized that the vital interests of the democratic state are often those of the dominant class. With Marx and Rauschenbusch, Niebuhr believed that "the creeds and institutions of democracy have never become fully divorced from the special interests of the commercial classes who conceived and developed them."[27] The economic power of the commercial classes either "deifies the authority of the state or it bends the institution of the state to its own purposes," with the result that political power, even in democracies, answers to economic power.[28] Still, tainted democracies are democracies, albeit ones in need of reformation, that is, the shifting of the balance of powers.

The balance of powers is the last topic King addressed in his rather undeveloped section entitled "The Inevitability of Government." In the beginning of his discussion, King quoted one of Niebuhr's famous comments on politics, justice, and power. "The very essence of politics is the achievement of justice through equilibria of power. A balance of power is not conflict, but a tension between opposing forces underlies it. Where there is tension there is potential conflict, and where there is conflict there is potential violence."[29]

For Niebuhr, it is not the responsibility of the state (or, for that matter, any other entity) to establish love, perfect love, for that is impossible in a world of sin. In *Moral Man and Immoral Society*, King would have read of Niebuhr's belief that love, or, more particularly, Christian love, is an ideal that absolutizes "disinterestedness" and imparts "transcendent worth to the life of others."[30] Wholly unselfish, love "submits to any demands, however unjust, and yields to any claims, however inordinate, rather than assert self-interest against another."[31] Moreover, love even denies the validity of assertions on behalf of others. As Harlan Beckley puts it in his summary of Niebuhr's ideal, "Love is interested in the well-being of others, but it cannot assert itself on behalf

---

[26] Ibid.

[27] Niebuhr, *Moral Man and Immoral Society*, 14.

[28] Ibid., 15.

[29] Niebuhr, *An Interpretation of Christian Ethics* (New York: Meridian Books, 1956) 189.

[30] Niebuhr, *Moral Man and Immoral Society*, 71.

[31] Ibid., 264.

of their interests."[32] Wholly unselfish and wholly nonresistant, this ideal transcends what is possible within a sinful world.

Nevertheless, Niebuhr argued that it is possible to approximate love in society, that approximating love is the role of justice, and that achieving justice is the proper work of the state. As Beckley notes about Niebuhr's view, "Justice is…a *strategy for approximating the social ideal of love*."[33] King noted the difference between love and justice in Niebuhr's thought in a couple of paragraphs he devoted to the topic.

> Niebuhr freely admits that justice is morally inferior to equality in love…Justice is a thisworldly value; *agape* is an eternal value which only the initiated understand and strive for.
>
> Niebuhr makes it quite clear, however, that justice is never discontinuously related to love. Justice is a negative application of love. Whereas love seeks out the needs of others, justice limits freedom to prevent the infringement upon the rights and privileges of others. Justice is a check (by force, if necessary) upon ambitions of individuals seeking to overcome their own insecurity at the expense of others. Justice is love's message for the collective mind.[34]

. For Niebuhr, love needs justice in order to affect a deeply sinful world. "Yet," as Lebacqz writes on Niebuhr, "love also transcends, fulfills, negates, and judges justice."[35] Just so, love also transcends, fulfills, negates, and judges the proper work of the state—achieving justice. The proper work of the state is not to establish perfect justice, for that is nothing less than perfect love. But the proper work of the state does entail establishing a relative justice that includes concrete standards, including social equality. For Niebuhr, equal justice is the most important, and best possible, goal that a state can have, even more important than peace.[36] The importance of equal justice as a political goal is grounded in its

---

[32] Harlan Beckley, *Passion for Justice: Retrieving the Legacies of Walter Rauschenbusch, John A. Ryan, and Reinhold Niebuhr* (Louisville: Westminster/John Knox Press, 1992) 202.

[33] Ibid., 210.

[34] King, Jr., "Reinhold Niebuhr's Ethical Dualism," *Papers*, 2:145.

[35] Karen Lebacqz, *Six Theories of Justice: Perspectives from Philosophical and Theological Ethics* (Minneapolis: Augsburg, 1986) 86.

[36] Reinhold Niebuhr, *Moral Man and Immoral Society*, 235.

inextricable connection to love, "for equal justice is the approximation of brotherhood under the conditions of sin."[37]

On a practical level, equal justice is a matter not of giving to each according to her or his need but of prescribing, in Beckley's words, "whose interests are to be constrained in order to satisfy other interests."[38] In society, the unequal distribution of goods yields groups with more power (those with the most and most-valued goods) and those with less power (those with the fewest and least-valued goods), creating instability and volatility.[39] This unstable and volatile situation, in Niebuhr's view, requires "an organizing center" that must arbitrate, manipulate, and coerce the various sources of power.[40] For Niebuhr, the state is the proper organizing center.

As the organizing center, the state must be able and willing to use the means required to establish equal justice. Niebuhr argued that not all means work. Reason, for example, is far from sufficient in establishing justice, partly because it is tainted by sin and partly because it addresses only part of life. Religion is also extremely limited, though for different reasons, in its ability to establish equal justice. Given the historical failure of reason and religion to counter the selfishness of humanity, as well as the inevitability of social conflict, the state can establish a tolerable equilibrium only by relying on forcible means. As a structure of justice, then, the state has the responsibility to recognize the limitations of reason and religion and to rely on power and coercion when establishing "a tolerable equilibrium" of power among contending groups.[41]

King reported on a number of themes from Niebuhr's understanding of the state, but, unfortunately, his closing critical evaluation of Niebuhr, only two-paragraphs long, skimmed over most of these topics. But King did offer a few general critical comments worth highlighting. First, he praised Niebuhr: "The strength of Dr. Niebuhr's position lies in its critique of the easy conscience and complacency of some forms of perfectionism. He is right, it seems to me, in insisting that we must be realistic regarding the relativity of every moral and ethical choice. His analysis of the complexity of the social situation is profound indeed, and

---

[37] Reinhold Niebuhr, *The Nature and Destiny of Man*, 2:254.

[38] Beckley, *Passion for Justice*, 213.

[39] Ibid., 2.

[40] Niebuhr, *The Nature and Destiny of Man*, 2:266.

[41] Ibid., 2:265.

with it I would find very little to disagree."[42] King lifted the first sentence directly from an article by Walter Muelder, but the sentiment—an appreciation for Niebuhr's call to Christians to be responsible for engaging the world directly and consistently—is certainly in line with the preaching King heard as a youngster.[43] Especially noteworthy in the passage, though, is King's apparent embrace of Niebuhr's ethics, an embrace that led King to follow Niebuhr in refusing an absolute prohibition against the use of coercion when discussing the responsibilities of the state to a sinful world.

The last sentence of King's evaluation, though not especially clear, seems to indicate at least two points. First, given his introduction to the paper, King's affirmation of Niebuhr's analytical work seems to imply appreciation for Niebuhr's analysis of the economic injustices of modern civilization—the pro-socialist sentiment expressed in *The Contribution of Religion to Social Work*.[44] The young Niebuhr's socialist tendencies were not new themes for King to ponder, but what Niebuhr offered was a heavily intellectual supplement to the earlier teachings of Chivers, Rauschenbusch, and others who commented on the relation between the state and the market.

Second, Niebuhr's realism also seems to be a target of King's appreciation in his last statement of praise. Given his earlier teachings and experiences, King would have felt an affinity for Niebuhr's realist interpretation of the state. King did not need Niebuhr to tell him that the state is far from sainthood, but what Niebuhr offered, especially in the chapter on the immorality of states, was a sophisticated intellectual analysis of the immorality of the state—an analysis that supplemented earlier lessons. Unlike King's earlier teachers, Niebuhr explained, on an intellectual level, reasons for the state's pride, contempt, hypocrisy, and false sense of independence.

Further, King would have appreciated Niebuhr's understanding of the state as divinely ordained. Like Niebuhr, King was aware of the

---

[42] King, Jr., "Reinhold Niebuhr's Ethical Dualism," *Papers*, 2:150.

[43] The Walter G. Muelder article that King adopts is "Reinhold Niebuhr's Conception of Man," *The Personalist* 26 (July 1945): 291–92. See editor's fn.3 in "Reinhold Niebuhr's Ethical Dualism," *Papers*, 2:150.

[44] See Douglas Sturm, "Martin Luther King, Jr., as Democratic Socialist." *Journal of Religious Ethics* 18 (Fall 1990): 90. Sturm notes that King, Jr., in "Reinhold Niebuhr's Ethical Dualism," "appropriated ideas from some of Niebuhr's early, pro-socialist texts," and that King "appears to accept" Niebuhr's socialist diagnosis.

Christian-historical perspective that envisioned the state as a divinely ordained dike against sin; this much he hadlearned from his earlier studies, including those of Paul Ramsey. In addition, as one who had experienced oppression from sinful citizens, King would have affirmed Niebuhr's understanding of the state as a principle of order. But Niebuhr offered something new here: a detailed theological underpinning that supported the need for the state as a principle of order. King did not need Niebuhr to tell him that the state should be a dike against sin because humanity is sinful; King's own experiences had encouraged the adoption of a realist perspective on the state's need to address human sin. But Niebuhr must have helped King clarify, on an intellectual level, the type and degree of sin that requires the state to be a principle of order.

Niebuhr's realist view of human nature, which King had first experienced at Crozer, was not lost on King, either. In fact, in an early Boston paper, a Niebuhrian King faulted liberal Christian theologians for failing to recognize the depth and pervasiveness of human sinfulness.[45] Indeed, in a later paper, King portrayed Niebuhr's view of human nature, with its focus on sin, as "the necessary corrective" to liberalism's optimism. To back his point, King pointed to "the brutal logic of events" he witnessed in history. "Instead of assured progress in wisdom and decency, man faces the ever present possibility of swift relapse not merely to animalism but into such calculated cruelty as no other animal can practice."[46] The graduate student also noted, in his doctoral qualifying exams, that the Bible itself refuses to downplay the importance of sin. "Concerning the extent of sin," King wrote, "the Bible is almost unanimous in affirming its universality."[47]

King also would have appreciated Niebuhr's understanding of the state as both immoral and necessary—a dialectical attitude that Niebuhr grounded in his theological interpretation of humanity and in his understanding of the Bible. Ever since "The Negro and the Constitution," King himself had expressed a similarly dialectical attitude towards the state—a "yes" to the state that carries out its proper work, and a "no" to the immoral state that exceeds its boundaries. On a related note, King would have affirmed Niebuhr's dialectical response to democracy,

---

[45] King, Jr., "Contemporary Continental Theology," *Papers*, 2:137.

[46] King, Jr., "The Theology of Reinhold Niebuhr," *Papers*, 2:278.

[47] King, Jr., "Qualifying Examination Answers, Theology of the Bible," *Papers*, 2:209.

including its recognition that historical democracies are classist. But, again, Niebuhr supplemented this familiar dialectical response with a sophisticated theological anthropology new to King.

Also new to King was Niebuhr's intellectual discussion of the balance of powers, along with its account of love, justice, and power. Given King's cultural background, including his embrace of civic republicanism, it is little wonder that he found little to quarrel with Niebuhr's belief that the proper work of the state is to achieve equal justice through the equilibria of power. Like Niebuhr, King understood the state as more than a dike against sin—as a catalyst for justice. Also like Niebuhr, along with his family and earlier teachers, King had fully accepted the need for the state to rely on power and coercion when establishing justice. King knew all too well about the obstinacy of those with power. But King was not an uncritical supporter of the role that Niebuhr granted love in the state's efforts to establish justice. King offered a critique of Niebuhr exactly on this point:

> But there is one weakness in Niebuhr's ethical position which runs the whole gamut of his writings. This weakness lies in the inability of his system to deal adequately with the relative perfection which is the fact of the Christian life. How can one develop spiritually; by what powers Christian values are conceived in personality; and how the imminence of *Agape* is to be concretely conceived in human nature and history—all these problems are left unsolved by Niebuhr. He fails to see that the availability of divine *Agape* is an essential affirmation of the Christian religion.[48]

King's deep dissatisfaction with Niebuhr's understanding of the role of love in history is crucial, because it also points to dissatisfaction that King must have felt with Niebuhr's understanding of the relationship between love and the state. It is helpful to remember here that, while a Crozer student, King argued that a Christian state could exercise love by meeting its neighbor's needs, including one attacked by an oppressor. That view runs counter to Niebuhr's, which understands state-sponsored power and coercion not as the work of love but as the work of justice. Given King's studies at Crozer, his dissatisfaction with Niebuhr's

---

[48] King, Jr., *Papers*, 2:150.

understanding of love makes sense. What is more, his dissatisfaction also makes sense in light of his exposure to Boston personalism.

Countering Realism: The Politics of Personalism

In the early- to mid-twentieth century, Boston University was home to a school of thought known as Boston personalism. Simply stated, the personalists of the Boston tradition grounded their theology and metaphysics in the human personality. As Paul Deats puts it, "Personalism is a philosophical perspective for which the person is the ontological ultimate and for which personality is the fundamental explanatory principle."[49] Though heavily metaphysical, Boston person-alism also attended to the social implications of its metaphysics. The Boston University professors—including Border Parker Bowne, A. C. Knudson, Edgar Sheffield Brightman, L. Harold DeWolf, and Walter Muelder—commented directly on a variety of social issues, including the life of the state. Indeed, in their teachings and writings, the Boston professors advanced a distinctively personalist interpretation of the state. King's political thought would both converge with and diverge from this interpretation.

Like Maritain, Boston personalism held that the state has its origins in the human personality, a view most clearly expressed in A. C. Knudson's claim that the state is an "order of creation"[50] that has its "rootage in our instinctive human nature." Following Aristotle, Knudson understood the human as "a political animal" with "state-forming dispositions that are deeper than volition."[51] Two of these dispositions stand out in particular—the need for community and the need for justice.[52] Because the state has its ultimate roots in these instinctive needs for community and justice, the state is ultimately a natural institution, a part of human nature.[53] This claim—that the state emerges out of the sociality of the

[49] *The Boston Personalist*, 2.

[50] Albert C. Knudson, *The Principles of Christian Ethics* (Nashville: Abingdon-Cokesbury Press, 1943) 212.

[51] Ibid., 213.

[52] Ibid., 214.

[53] Other personalists offered similar arguments about the origin of the state. See Bordon Parker Bowne, *The Principles of Ethics* (New York: Harper & Brothers, 1892) 251; and Walter G. Muelder, *Foundations of the Responsible Society* (Nashville: Abingdon Press, 1959) 61.

human personality—would appear in King's later works, though he would never be as exact as Knudson had been.

King would also adopt personalist claims about the character of the state. The personalists considered the human needs in which the state was grounded as ones to be affirmed and celebrated as natural parts of the human creation. This positive grounding of the state directly affected the personalists' understanding of the character of the state itself. One would have to search personalist writings long and hard to find the type of withering critique of the state that Niebuhr had offered; they simply wrote no chapters on the immorality of states. On the contrary, Knudson in particular criticized Niebuhr's "pessimistic" view of the state and his dichotomy of "moral man" and "immoral society," claiming that the state, just like the individual, is capable of being moralized. "Even as it is," Knudson wrote, "the state is obviously a moral agent. It is both a providence and a stern judge."[54]

Like the personalists, King would never lose sight of the potential goodness of the state, primarily because he always acknowledged the goodness of humanity. Commenting on Jeremiah 4:22, King responded to his own question of whether the human can become so corrupt that he or she might have no conception of the good. "I think not," King wrote. "It seems to be that no matter how low an individual sinks in sin, there is still a spark of good within him."[55] King then carried this point further in a criticism of the anthropologies of Calvin and Luther. "Certainly we must agree that the image of God is terribly scarred in man," he wrote, "but not to the degree that man cannot move toward God." Further, Jesus taught that "humanity remains conscious of its humble dependence upon God, as the source of all being and all goodness." Even in his relations with the worst of humanity, Jesus Christ "constantly made appeal to a hidden goodness in their nature."[56] As a follower of Jesus Christ, King insisted on doing the same not only with people in general but also with their political institutions.

With their positive understanding of the character of the state, the personalists also set forth a positive view of the functions of the state. More particularly, they attempted to steer clear of the negative emphasis

---

[54] Knudson, *The Principles of Christian Ethics,* 217.

[55] King, Jr., "Notecards on Books of the Old Testament," *Papers,* 2:166.

[56] King, Jr., "A Comparison and Evaluation of the Theology of Luther with That of Calvin," *Papers,* 2:190.

on coercive power that was so evident in Niebuhr's writings. To be sure, the personalists did not deny the negative function of the state in exercising power. Border Parker Bowne, for example, stressed the need for the state to be a "supervising, restraining, and coercive power."[57] Beyond that, most of the major personalists also agreed that the state must sometimes resort to and execute war.

In general, however, the personalists sought to downplay the role of power in the life of the state. Knudson thus argued that the essence of the state is not in power but in justice. Knudson conceded that meeting the human need for justice requires the state to exercise power. "But the power came second, not first. It was not power that created right but rather right that created power."[58] Following Knudson, Muelder claimed that overemphasizing power precludes humanity from conceiving ways in which the state can be developed as a "servant of justice and freedom, perhaps even of love."[59] For Muelder, the human person is much more than a nonrational, egocentric, and lustful being in need of restraint; the human person is primarily a free and rational being who can willingly participate in creating authority that focuses on self-actualization, justice, and the common good. In accord with Muelder, L. Harold DeWolf, King's theological mentor at Boston, maintained that, although the preservation of law and order is a fundamental function of the state, the overarching purpose of the state is to make "possible the fulfillment of all the existential ends of its citizens."[60] DeWolf even argued that, by leading citizens to self-actualization, the state carries out the requirements of love. Like other personalists, DeWolf refused to draw a radical distinction between love, particularly the *agape* of the New Testament, and the work of the state. In DeWolf's view, love requires the state, primarily, to establish the positive conditions required for the human personality to flourish (for example, the human rights detailed in the "Universal Declaration of Human Rights") and, secondarily, to minimize the force required for order.[61]

---

[57] Borden Parker Bowne, *The Principles of Ethics* (New York: Harper & Brothers, 1892) 250.

[58] Knudson, *The Principles of Christian Ethics*, 216.

[59] Muelder, *Foundations of the Responsible Society*, 108.

[60] L. Harold DeWolf, *Responsible Freedom: Guidelines to Christian Action* (New York: Harper & Row, 1971) 312.

[61] Ibid., 310–15.

King would never downplay the political value of order as much as had the personalists. Throughout his public life, King would always rely heavily on the negative function of the state in using physical force to restrain his political foes. Neither would he denigrate the state's role in maintaining order, internal or external, primarily because his view of human nature would not allow him to do so. The personalist King was too Niebuhrian to let the political implications of human sin fall by the wayside. Still, King would join the personalists in emphasizing the role of the state in establishing freedom, rather than in maintaining order, for the human personality in community. Like the personalists (and Maritain), King would argue that the state is for the free human personality; the free human personality is not for the state.

The central foundation of King's thought at Boston was the freedom of the human personality. In an early Boston paper in which King criticized the views of J. M. E. McTaggert, King argued that freedom, not sin, is "the most important characteristic of personality." Freedom is necessary in order for humanity to make moral choices in a reasonable way.[62] King expanded this point in a criticism he offered in a paper on the theologies of Calvin and Luther. Criticizing doctrines of predestination, King questioned, rhetorically, how either responsibility or reason could ever exist without freedom. "Freedom," he wrote, "is both a moral and metaphysical necessity."[63] More, in his dissertation, King criticized Tillich on this same point. King believed that Tillich's monism, with its claim that finite human beings "issue forth from [the Infinite's] being by a kind of logical necessity," made human freedom "nonexistent." "In order for freedom to exist," King wrote, "there must be distinct individuality and independence on the part of the finite soul."[64]

As a graduate student, King learned that freedom is the essence of the human person. He had learned as much at home and on the streets; he did not need the liberal personalists to instruct him about the centrality of human freedom. But what the Boston personalists offered

---

[62] King, Jr., "The Personalism of J. M. E. McTaggert Under Criticism," *Papers*, 2:73.

[63] King, Jr., "A Comparison and Evaluation of the Theology of Luther with That of Calvin," in *Papers*, 2:190–91.

[64] King, Jr., "A Comparison of the Conceptions of God in the Thinking of Paul Tillich and Henry Nelson Wieman" (Ph.D. dissertation, Boston University, 1955), *Papers*, 2:533. In this part of his dissertation, King borrowed, without citation, from the work of Jack Stewart Boozer, "The Place of Reason in Paul Tillich's Conception of God" (Ph.D. diss., Boston University, 1952).

King was additional exposure to a developed theological and philosophical system that made a theoretical case for the centrality of freedom. In effect, they added theory to what King had learned experientially.

The personalists also added substance to the democratic socialism King had experienced at Crozer. For the personalists, freedom was a matter of political economy. Of those already mentioned, Bowne was perhaps the least enthusiastic about the state's role in the market. He criticized those who prescribed a "socialistic cure-all" that called for the state to control the instruments and forces of production. For Bowne, "nothing could be more insane than the fancy that society is to be redeemed by removing the motives to individual effort which lie in private property and private ambition."[65] Bowne did not mean to suggest that the state should have no role to play in the economic life of society but only that the state should play an indirect role.[66] Knudson went further than Bowne had. For Knudson, the state has a direct responsibility to supplement the efforts of private charity to assist the poor of society.[67] Rather than sharply criticizing socialism, as Bowne had, Knudson offered a synthetic view of capitalism and socialism, arguing that "the road to progress lies in the fusion of these truths rather than in the partisan adoption of one system to the exclusion of the other." In particular, Knudson wanted to fuse capitalism's emphasis on free enterprise, individual responsibility, and adequate incentives with socialism's emphasis on cooperation, social responsibility, and ethical incentives.[68]

Muelder, a devotee of Rauschenbusch, spoke even more forcefully about the state's role in the economic life of society than had either Bowne or Knudson. According to Muelder, Rauschenbusch was "undoubtedly working along the correct line" when he called for nationalization of the economic resources on which society depends (for example, minerals, forests, waterpower, and more).[69] Muelder appreciated the socialistic tendencies of Rauschenbusch, and called as well for the

---

[65] Bowne, *The Principles of Ethics*, 264.

[66] Ibid., 267.

[67] Knudson, *The Principles of Christian Ethics*, 270.

[68] Ibid., 280.

[69] Walter Muelder, *Religion and Economic Responsibility* (New York: Charles Scribner Sons, 1953) 158.

state to play a leading role in organizing economic power so that human needs may be met. Muelder's hope was for a "democratic planned economy,"[70] in which the political community "must have the ultimate authority in handling economic power relationships."[71] He did not mean to suggest "that productive property must all be state owned and operated." Rather, he proposed "a mixed economy, with ample room for experimentation."[72]

Muelder's *Religion and Economic Responsibility* proved to be an influential work for L. Harold DeWolf.[73] Like Muelder, DeWolf believed that the state has a vital role to play in the economic life of society. The conversion of individuals is necessary but insufficient, he argued, for rectifying the economic problems faced by society. "Most major injustice and other evil in our economic order," he wrote, "requires concerted attack with carefully-planned, well-informed, and systematic effort."[74] DeWolf saw such an attack as a response to the demands of love,[75] which include useful and creative work by all during their productive years; adequate food, clothing, shelter, and medical care from birth through old age; security against natural and human disaster; protection of the environment; education of all according to their ability and desire; time and resources for rest and recreation for all; freedom to pursue spiritual values; and the opportunity for all to participate in decision-making about economic goals.[76] It is no wonder at all why King found a mentor in DeWolf.

The Boston personalists also grounded their thoughts about the form of the state in the human personality. This is especially evident in the work of Edgar Sheffield Brightman. "Belief in democracy in some form," he wrote in 1925, "follows from the fact that every person is an autonomous moral agent and, as such, worthy of respect."[77] Because the human personality is worthy of respect, and because democracy respects the human personality, democracy is the best form of the state. Brightman further believed that, unlike totalitarianism, democracy

---

[70] Ibid., 167.

[71] Ibid., 169.

[72] Ibid., 170.

[73] DeWolf, *Responsible Freedom*, 261.

[74] Ibid., 260.

[75] Ibid., 259.

[76] Ibid., 261.

[77] Edgar Sheffield Brightman, *Religious Values* (New York: Abingdon, 1925) 66.

encourages associations other than the state, grants freedom to the artistic and religious communities, promotes the value of truth, and allows for the expression of free moral autonomy.[78]

Muelder also made the personalist case for democracy as the best form of state possible. Following Niebuhr, Muelder claimed that a realistic view of human sin calls for democracy, but Muelder focused more on building a positive case for democracy based on freedom.[79] "The spirit of democracy," Muelder wrote, "is an eager sensitivity to let the people 'play the music' which God has put in their natures and to devise the institutions which make possible its effective utterance." To build his case for democracy, Muelder also highlighted the importance of free discussion—an importance grounded in his Christian belief that people are in need of conversion, correction, and self-actualization within community.[80] Beyond that, Muelder claimed that democracy, just like Christianity, challenges entrenched social hierarchies and establishes checks and balances on human sin. Muelder's work, then, added substantive depth to the connection between Christianity and democracy that King had already begun to make.

Finally, the Boston personalists held that, even though democratic states are the best form, they do not exist apart from the moral order of the universe. Neither a democratic state nor any other state is free to be and do what it wants to be and do. Above all states is "the fixed nature of things, the moral law, the natural rights of the person, and the constitution of the objective world." All that the state does "must finally be referred to these as [its] warrant and foundation."[81]

Boston personalists believed in universal principles that comprise the moral order of the world. Building on the moral laws of Bowne and Brightman,[82] Walter Muelder sketched no fewer than fifteen universal principles inherent in the moral order, arguing that there is in fact an "ultimate right and wrong to every situation despite the difficulties, confusions, perplexities, ambiguities, and compromises which objectively

---

[78] Edgar Sheffield Brightman, *Is Democracy Right?* (Pamplet reprinted from *World Affairs Interpreter* 9/3 [October 1938]) 272.

[79] Muelder, *Foundations of the Responsible Society*, 116.

[80] Ibid., 117.

[81] Bowne, *The Principles of Ethics*, 251.

[82] Edgar Sheffield Brightman, *Moral Laws* (Nashville: Abingdon Press, 1933).

inhere in the situations."[83] The moral order, however, consists of more than fifteen universal principles; it also consists of the natural rights of the human person—rights that must never be violated. For Bowne, "The rights to life, property, freedom, reputation, and those arising from contract are the elementary rights in the community."[84] Each of these rights, he believed, must be formulated and enforced by the state. Muelder, too, focused on personal and social rights, including the rights to survival and physical well-being, fellowship, enlightenment, freedom, justice, and many more.[85]

Consisting of universal principles and human rights, the moral order of the universe, itself a creation of God, is the standard for human life, including the life of the state. No state can exist apart from the demands of the created moral order. These demands are, as Bowne put it, "the law of nature, the higher law, antecedent and fundamental to all statute law...and so far as society departs from this law it loses all justification."[86] Knudson continued this line of argument by claiming that though the state is the "supreme authority in human society," the state does not rightly possess "absolute and unlimited power." The state is always subject to the universal "rule of reason and conscience."[87] The truly sovereign state, in Knudson's view, encourages the protection and development of the rights and laws existent in the moral order. Like Knudson, DeWolf also argued for the limited state. The state is not endowed with "supreme authority," according to DeWolf, but "only with the most inclusive human authority in the area of its jurisdiction"—a jurisdiction delineated in part by the "Universal Declaration of Human Rights."[88] Muelder seemed to state the argument in even stronger terms when he referred to the institutions and laws of the state as, ideally, the historic concretization of the moral order—an order that includes the right of revolution.[89]

The personalist emphasis on moral order leads directly to "Rediscovering Lost Values," a sermon King delivered, in February 1954, at

---

[83] Walter Muelder, *Moral Law in Christian Social Ethics* (Richmond: John Knox Press, 1966) 87–88.

[84] Bowne, *The Principles of Ethics*, 229.

[85] Muelder, *Foundations of the Responsible Society*, 134–38.

[86] Bowne, *The Principles of Ethics*, 251.

[87] Knudson, *The Principles of Christian Ethics*, 218.

[88] DeWolf, *Responsible Freedom*, 312.

[89] Muelder, *Foundations of the Responsible Society*, 109.

Detroit's Second Baptist Church. Before exploring the sermon, which is significant for tracing King's emerging political views, it is necessary to address his doctrine of God as it appeared at Boston University.

At Boston, King emphasized his belief in a personal God. King, of course, did not learn about a personal God only at Boston; his family, college, and seminary had taught him that God is personal. Nevertheless, at Boston, King clearly stated and stressed a developed theological personalism.

In an exam for a course taught by Brightman, King defined his professor's understanding of "the finite God" as "a conscious Person of eternal duration"—a definition with which King was "quite sympathetic."[90] But his strongest statements on his belief in the personality of God are found in his dissertation. Critiquing Tillich's doctrine of God, King argued: "In the world of experiences the basic source of personality production and sustenance has been personality. Now when we are confronted with the fact of personality production and sustenance on a cosmic scale, why not ascribe the source to cosmic personality?"[91] King did not like Tillich's "supra-personal" God, who was without consciousness and rationality. For King, God is nothing if not personal, that is, self-conscious and self-directed: "The idea of personality is so consistent with the notion of the absolute that we must say with Bowne 'that complete and perfect personality can be found only in the Infinite and Absolute Being, as only in him can we find that complete and perfect selfhood and self-expression which is necessary to the fulness of personality.'"[92] Rejecting a personal God has disastrous consequences, for God's love and goodness have personality as their "presupposition." "There can be no goodness in the true ethical sense," King wrote, "without freedom and intelligence"—characteristics of a personal God.[93] Moreover, real love can happen only between persons. Given these consequences, impersonal conceptions of God, like those affirmed by the theologians Tillich and Wieman, simply fail. "They provide neither the conditions for true fellowship with God nor the assurance of his goodness."[94]

---

[90] King, Jr., "Final Examination Answers, Philosophy of Religion," *Papers*, 2:109.

[91] King, Jr., "A Comparison of the Conceptions of God in the Thinking of Paul Tillich and Henry Nelson Wieman," *Papers*, 2:510.

[92] Ibid., 2:511.

[93] Ibid., 2:513.

[94] Ibid., 2:514.

As a graduate student, King was especially intent on preserving his belief that the personal God also loves. In the paper on the theologies of Calvin and Luther, King took the reformers to task for their emphasis on the sovereignty of God. "God," King wrote, "is first and foremost an all loving Father, and any theology which fails to recognize this, in an attempt to maintain the sovereignty of God, is betraying everything that is best in the Christian tradition." King was especially disturbed by the prominence of justice and power in Calvin's God, which King described as "a monster of iniquity."[95] For King, God is first and foremost a loving person who affirms and respects humanity everywhere.

In addition, God is not a distant sovereign, a ruler who sits behind an impenetrable fortress located far from the world. The loving person— God—is with humanity and the world, sustaining both in brilliant creativity. As King put it in his criticism of Karl Barth, God is "immanent, expressing his creative genius throughout the universe which he is ever creating and always sustaining as well as through the essential goodness of the world and human life." God is not foreign to human experience, then, but is "in the beauty of the world, in the unpremeditated goodness of men, and in the moral order of reality."[96]

King's belief in God's presence in a moral order, which is crucial for understanding his view of God and the state, appeared in greater detail in the sermon mentioned above. In that sermon, King argued that the problem with the world is that it has forgotten the spiritual ends for which it exists. "The real problem," he preached, "is that through our scientific genius we've made of the world a neighborhood, but through our moral and spiritual genius we've failed to make of it a brotherhood." We need to correct the problem by returning to "mighty precious values that we've left behind."[97]

The first precious "value that we need to rediscover is this—that *all* reality hinges on moral foundations." According to King, the universe consists not only of physical laws, such as the law of gravity, but also of moral laws. These moral laws are absolute, not relative. For King, "some

---

[95] King, Jr., "A Comparison and Evaluation of the Theology of Luther with That of Calvin," *Papers*, 2:188.

[96] King, Jr., "Karl Barth's Conception of God," *Papers*, 2:104. King's uncited source for this statement, and the following one in the text, is George W. Davis, "Some Theological Continuities in the Crisis Theology," *Crozer Quarterly* 27/ 3 (July 1950): 218.

[97] King, Jr., "Rediscovering Lost Values," *Papers*, 2:249.

things are right and some things are wrong. Eternally so, absolutely so." For example, it is always wrong to hate and to "throw our lives away in riotous living." It is always right to be "honest and loving and just with all humanity." Though relativism and pragmatism are prevalent throughout society, "Some things in this universe are absolute. The God of the universe has made it so."[98]

The second precious value we need to rediscover is "that all reality has spiritual control."[99] The world has unconsciously left God behind, but God has not left the world behind. God is immanent, in the world and its nature and history, creating and sustaining honesty, love, and justice. And it is necessary for all of humanity, if it is to move forward, to rediscover the personal God who created reality with moral foundations and who continues to control all historical processes.

To rediscover the personal God behind the process, King preached, is nothing less than to encounter the right object of our ultimate allegiance. Only God will endure, and nothing can stop God from enduring. "All of the P-38s in the world can never reach God. All of our atomic bombs can never reach him." The God who will endure—the personal God active in history—"is the God that *demands* and *commands* our ultimate allegiance."[100]

Here is the significant part of the sermon for King's developing interpretation of the state. The state (or, for that matter, any other human institution) is not immune from King's call of accountability to a personal God. King did not conceive of God as an impersonal being far removed from the historical state; nor did he conceive of the state as an entity separate from, and not responsible to, a personal God who creates and sustains the universe moment by moment. For King, God is immanent in history, and just so, immanent in the historical life of the state. The state is thus responsible to, and so owes its allegiance to, the God of and in the universe. Indeed, owing its allegiance to God, the state must recognize and obey the moral laws of the universe that God created—laws that affirm justice and love. Like the personalists, King would refuse to argue that love has no direct role to play in the life of the state. Especially like DeWolf, his theological mentor, King would refrain

---

[98] Ibid., 2:251.
[99] Ibid., 2:253.
[100] Ibid., 2:255.

from drawing a radical distinction between the requirements of love and the work of the state, even regarding the issue of war.

Following Bowne, Brightman, Knudson, Muelder, and DeWolf, King would affirm the existence of a divinely created moral order that the state must never violate. If the state were to violate it, King would hold, the citizenry has an obligation to obey the will of God in the handiwork of creation rather than the sinful ways of the state. Like the personalists, King would believe that humanity has an inherent right (and obligation) to disobey a state that is contrary to the moral order created by a personal God who would hold all accountable.

Summary

During his doctoral studies at Boston University, King studied the Christian realism of Reinhold Niebuhr more deeply, and embraced the theological (and philosophical) personalism of the Boston professors. King synthesized lessons from both of these sources.[101]

Regarding the internal functions of the state, King affirmed the democratic socialism of the early Niebuhr. Thus, the graduate student continued to insist that the state should be much more than a mere night watchman. At Boston, King affirmed a state that assumes an active role in safeguarding and serving economic justice for all of its citizens. Doing so, King simply followed the ways of his own democratic-socialist teachers at Boston University, especially Muelder and DeWolf, as well as of his earlier teachers, especially Benjamin Mays, all of whom had a common connection in their appreciation for the democratic socialism, and the underlying relational and solidaristic anthropology, of Walter Rausch-enbusch. But King's vision of a social democracy continued to remain undeveloped at Boston. Even though some Boston personalists commented on the virtues of participatory socialism, the graduate student chose not to explicate on state strategy for achieving economic justice.

---

[101] L. Harold DeWolf, "Martin Luther King, Jr., as Theologian," *Journal of the Interdenominational Theological Center* 4 (Spring 1977), argues: "Neither the thesis of liberal optimism nor of Niebuhrian 'realism' would do" (8). As the conclusion and the remainder of my study show, however, DeWolf would have been more accurate to state that King drew from the theses of liberal optimism and Niebuhrian realism throughout the rest of his life.

King also synthesized the personalists' focus on the state's role in enhancing the free human personality with Niebuhr's focus on the state's role in balancing powers and keeping order for a purpose. The graduate student did not focus either on establishing justice to the exclusion of keeping order or on keeping order to the exclusion of establishing justice; he affirmed both justice and order as important political values for the state to safeguard and enhance. (The later King would clearly speak of justice as a greater political value than order.)

Regarding the external functions of the state, King encountered arguments that allowed the justifiability of certain wars from nearly all his teachers, Niebuhr primary among them. The only indication that the student embraced the realists' claim that war is justifiable under certain circumstances, as he had in earlier years, is his stated appreciation for Niebuhr's ethics—a dimension that led Niebuhr to refrain from accepting an absolute prohibition against the use of coercion when discussing the responsibilities of the state to a sinful world. Even when he disagreed with Niebuhr's refusal to apply love directly to state issues, King merely argued that it is important to affirm the love ethic. In King's mind, one can affirm both the love ethic that Muelder stressed and the power politics that Niebuhr and other realists championed, including the power politics of war. The graduate student continued his resistance to pacifism.

King's years at Boston also led him to systematic analyses of a wide variety of theological works—a task that enabled him to hone his own theological understanding of the state. His emerging views during these years included a synthesis of the liberalism of the personalists and the realism of the neo-orthodox Niebuhr. Niebuhr helped King understand, in theological terms, the depth of the pathology of the state, and the personalists (and a small part of Niebuhr) helped King understand that the character of the state was not all evil, thus ensuring a continuation of the dialectical attitude towards the state that King had expressed even as a student in high school. Both Niebuhr and the personalists, however, encouraged King to remember that the state is accountable to God. The personalists, in particular, helped King to think of a personal God who holds the state accountable in history. These were not entirely new lessons—indeed, they continued the themes King learned at home, at college, and at seminary—but they were new in the sense that they explained old lessons in greater detail and in the new language and categories of realism and personalism.

5

AGAINST US, BUT FOR US

1954–1963

With his dissertation work in hand, King preached a trial sermon at Dexter Avenue Baptist Church in Montgomery, Alabama, and became so enamored of the church that he accepted the call to pastoral ministry there on 14 April 1954. This decision turned out, in retrospect, to be one of the most momentous decisions in US history and, on a smaller scale, in the ongoing development of King's understanding of the state. The context of King's ministry in Montgomery and beyond required him to articulate, on nothing less than the world stage, the substantive content of his theological interpretation of the state, not only through the spoken word but also in concrete actions.

A Deepening Realism

As a member of the King family, a product of the black church and black schools, and a student of realism, King was no stranger to views that strongly emphasized the immorality of the state. In this first period of his career, King emphasized the same, but in terms stronger than those he had learned from his teachers. Parting ways especially with the Boston personalists, who held a largely optimistic view of the state, King highlighted the sinfulness of the state, even while nodding towards its goodness.[1] King portrayed the state as deeply sinful especially because of its sanctioning of segregation but also because of its support of capitalism and its willingness to resort to total nuclear war.

King's realistic emphasis on the immorality of the state is especially visible in a speech he made at the very first meeting of the Montgomery Improvement Association (MIA), called in response to the arrest of Rosa Parks. In this rousing speech, King claimed that the just God was on the brink of punishing the nation for having disobeyed the divine will. What made the nation, including the state, so sinful on this particular evening, according to King, was its willingness to sanction Montgomery City Lines's discourteous treatment of its black riders, Rosa Parks among them. At this point, King publicly portrayed the sinfulness of the state not as the injustice of sanctioning the system of segregation, but as the injustice of supporting an arrogantly racist bus company. But the young pastor had felt for years that the sinfulness of the state ran much deeper than its willingness to overlook a bus company's treatment of black citizens. Correlatively, as "The Negro and the Constitution" showed, he had believed for years that the mandates of divine justice required much more than the courteous treatment of blacks. This deep-seated belief, coupled with increasingly difficult events in the ongoing struggles in Montgomery, pushed King to deepen his realism and to preach that what made the state so sinful, so unjust, was its sanctioning of bus segregation.

King expressed this evolving sense of state sin by intensifying his public rhetoric. When the governing authorities in Montgomery chose not to negotiate, but rather to grow increasingly recalcitrant,[2] King began to use the realistic language of opposition when referring to the state. "Our opponents," he said, "I hate to think of government officials as opponents, but they are, have tried all sorts of things to break us up, but we still hold steadfast."[3] Like Niebuhr before him, King discovered the

---

[1] When assessing the US government in particular, King made moral distinctions between its different levels, and often applauded the federal government for countering the sins of state and local governments.

[2] Reflecting on meetings held between Montgomery leaders and the MIA, King believed "that we would have come to a solution had it not been for the recalcitrance of the city commission." See Martin Luther King, Jr., *Stride Toward Freedom: The Montgomery Story* (New York: Harper & Row, 1958) 122.

[3] Willie Mae Lee, "Notes on MIA Mass Meeting at First Baptist Church, by Willie Mae Lee," in *Birth of a New Age, December 1955–December 1956*, vol. 3 of *The Papers of*

state to be selfish, deceptive, and hypocritical, especially in its tactical dealings with the MIA. With these experiences came a hardened realism—so hardened, in fact, that King would also use the word "evil" when describing the state that he experienced.[4]

Encouraged by others, especially Bayard Rustin, King's deepening realism during the Montgomery era also moved beyond a mere focus on the sinfulness of state-sanctioned bus segregation. Without anyone's prompting, King knew that an attack on bus segregation was an attack on segregation itself, and thus he also publicly acknowledged that justice within a segregated system could never be real justice. Along with his advisers, then, King eventually envisioned the desegregation of buses in Montgomery as the initial step towards desegregation in total—a goal to which the Southern Christian Leadership Conference (SCLC) committed itself at its formation in 1957.

This publicly expanding view of the sinfulness of the state led King, as president of the SCLC, to decry segregation in areas well beyond Montgomery. Working on behalf of the SCLC in local campaigns in Albany, Birmingham, and St. Augustine, King proclaimed his firm and unwavering opposition to state-sanctioned segregation in voting booths, education, public and private housing, and all transportation areas, as well as to any form of racial discrimination, including the discrimination evident in the awarding of federal contracts. The SCLC president's focus also moved beyond the United States to decry British and French colonialism, the international equivalent of American segregation. Colonialism and segregation, as King put it, "are nearly synonymous; they are legitimate first cousins because their common end is economic exploitation, political domination, and the debasing of the human personality."[5]

King portrayed the state as deeply sinful not only because of its support for segregation and its related partner, colonialism, but also because of the means used by the state to further segregation—namely, "naked state power"[6] and sheer neglect. The violent side of the sinful state

---

Martin Luther King, Jr., ed. Clayborne Carson, Stewart Burns, Susan Carson, Peter Holloran, and Dana L. H. Powell (Berkeley: University of California Press, 1997) 113.

[4] King, Jr., "The Death of Evil upon the Seashore," *Papers*, 3:258–62.

[5] Martin Luther King, Jr., Statement of Dr. Martin Luther King, President, Southern Christian Leadership Conference, at the American Negro Leadership Conference on Africa, 24 November 1962, MLKJP, GAMK, 1.

[6] Martin Luther King, Jr., "The Burning Truth in the South," in James M. Washington, ed., *A Testament of Hope* (San Francisco: Harper & Row, 1986) 97.

manifested itself most clearly, in the first part of King's career, in the person and work of Eugene "Bull" Connor, Birmingham's public safety commissioner. Unlike the public officials in Albany, who exercised physical restraint of state power and thus did not sensationalize the story there, Connor brought out the big guns of state power on the local level: he sicced vicious police dogs on peaceful protestors, turned high-powered fire hoses on the backs of fleeing activists, ordered mass arrests of school-age children, and even sent an armored vehicle into the streets of Birmingham. Connor's violent tactics in Birmingham were exactly what King had in mind when he would derisively refer to "the police state" that he and other blacks had to confront on a daily basis in the South.[7]

King privately acknowledged, with some pleasure, that Connor was an unwitting tool in the hands of civil rights activists—his violent tactics, televised and heavily publicized, led much of the country to support the activists—but King always believed that Connor's use of force was deeply sinful.[8] King had this sense even in 1962, well before he became fully active in Birmingham, when bombs exploded at a city Baptist church known to be the home of mass rallies for the Alabama Christian Movement for Human Rights. Believing that Connor and his police force had contributed to this bombing by having created a culture of violence and brutality against blacks, King dispatched a telegram to President Kennedy requesting federal action against "the Gestapo-like methods of Connor's city police."[9] In King's view, Connor was like a fascist who wielded power and force, without principled restraint, to support a system of sin of the worst kind.

But it was not just the use of "naked state power," especially as Connor manifested it, that King identified as a sinful characteristic of the state; the state's sheer neglect of the demands of civil rights activists also deepened his realism during this period. King's frustration with the sin of neglect intensified as he experienced the state more and more throughout the first part of his career. Consider his time in Montgomery alone. In the beginning, King was frustrated with the Montgomery city police for, among other things, not protecting him and his followers. Then he became frustrated with Governor Folsom for not addressing the lack of

---

[7] Martin Luther King, Jr., "Hammer on Civil Rights," in *A Testament of Hope*, 172.

[8] See David J. Garrow, *Bearing the Cross: Martin Luther King, Jr., and the Southern Christian Leadership Conference* (New York: Vintage Books, 1986) 251.

[9] Ibid., 225.

protection provided by Montgomery to its black residents. Then he became frustrated with the federal officials who did not provide the aggressive leadership he deemed necessary for success in Montgomery and the South. King expressed his frustration on 17 May 1957 at the Prayer Pilgrimage for Freedom in Washington, DC, when he called the executive branch "all too silent and apathetic" and referred to the legislative branch as "all too stagnant and hypocritical."[10] These tough words reflected exactly what King believed he encountered throughout the first part of his career—an absence of constructive leadership from the city to the federal levels of the state.

There is no doubt that, in the first part of his career, the realistic King portrayed the state as deeply sinful mostly because of its sanctioning of segregation and because of the means it used to support segregation. Segregation, in short, was *the* hallmark sin. But, on occasion, King identified another sin that, in his mind, marked the state as fallen—namely, the sin of sanctioning a capitalistic system that made war on the poor. The two sins, in King's view, are not at all unrelated. As he put it in his reflections on the Montgomery story, "the inseparable twin of racial injustice is economic injustice."[11]

"I never intend," King stated in June 1956, "to adjust myself to the tragic inequalities of an economic system which takes necessities from the masses to give luxuries to the classes."[12] King believed that state-sanctioned capitalism resulted in the sinful condition of one group of people living in "superfluous wealth" and another group living in "abject poverty."[13] The gap between these two groups was especially sinful, in King's mind, because it existed in a "historic period of prosperity," and the gap was doubly sinful when one considered that in "'the affluent society,' the Negro has remained the poor, the underprivileged, and the lowest class."[14]

---

[10] Martin Luther King, Jr., "Give Us the Ballot—We Will Transform the South," in *A Testament of Hope*, 198.

[11] Martin Luther King, Jr., "Pilgrimage to Nonviolence," in *A Testament of Hope*, 37.

[12] Martin Luther King, Jr., "The 'New Negro' of the South: Behind the Montgomery Story," *Papers*, 3:286.

[13] Martin Luther King, Jr., "Paul's Letter to American Christians," *Papers*, 3:416.

[14] Martin Luther King Jr., "The Burning Truth in the South," in *A Testament of Hope*, 96.

King did not publicly make the same point that he had made on note cards while a student at Crozer—that "capitalism has seen its best days in America, and not only America, but the entire world"—but his belief that capitalism "has failed to meet the needs of the masses" definitely found its way into his public comments. Having lived with Daddy King, studied with Chivers and Williams, and read the pro-socialist works of Rauschenbusch and Niebuhr, King found it natural to critique the state for supporting an economic system that neglected to provide basic life necessities for all people.

Yet another sin, according to King, pushes the state far from sainthood—its willingness to resort to total nuclear war. While a seminary student, King had argued that, given the human inclination to sin, war is justifiable under certain circumstances. But now, in the first period of his career, King moved away from offering justifications, primarily because he had begun to equate war with total nuclear war. On the issue of nuclear war, King stated that he could "see no moral justification for that type of war. I believe absolutely and positively that violence is self-defeating."[15] Two years later, in an article on the social organization of nonviolence, King declared nuclear war to be "the most colossal of all evils."[16]

King detailed some of the reasons for the evolution in his thinking in "Pilgrimage to Nonviolence," noting that in his student days he had "felt that while war could never be a positive or absolute good, it could serve as a negative good in the sense of preventing the spread and growth of an evil force." But no longer did he feel the same, for he had concluded "that the potential destructiveness of modern weapons of war totally rules out the possibility of war ever serving again as a negative good." Interestingly, King's argument here is against unlimited nuclear war, not a limited war without the use of nuclear weapons. Believing that the only option is between "nonviolence and nonexistence," King chose nonviolence in international relations.[17]

Throughout the first part of his career, King's realism deepened and intensified as he encountered different manifestations of state sin. Indeed, his realist emphasis on the immorality of the state became even more

---

[15] Martin Luther King, Jr., "When Peace Becomes Obnoxious," *Papers*, 3:208.

[16] Martin Luther King, Jr., "The Social Organization of Nonviolence," in *A Testament of Hope*, 34.

[17] King, Jr., "Pilgrimage to Nonviolence," in *A Testament of Hope*, 39.

realistic than Reinhold Niebuhr's: King's language was stronger than Niebuhr's, and the conditions in which he lived provided King the opportunity to comment more frequently on the immorality of the state than had Niebuhr. It is fitting to mention Niebuhr here especially because, in January 1958, King preached a Niebuhrian sermon in which he sought "to work out a realistic doctrine of man."[18] The sermon reveals King's Niebuhrian belief that the state is morally inferior to the individual person. "When man interacts in his societal existence," King preached, "his sin rises to greater dimensions. See how we live! Nations trample over other nations with the iron feet of oppression."[19] King expressed his realistic inclinations even more strongly by claiming that the collective life, including the life of the state, is growing "progressively evil." King then went beyond the ambiguity of Niebuhr's realism when he said, "I can see nothing but the fact that man in his individual and collective life is a sinner, in need of God's divine grace."[20]

Against Us:
A Theological Understanding of State Sin

King described the state as sinful because he thought theologically about segregation, capitalism, and war. More than a political thinker, King understood segregation, economic injustice, and war as actions or conditions that desecrate the God-given status, rights, freedom, and interconnectedness of humanity.

Having been taught that he was "somebody," King believed that every person is created in "the image of God," that every person "has etched in his personality the indelible stamp of the Creator," and that "the image of God is universally shared in equal portions by all." God the Creator did not make the individual into a thing, merely a tool to be used and discarded. Rather, God conferred sacredness upon the human personality by creating every person in the divine image and by giving each person sacred rights, among them the rights to "life, liberty and the pursuit of happiness." The connection here between King's theological beliefs and his republican beliefs is obvious, and he stated it clearly. "The

---

[18] Martin Luther King, Jr., "What is Man?" An Address Delivered before the Chicago Evening Club, 12 January 1958, MLKJP, GAMK, 1.

[19] Ibid., 3.

[20] Ibid.

idea of the dignity and worth of the human personality is expressed eloquently and unequivocally in the Declaration of Independence." Affirming the language of inalienable rights, King argued: "Never has a socio-
political document proclaimed more profoundly and eloquently the
sacredness of the human personality."[21]

King also held that freedom is the very essence of the human person
created in the image of God. "Under God," King preached, "we were
born free."[22] By freedom, he meant "one's capacity to deliberate, decide
and respond" for oneself. King did not mean to refer simply to the
freedom of the will. "So," he said, "I am speaking of freedom of man, the
whole man, and not one faculty called the will." That King's intent here
was to include the notion of freedom of the body, that is, the capacity to
move unhindered from one place to another, is evident in his description
of the absence of freedom. "The absence of freedom is the imposition of
restraint on my deliberation as to what I shall do, where I shall live, how
much I shall earn, the kind of tasks I shall pursue."[23]

Further, King claimed that the individual, created in the image of
God to be free, is also inextricably connected with other people. "All men
are caught in an inescapable network of mutuality, tied in a single
garment of destiny."[24] The words reflect exactly what he had learned at
Morehouse College from Benjamin Mays, who taught his students that
humanity is "tied together," and that "what affects one, affects all."

Armed with this view of humanity, King critiqued the state for its
support of segregation, capitalism, and war. "The tragedy of segregation,"
King argued, "is that it treats men as means rather than ends, and thereby
reduces them to things rather than persons."[25] Segregation also opposes
human freedom by cutting off "one's capacity to deliberate, decide and
respond."[26] Finally, segregation disobeys the moral laws of God's
universe, more particularly, the law that requires recognition of and
proper response to the network of mutuality. The theological sin of
capitalism is its failure to recognize the physical and material conditions

---

[21] Martin Luther King, Jr., "The Ethical Demands for Integration," in *A Testament of Hope*, 119.

[22] Martin Luther King, Jr., "Who Speaks for the South?" in *A Testament of Hope*, 92.

[23] King, Jr., "The Ethical Demands for Integration," in *A Testament of Hope*, 120.

[24] Ibid., 122.

[25] Ibid., 119.

[26] Ibid., 120.

required for the flourishing of full human freedom, including such basic necessities as education, jobs, livable housing, food, and more. "God," King declared, "intends for all his children to have the basic necessities of life, and he has left in this universe 'enough and spare' for that purpose." A sinful capitalism, however, has affected the redistribution of life's basic necessities so that now one group lives in "superfluous wealth" while another lives in "deadening poverty."[27] To state the point theologically, state-sanctioned capitalism has disobeyed God's moral laws, as discovered through the created universe, which allow and call for the provision of life's basic goods to all God's children. The theological sin of total nuclear war is its opposition to the principle of the sacredness of human personality, more particularly, the God-given (and sacred) right to life. King stated this theological belief most explicitly: "If we assume that life is worth living and that man has a right to survival then we must find an alternative to war."[28]

Exactly because segregation, capitalism, and war are sins against God and humanity, King portrayed the state as a force for evil. The state is a force for evil not because its politics are pragmatically askew, or because it is either too liberal or too conservative, but because it sins against God by supporting systems that oppose the sacredness of the human personality in community. The state relegates some of its citizens to the status of things, refusing to recognize their dignity and worth in the image of God, and acting as if God created individuals simply to be things used by the state.

Resisting the Sinful State:
A Theological Understanding of Political Authority

"We must obey God rather than any human authority."[29] Peter and the apostles, according to the author of the Book of Acts, spoke these words upon being questioned by the high priest of Jerusalem at their arrest for having taught in the name of Jesus Christ. Standing before the official Jewish court, Peter and the apostles proclaimed that their ultimate allegiance belonged not to the Jewish leaders but to God alone. In their religious view, the proper object of loyalty is the God who raised Jesus

---

[27] King, Jr., "Paul's Letter to American Christians," *Papers*, 3:416.

[28] Martin Luther King, Jr., *Strength to Love* (Philadelphia: Fortress Press, 1981) 41.

[29] Acts 5:29.

from the dead so that Israel might experience repentance and the forgiveness of sins.

In the first part of his career, and indeed throughout his life, King followed in the footsteps of Peter. Like Peter, he claimed that humanity should place its ultimate faith in God alone. As noted in the previous chapter, King had made this point early in his ministerial career, while a student at Boston University, in a sermon he delivered at Detroit's Second Baptist Church. King took the basic point he had made in the sermon—that God, not things, should be the object of our ultimate loyalties—and revised it, during this part of his career, to claim that when human authority conflicts with divine authority, Christians must ultimately subject themselves to God. For King, the unassailable sovereignty of God means that when human authority conflicts with God, God is the proper object of devotion.

This theological claim is especially clear in King's recounting of one of the meetings he held with Montgomery officials in order to resolve the bus boycott. At this particular meeting, G. Stanley Frazier, one of Montgomery's segregationist ministers, stated that Christian ministers should busy themselves with saving souls, not with addressing social issues. King responded to Frazier in part by arguing that Christians have a responsibility to give their ultimate allegiance not to humanity and its customs, however cherished they may be, but to God alone. King held that the issues posed by Montgomery's practice of segregation required Christians to choose between giving allegiance either to unjust human customs, which restrict human freedom, or to God, who wills the freedom of all people. For King, the choice was clear. "As Christians," he stated, "we owe our ultimate allegiance to God and His will rather than to man and his folkways."[30]

Noticeably absent from King's comments on political authority during this period is any affirmation of the Apostle Paul's claim, in Romans 13:1-7, that Christians should subject themselves to the governing authorities. Paul called for subordination because he believed that the governing authorities derive their authority from God and that they properly carry out the divine work of executing the wrongdoer. To resist the governing authorities, in Paul's view, is to resist the will of God and to risk the judgment and wrath of God. And so if Christians hope to

---

[30] King, Jr., *Stride Toward Freedom*, 117.

be true to conscience, and to avoid the divine wrath, they should be subject to the political authorities. For example, they should pay taxes and offer the government their respect and honor.

King responded to this biblical text by claiming that Paul's thought about the governing authorities was conditioned by a belief that the end of the world was just days away. "Feeling that the time was not long the Apostle Paul urged men to concentrate on preparing themselves for the new age rather than changing external conditions."[31] King further claimed that, though early Christianity knew the existing social order to be less than faithful, it offered no prescription for making the world a better place. "It taught its adherents neither to conform to the external framework of their time, nor to seek directly to alter it, but to live within it a life rooted in a totally different order." King acknowledged that his own practice of nonviolent resistance broke away from this teaching, and he readily justified the break: "Today we live in a new age, with a different theological emphasis; consequently we have both a moral and religious justification for passively resisting evil conditions within the social order."[32] Unfortunately, King did not expound on this point, but it is clear that he had no interest in blindly accepting Paul's understanding of political authority and in embracing his ethic of subjection.

King clarified his view of political authority in his famous *Letter from Birmingham Jail.* King interpreted his Birmingham incarceration as a mere continuation of the early church's efforts to be faithful to the sovereign God it discovered in Jesus Christ. The early Christians were persecuted by political and religious authorities for their efforts to transform society, King wrote, but they persevered "with the conviction that they were a 'colony of heaven,' and had to obey God rather than man."[33] King also clarified, in the same letter, the circumstances under

---

[31] Martin Luther King, Jr., "Advice for Living," in *Symbol of the Movement, January 1957-December 1958,* vol. 4 of *The Papers of Martin Luther King, Jr.,* ed. Clayborne Carson, Susan Carson, Adrienne Clay, Virginia Shadron, and Kieran Taylor (Berkeley: University of California Press, 2000) 280.

[32] Ibid., 281.

[33] Martin Luther King, Jr., "Letter from Birmingham City Jail," in *A Testament of Hope,* 300. King made a similar statement two years later to interviewers from *Playboy.* Against "the resident power structure," King argued, "the early Christians insisted on spreading the love of God, convinced that they were 'a colony of heaven' on this earth who were missioned to obey not man but God." See *"Playboy* Interview: Martin Luther King, Jr.," in *A Testament of Hope,* 349.

which he would obey God rather than the state by describing the difference between just laws and unjust laws. In King's view, grounded in part in his reading of Thoreau while a college student, just laws are in accord with natural and divine law, both of which serve and uplift human personality, and are willingly assented to and followed by all the citizenry.[34] Unjust laws, conversely, are in discord with natural and divine law and so distort the human soul and degrade the human personality. Further, they are codes that a majority does not follow itself but inflicts instead upon a minority of citizens who have no right to vote or no legal means of redress.[35] According to King, citizens have a legal and a moral obligation to obey just laws. When the state's law supports and serves the eternal law, and the divinely created natural law, the citizenry is obliged to support the state. But, at the same time, the citizenry has a moral responsibility to disobey unjust laws. Unjust laws do not possess any moral authority, and thus disobeying them becomes a moot point.[36]

Beyond appealing to natural and divine law, King also referred to the US Constitution, arguing that when the Constitution conflicts with other laws, the citizen has an obligation to obey the Constitution. King appealed to the Constitution especially when he felt that he was a victim of an apparently just law that was unjustly applied. For example, he argued that the apparently just law requiring permits for parades, when applied to civil rights marches with the intention of preventing the marches, denied him and his followers their First Amendment privilege of peaceful assembly.[37] King made a similar appeal to the First Amendment when he and his followers openly disobeyed a court injunction directing them to cease their marches.[38]

Given King's ongoing direct confrontation with political authority, it would have made sense for him to have substituted the word "state" for

---

[34] King, Jr., "Letter from Birmingham City Jail," in *A Testament of Hope*, 293. For a detailed analysis of the sources behind King's stance on civil disobedience, as well as his understanding of law, see Ansbro, *The Making of a Mind*, 110–62. For more on King's notion of divine law, see Luther D. Ivory, *Toward a Theology of Radical Involvement: The Theological Legacy of Martin Luther King, Jr.* (Nashville: Abingdon, 1997) 50–52. Ivory's excellent study explicates King's theological views on God, people, and history.

[35] Ivory, *Toward a Theology of Radical Involvement*, 293–94.

[36] Ibid., 293.

[37] Ibid., 294.

[38] Martin Luther King, Jr., *Why We Can't Wait* (New York: Harper, 1963) 70.

"human authority" when paraphrasing Peter's and the apostles' claim. This point was not lost on King, who proclaimed explicitly, in one of his more widely-known sermons, that the ultimate allegiance of American Christians "is not to the government, not to the state.... The Christian owes his ultimate allegiance to God, and if any earthly institution conflicts with God's will it is your Christian duty to take a stand against it."[39] For King, political authority is a profoundly theological issue. Christians, he believed, "have a dual citizenry," living "both in heaven and earth." As part of the colony of heaven, Christians have a responsibility to ensure that their "ultimate allegiance is to the empire of eternity," where the sovereign God rules over all.[40]

Resisting the Sinful State: Christian Love

But King, a principled preacher, did not want his followers to adopt just any means in expressing their opposition to political authority. He wanted Christian principles, especially love, to guide the adoption of means. King's insistence on moral means was present even at the first MIA meeting in Montgomery, when he stated that the teachings of Jesus stood opposed to violence.[41] At this meeting, King did not expound on his theological reasoning for adopting nonviolence, but his reasoning was already within his mind, especially because of the work he did in seminary and graduate school, and then developed progressively during this first period of his career. At the center of his theological understanding of the proper means was a doctrine of God that emphasized love as revealed in the life and teachings of Jesus.[42]

"Beloved, let us love one another, because love is from God; everyone who loves is born of God and knows God."[43] These words, from the

---

[39] King, Jr., "Paul's Letter to American Christians," *Papers*, 3:416.

[40] Ibid.

[41] Martin Luther King, Jr., "MIA Mass Meeting at Holt Street Baptist Church," *Papers*, 3:72. James Cone overlooks this emphasis in his argument that King allowed justice to trump love at the beginning of the Montgomery campaign.

[42] There is an underlying continuity in the understanding of God that King set forth throughout his years in public ministry. For example, King understood God as a loving parent not only in the early days of his ministerial career but also in the latter days, even up until the tragic day in Memphis. See Thomas Mikelson, "The Negro's God in the Theology of Martin Luther King, Jr." (Th.D. dissertation, Harvard University, 1988).

[43] 1 John 4:7–8.

author of I John, were among King's favorite words from scripture, and he cited them on numerous occasions throughout the first period of his career. For example, near the end of the Montgomery campaign, when the spirit of the MIA was at an all-time low, King preached on the need for love, proclaiming that the principle of love "stands at the center of the cosmos. As John says, 'God is love.' He who loves is a participant in the being of God. He who hates does not know God."[44] King's call for love was different from the biblical author's, in the sense that the latter was speaking merely about love within the Christian community, but both King and the author meant to claim that love is part of the essence of God and that love is the appropriate human response to God.[45] To explain what he meant by love, King turned primarily to the cross of Jesus, revealing his view on love to be cruciform at its core.

One of King's earliest written statements on love is found in the seminary paper titled "A View of the Cross Possessing Biblical and Spiritual Justification," in which he wrote that "the death of Christ is a revelation or symbol of the eternal sacrificial love of God." The love of God, to be mirrored by disciples, is a matter not of holding onto one's own life at all costs but of surrendering one's life for others. As King put it, "The divine love, in short, is sacrificial in nature."[46]

King also argued that, as revealed in the cross of Jesus, the love of God is forgiving. Through the cross, God intended for Jesus' death to effect divine forgiveness of a sinful humanity. In the first part of his career, King explicated on this point in *Strength to Love* by claiming that the famous words of Jesus on the cross—"Father, forgive them; for they

---

[44] Martin Luther King, Jr., "The Most Durable Power in the World," in *A Testament of Hope*, 11.

[45] Keith Miller has also argued in some detail that King's understanding of love is largely indebted to the work of African-American preachers and scholars. For example, some of King's comments on love are directly traceable to the works of William Stuart Nelson and George Kelsey. This is not to say that white preachers, theologians, and ethicists did not influence King's thoughts about love. The works of Harry Emerson Fosdick and Paul Ramsey, for example, were sources King relied on very heavily when writing and talking about love. But it is necessary to note that the black church played the formative role in King's view of God as love. See Keith Miller, *Voice of Deliverance: The Language of Martin Luther King, Jr. and Its Sources* (New York: The Free Press, 1992) 59–60.

[46] Martin Luther King, Jr., "A View of the Cross Possessing Biblical and Spiritual Justification," *Papers*, 1:267.

do not know what they are doing"[47]—show "love at its best."[48] Jesus'
words of forgiveness revealed what the love of God is essentially about:
the forgiveness of humanity for acting as if God has no place in life.

King did not believe that God gives and forgives without purpose, as
if sacrifice and forgiveness are good in themselves. Rather, King
maintained that God gives and forgives so that reconciliation may result.
In the seminary paper just mentioned, King wrote: "The cross represents
the eternal love of God seeking to attract men into fellowship with the
divine."[49] Divine sacrifice and forgiveness, then, have a purpose—the
reconciliation between God and humanity. Such reconciliation also
means the coming together of humanity itself, a reconciliation among all
people. Rather than being parochial, then, love is not limited to either
Jew or Greek, slave or free, male or female, but is universal in its embrace.

Further, King cited Anders Nygren, whose use of the word *agape*
King adapted throughout his lifetime, to suggest that the presence of the
universal love of God, far from dependent upon human worth, is
"spontaneous" and "unceasing."[50] In his reflections on the Montgomery
story, King then expounded on *agape* by claiming that it surpasses both
eros and *philia* in terms of quality. "*Agape* means understanding, redeeming good will for all men. It is an overflowing love which is purely
spontaneous, unmotivated, groundless, and creative."[51]

King continued, in this text and others, to use the themes that he
had begun to develop in his seminary papers. "*Agape*," he wrote, "is

---

[47] Luke 23:32.

[48] Martin Luther King, Jr., *Strength to Love*, 36.

[49] King, Jr., "A View of the Cross Possessing Biblical and Spiritual Justification,"
Papers, 1:266.

[50] Ibid., 1:267.

[51] King, Jr., *Stride Toward Freedom*, 104. It is important to note that although
King's use of the word *agape* stuck with him as he continued to explain the love of God,
King largely left behind Nygren's work. Miller, *Voice of Deliverance*, 59–60, reports that
King actually borrowed from Fosdick's *On Being Fit to Live With* (New York: Harper,
1946), not Nygren's *Agape and Eros*, when distinguishing between the three different
types of love. In addition, Miller argues that King's love passages in *Stride*, 102–105, are
directly traceable to William Stuart Nelson, "Satyagraha: Gandhian Principles of
Nonviolent Noncooperation," *Journal of Religious Thought* (Autumn–Winter,
1957–1958): 17–18; George Kelsey, "The Christian Way in Race Relations," in *The
Christian Way in Race Relations*, ed. William Nelson (New York: Harper, 1948) 40; and
Paul Ramsey, *Basic Christian Ethics* (New York: Charles Scribner's Sons, 1950; Chicago:
University of Chicago Press, 1980) 92–99.

disinterested love." It is a matter of sacrificing for the sake of the beloved, not a matter of taking from the other in order to satisfy the self.[52] Love also expresses a willingness to forgive seventy times seven, with the purpose of restoring community. "*Agape* is love seeking to preserve and create community."[53] But King added some new, related themes in this text and others. For example, he spoke of *agape* as "a recognition of the fact that all life is interrelated." The love of God knows that "humanity is involved in a single process, and all men are brothers." King also wrote with renewed emphasis on the devotion and commitment of love. "*Agape* is a willingness to go to any length to restore community." Once again, he turned to the cross to explain his point: "The cross is the eternal expression of the length to which God will go in order to restore broken community."[54]

Most significant, however, King began to stress that love, as revealed in the cross of Jesus, entails a willingness to suffer for the end of reconciliation. Love is a matter of facing evil, suffering through evil, and attempting to overcome it, even unto death. As King put it, love is "facing evil with an infinite capacity to take it without flinching."[55] The cross of Jesus, in this view, reveals that love suffers nonviolently for the sake of reconciliation. When Jesus was hanging on the cross, he could have called upon God to "let loose the mighty thunderbolts of righteous wrath and destroy" his persecutors. But Jesus did not strike his enemies, he did not call upon his followers to take up arms, and he did not call upon God to kill. Rather than calling for violence, Jesus suffered nonviolently and thus subjected himself to "inexpressible agony" and "excruciating pain."[56]

It was King's evolving, cruciform understanding of love that led him on that first night in Montgomery and thereafter to insist that he and his followers refuse violence. The use of forcible means that threaten or use

---

52 Ramsey, *Basic Christian Ethics*, 92–99. Ira Zepp is the one who discovered that King's words here are directly traceable to Paul Ramsey's *Basic Christian Ethics*. King used this book in an ethics course at Crozer Theological Seminary. Zepp, *The Social Vision of Martin Luther King, Jr.* (Brooklyn: Carlson Publishing, 1989) 108–12.

53 King, Jr., *Stride Toward Freedom*, 105. Zepp has shown that King borrowed heavily from Ramsey when depicting love as the creation and preservation of community. Zepp, *The Social Vision of Martin Luther King, Jr.*, 111.

54 King, Jr., *Stride Toward Freedom*, 106.

55 Martin Luther King, Jr., Address at the Conference on Religion and Race, Chicago, Illinois, Edgewater Beach Hotel, 17 January 1963, MLKJP, GAMK, 13.

56 King, Jr., *Strength to Love*, 36.

violence, in King's view, is the exact opposite of Jesus' example of "facing evil with an infinite capacity to take it without flinching." King's view of cruciform love also led him to adopt Gandhi's method of nonviolent resistance to the state. King was fond of saying that "Christ furnished the spirit and motivation for the movement, while Gandhi furnished the method."[57]

According to King, the general method of nonviolent resistance, as he used it, consists of six "basic facts." First, nonviolent resistance resists. The method of nonviolence "is not passive non-resistance to evil, it is active nonviolent resistance to evil." Second, nonviolence "does not seek to defeat or humiliate the opponent, but to win his friendship and understanding." Third, a nonviolent "attack is directed against forces of evil rather than against persons who happen to be doing the evil." Fourth, nonviolent resistance "is a willingness to accept suffering without retaliation, to accept blows from the opponent without striking back."[58] Fifth, nonviolent resistance "avoids not only external physical violence but also internal violence of the spirit."[59] Sixth, nonviolent resistance operates with "the conviction that the universe is on the side of justice"; God works through nonviolence "to bring the disconnected aspects of reality into a harmonious whole."[60] Like Christian love, then, nonviolent resistance, as embraced by King, is sacrificial, forgiving, reconciling, and peaceful.

Nevertheless, King had more than theological reasons for adopting the means of nonviolence in resisting a sinful state. The Niebuhrian King also rightly recognized that the power and force available to the civil rights activists in no way compared favorably with the power and force available to the state. This meant, for King, that the use of violence was purely and simply "impractical": the state would slaughter the activists in any armed battle.[61]

To say that King adopted nonviolent resistance is necessary (and painfully obvious) but not sufficient in an analysis of the methods that King used to oppose the state. Nonviolence, for King, was a general style

---

[57] King, Jr., "Pilgrimage to Nonviolence," in *A Testament of Hope*, 38.

[58] Martin Luther King, Jr., "An Experiment in Love," in *A Testament of Hope*, 18.

[59] Ibid., 19.

[60] Ibid., 20.

[61] Ibid., 17.

of resistance within which he adopted specific tactics for fighting the sinful state.

Throughout the first part of his career, King embraced a variety of tactics in the fight against state-sponsored segregation. In the very beginning, even before the Rosa Parks incident, King, as the ordained minister at Dexter, formed a political and social action committee designed to educate his members about political issues and to stress the importance of voting.[62] After the arrest of Rosa Parks, however, King moved beyond a simple focus on education to an emphasis on boycotts, stressing the need to damage the political economy in order to effect real change. As head of the SCLC, and in the footsteps of his father, King then encouraged his followers to fight the state by exercising their right to vote. "Until we gain political power through possession of the ballot," King stated earlier, "we will be convenient tools of unscrupulous politicians."[63] Then, during Birmingham, when he helped to engineer the mass movement of adults and children, King became even more convinced of the effectiveness of direct action campaigns, especially those with huge numbers of nonviolent participants, in fighting the state.[64] As King understood them, all of these methods, the use of which he determined according to his context, were sacrificial, forgiving, and reconciling in nature, and thus reflective of cruciform love.

Beyond these methods, all of which have been thoroughly studied, King suggested other, equally significant tactics for resisting the state. For example, King encouraged his followers to pray for those who fight against the state. "We ask people everywhere," King wrote, "to pray that God will guide us, pray that justice will be done and that righteousness will stand."[65] King counted on prayers to strengthen the activists and to make them feel "the unity of the nation and the presence of the Almighty God."[66] King also encouraged his followers to pray for the segregationists who held political offices. "We must pray for a change in attitude in all those who violate human dignity and who rob men, women, and little children of human decency."[67] For King, prayers of Christian love were a

---

[62] King, *Stride Toward Freedom*, 30.

[63] Martin Luther King, Jr., "Facing the Challenge of a New Age," *Papers*, 3:460.

[64] See Garrow, *Bearing the Cross*, 273.

[65] King, Jr., "Walk for Freedom," *Papers*, 3:279.

[66] Ibid., 280.

[67] King, Jr., "Who Speaks for the South?" in *A Testament of Hope*, 92.

necessary part of the spiritual struggle to effect changes in the state and its active support of sins.[68]

Another little-known tactic that King encouraged was the nurturing of "intelligent, courageous and dedicated leadership" within the black community—leaders who would fight for the elimination of segregation. King felt a "dire need" for the black community to develop a set of leaders who would embrace neither "hot-headedness" nor "Uncle Tomism," but who would be lovingly resistant to sin.[69] King had in mind not only leaders who would be civil rights activists but also those who could win political office.

Beyond his call to everyone for prayers, and beyond his call to the black community for moral politicians, King adopted yet another tactic that is rarely discussed among scholars—lobbying. In Montgomery, Albany, and Birmingham, King met face-to-face with all types of representatives from the state, from safety commissioners to mayors to governors to presidents. King met with local political authorities to persuade them, partly through moral arguments, to end their support for the sin of segregation, and he met with legislators and presidents to promote desegregation-friendly legislation and executive orders, to encourage the use of bully pulpits and the moral power of their offices, and to ensure the implementation of legislation already in place.

Nevertheless, in this first period, King came to realize that, given the intransigence of the state, nonviolent direct action campaigns, especially those filled by masses of people, were the best tactics for resisting the state, domestically and internationally.[70] Interestingly, he also came to realize that the civil rights movement needed to avail itself of the potentially violent power of the state itself in the fight to end state-sanctioned sins.

---

[68] There were times in his life, especially when President Lyndon B. Johnson called for a day of prayer, that King emphasized the necessity for the church to undertake actions in addition to prayer. But, even in his most revolutionary moments, King never dismissed the value of prayer. It is important to keep this in mind when reading Rathburn, who characterizes King's position as holding that there is no time "for taking refuge in prayer." See Rathbun, "Martin Luther King: The Theology of Social Action," *American Quarterly* 20 (Spring 1968): 49.

[69] King, Jr., "Facing the Challenge of a New Age," *Papers*, 3:461.

[70] King actually believed that nonviolent direct action campaigns "must be applied in international affairs," especially regarding the issue of nuclear disarmament. See Martin Luther King, Jr., "Gandhi and the World Crisis," January 1962, MLKJP, GAMK, 24.

Divine Justice and the State

Although King emphasized his belief that the state is sinful, he also flatly refused to dismiss the state unreservedly and without qualification. Rather, King acknowledged, in word and deed, that the state is necessary on earth for setting free the human personality, every human personality, so that it can flourish in community. Thus, King encouraged the state to be a divine tool of justice—God's minister for preserving and serving human freedom—and affirmed it wholeheartedly when it acted so.[71]

"But let justice roll down like waters, and righteousness like an everflowing stream."[72] King had studied Amos 5:21-24 as a student in Harold DeWolf's Boston University class on religious teachings of the Old Testament, and he had noted his own agreement with Amos on a class note card on the passage.[73] King's agreement meant that he understood God as one who despises those who trample on the poor and push aside the needy in order to amass property and wealth. In Amos's (and King's) view, the just God demands and commands that life's basic necessities be provided to the poor and that the needy receive honest and fair treatment. Rather than trampling the poor and the needy, the just God joins their efforts to seek and maintain the basic material necessities required for their livelihood.

But, in this first period, there is also another dimension of King's understanding of divine justice—a dimension he expressed explicitly at the first meeting of MIA:

> The Almighty God himself is not the only…God just standing up saying through Hosea, 'I love you, Israel.' He's also the God that stands up before nations and said: 'Be still and know that I am God, that if you don't obey me I will break the backbone of your power

---

[71] This section of the study, as well as other sections on justice, will show that Enoch Oglesby, "Martin Luther King, Jr.: Liberation Ethics in a Christian Context," *The Journal of the Interdenominational Theological Center* 4 (Spring 1977) 35, is wrong to suggest that King's ethics resembled "a kind of 'love-monism.'"

[72] Amos 5:24.

[73] On the note card, King wrote: "God is a God that demands justice and sacrifice can never be a substitute for it. Who can disagree with such a notion?" See Martin Luther King, Jr., "Notecards on Books of the Old Testament: God (Amos)," *Papers*, 2:165.

and slap you out of the orbits of your international and national relationships.[74]

More than a concern for the needy, divine justice is also a matter of legislating divine will and then judging and actually punishing those who disobey divine law. The just God has established moral laws in the universe that require human obedience, among them the law to attend to one another's basic needs, and the presence of a just God means that sinners will most assuredly experience checks upon their sinning. For King, the just God is not a soft sentimentalist but a judge who orders disobedient people (and their institutions) to repent of their sinful ways. If the sinners do not repent, the judge then becomes an executor who uses wrath and power to punish sinners.

King's understanding of divine justice, then, is two-dimensional: the just God (1) shows active concern for the welfare of the poor and needy, and (2) heaps judgment and punishment upon those who disobey the divine law. Further, these two dimensions are inextricably related in King's thought: the just God judges and punishes those who fail to care for the welfare of the needy and the poor.

The state, in King's theological view, does not and cannot escape the justice of God. Rather than existing in a sphere unto itself, the state exists in, with, and under the justice of God. King held that to obey the divine law, and thereby avoid incurring the wrath of a just God, the state itself must be a tool of the justice of God. King often prayed for the day when "justice would roll down like waters" from every city hall, every state house, and every form of federal government. This day, in King's mind, would exist when the state, recognizing its subordination to divine law, embraces a justice that has its perfect model in the justice of God.

---

[74] King, Jr., "MIA Mass Meeting at Holt Street Baptist Church," *Papers*, 3:73–74. With King's words in mind, I contend that it did not take King until after Selma to learn "to get angry at his opponents and send them to hell" (Richard Lischer, *The Preacher King: Martin Luther King, Jr. and the Word That Moved America* [New York: Oxford University Press, 1995] 11). Nor did it take until the last three years of his life for King to carry out "the more dangerous function of prophecy, namely, the exercise of speech that is received directly from God and hurled against God's opponents" (Lischer, *The Preacher King*, 180–81). Lischer and others seem to believe that King did not rely on prophetic rage until after Selma and before Vietnam. But my study shows that King was willing to threaten his opponents, including the state, with the damning words of a just God even in the first part of his career.

Like the just God, the just state would be legislator, judge, and executor. Throughout this first period, King stressed the need for legislation that would serve the freedom of humanity, especially blacks. "We must continue," King stated again and again, "to struggle through legislation,"[75] one of the "tools of justice."[76] Feeling the need to explain why he was moving beyond preaching and education, King argued that, though legislation has its limits in establishing love, it can control "the external effects of one's internal feelings."[77] Legislation can criminalize such things as lynching, segregation, and discriminatory hiring practices. For this reason alone (the ability to coerce and control the behavioral effects of feelings), King felt that the movement should push the state to do what a just state does—help establish human freedom by regulating physical behavior through legislation, executive orders, and judicial decrees.

But King increasingly realized that the ongoing presence of lynching, physical threats, nullification, and interposition, among many other obstructive tactics, meant that passing legislation, issuing executive orders, and ruling in court cases were necessary but insufficient measures for establishing justice in society. Thus, King held that the state, if it is to be just as God is just, must also enforce compliance with its just laws. Justice, in King's mind, became exactly that—enforced compliance with the just laws of the state.

One of the main problems King faced throughout his career, and especially in this first period, was the presence of local political authorities who willfully and flagrantly violated federal laws prohibiting segregation and discrimination. King responded to these intransigent authorities in part by calling upon the federal government to enforce compliance with its just laws, and he envisioned such compliance in at least two forms: the prosecution and punishment of those who break just laws, and the physical protection of law-abiding citizens in the midst of a civil disorder created by those who break just laws.

In King's view, to mirror the God of justice, the state must judge, prosecute, and punish those who disobey its just laws. If justice rules in

---

[75] King, Jr., "The 'New Negro' of the South: Behind the Montgomery Story," *Papers*, 3:284.

[76] King referred to legislation as a tool of justice as early as his first speech to the MIA. See King, Jr., "MIA Mass Meeting at Holt Street," *Papers*, 3:74.

[77] King, Jr., "The 'New Negro of the South," *Papers*, 3:284.

the state, as God intends, the state will actively search for lawbreakers and bring its full powers of prosecution and punishment to bear on them. In this part of his career, King emphasized this point especially in periods of intense crisis. For example, when segregationists in Birmingham engineered a church bombing that resulted in the deaths of four girls, King sharply denounced the intransigence of local political authorities and called upon the federal government, in particular the Justice Department, to move quickly to investigate and convict those responsible for the murders of the little girls.[78]

Moreover, King held that to mirror the God of justice, the state must also provide physical protection for law-abiding citizens, even if such protection requires the potential and actual use of violence. Again, King emphasized justice as physical protection especially in times of crisis. In Montgomery, for example, King approached Governor James Folsom to ask that the state of Alabama provide physical protection, by which King meant armed troops under Folsom's command.[79] In August 1956, King appeared before the Democratic National Committee and pleaded for "federal protection," arguing that without the armed protection "we will be plunged across the abyss of mob rule and tragic anarchy."[80] During a rally to support a 1961 freedom ride, in which hostile segregationists surrounded the church in which the rally took place, King and others survived in part because of the physical protection of armed federal marshals and national guardsmen.[81] In a violent Birmingham, King enjoyed the presence of a federalized Alabama National Guard and the close proximity of armed federal troops.[82]

King often registered regret about the need for forcible means in the search for justice, but he firmly believed that one of the state's proper domestic functions is to keep "law and order" through the intelligent use

---

[78] Martin Luther King, Jr., "What Killed These Four Little Girls?," SCLC Conference Closing Session, Seventh Annual Convention, Virginia Union Seminary, 27 September 1963, MLKJP, GAMK, 2.

[79] Martin Luther King, Jr., interview by Donald T. Ferron, *Papers*, 3:125.

[80] Martin Luther King, Jr., "Testimony to the Democratic National Committee, Committee on Platform and Resolutions," *Papers*, 3:337.

[81] See Garrow, *Bearing the Cross*, 158.

[82] Ibid., 261.

of police power.[83] Justifiable police power on the domestic front, according to King, differs morally from war making on the international front. Unfortunately, King never unpacked this point in great detail, but consider his comments on the volatile admission of James Meredith to the University of Mississippi:

> More than anything else, it is regrettable that United States marshals, a federalized National Guard and troops of the United States Army were the only means by which the admission of James Meredith could be secured. As a devotee of nonviolent discipline, I am also a pacifist. Though I regret the use of force in the Mississippi situation, nevertheless, in my humble judgment, it was necessary and justifiable. Whereas I abhor the use of arms and the thought of war, I do believe in the intelligent use of police power. Though a pacifist, I am not an anarchist. Mississippi's breakdown of law and order demanded the utilization of a police action to quell the disorder and enforce the law of the land. Armed force that intelligently exercises police power, making civil arrests in which full due process is observed, is not functioning as an army in military engagement, so I feel the presence of troops in Oxford, Mississippi, is a police force seeking to preserve law and order rather than an army engaging in destructive warfare.[84]

King's explanation reveals that he relied heavily on the forcible means of the state—its armed forces—to enforce the just laws of the state and to protect and support him and his followers in their nonviolent quest for human freedom.

King also believed that, like the just God, whose divine law commands that life's basic necessities be provided to the poor, the state must also seek to establish economic justice in society. King did not emphasize this point in the first period of his career, especially while he was in Montgomery, but neither did he ignore it.

This deeply grounded belief appeared a number of times throughout this first period, especially after Montgomery. For example, on his first

---

[83] Thus, Hanes Walton, Jr., *The Political Philosophy of Martin Luther King, Jr.* (Westport: Greenwood Publishing Corporation, 1971) 112, is wrong to argue that " King was silent on the right of the state to employ violence in carrying out its lawful functions."

[84] King, Jr., "Who Is Their God?" *The Nation* 195 (13 October 1963): 210.

trip to India, in early 1959, King commended India's government for throwing "its full weight behind the program of giving the Harijans an equal chance in society—especially when it comes to job opportunities, education, and housing."[85] In King's mind, the government of India rightly recognized that the twin of the injustice of social segregation is the injustice of economic segregation, and that both problems need to be the focus of state action.

Further, in 1960, King critiqued the US government for forming powerless commissions whose many "studies…continue to pose [racial and economic] problems without any concrete results that could be translated into jobs, education, equality of opportunity, and access to the fruits of an historic period of prosperity."[86] In 1961, King identified the needs of blacks as the same needs expressed by labor—"decent wages, fair working conditions, livable housing, old age security, health and welfare measures," and more—and called upon the labor movement to work in concert with the civil rights movement to push the state to meet these needs.[87] Two years later, in 1963, King called upon the government to level "obstacles of discrimination," to establish job training, create "new jobs by public works," liquidate ghettos, offer loans and grants to the poor, provide adult education, and construct integrated housing.[88] King directed his words here to the state, not to private industry. Although he certainly did not exclude the option of the state and private industry working in cooperation, King held that it was the state that could and should act aggressively, even through national planning, to transform the problems of capitalism into opportunities for society's poor. In King's view, the state is for the poor; the poor are not for the state.

Cruciform Love and the State

Because King encouraged the state to enforce compliance with just laws, even through the use of forcible means, he did not expect the state to exercise perfectly the unflinching love that Jesus revealed on the cross.

---

[85] Martin Luther King, Jr., "My Trip to the Land of Gandhi," in *A Testament of Hope*, 28.

[86] King, Jr., "The Burning Truth in the South," in *A Testament of Hope*, 96.

[87] Martin Luther King, Jr., "If the Negro Wins, Labor Wins," in *A Testament of Hope*, 203.

[88] Martin Luther King, Jr., "In a Word: Now," in *A Testament of Hope*, 168.

This is not to say, however, that King did not call upon the state, in this first period, to love as Jesus loved. Following in the footsteps of Morehouse's George Kelsey and of Boston personalists, and in concert with his earlier criticism of Reinhold Niebuhr's theological account of the state, King believed that the state must heed, at least in part, the mandates of divine love. Consider again the primary themes of King's understanding of divine love—giving, forgiving, reconciling, universal, and nonviolent—but this time in relation to the internal and external life of the state.

King made the bold suggestion, in this first period, that the state should be other-focused, sacrificial, and concerned about persons and things other than itself. King offered this suggestion in, among other places, "The Dimensions of a Complete Life," a sermon in which he argued that "life at its best" is the life that includes length (self-concern), breadth (concern for others), and height (concern for God).[89] These three dimensions, King claimed, "must meet in every individual life if that life is to be complete."[90] But King did not limit his subject to the life of individuals, particularly when addressing the breadth of life. "So often," King proclaimed, "nations of the world are concerned about the length of life, about perpetuating their nationalistic concerns, and their economic ends."[91] This selfishness lay at the root of global problems such as world poverty and diseases. "May it not be," he asked, "that the problem in the world today is that individuals as well as nations have been overly concerned with the length of life, devoid of the breadth?"[92] The question, of course, was rhetorical, and King recommended that both individuals and states begin to exhibit a "dangerous altruism."[93]

King also maintained that the state should practice forgiveness. Interestingly, however, he refrained from talking much about the state's responsibility to forgive, primarily because he held that only the wronged party can rightly initiate forgiveness and that rarely is the state the wronged party.[94] Nevertheless, he fully recognized that the state is not always

---

[89] Martin Luther King, Jr., "The Dimensions of a Complete Life," in *The Measure of a Man* (Philadelphia: Fortress Press, 1988) 36.

[90] Ibid., 37.

[91] Ibid., 44, 48.

[92] Ibid., 48.

[93] Ibid., 44.

[94] King, Jr., *Strength to Love*, 48.

(or merely) the perpetrator of injustices, and firmly believed that, when the state has been a victim, it would do well to forgive its enemies, once the unjust actions have been eliminated, and to pursue reconciliation.

"Forgiveness," wrote King, "is a catalyst creating the atmosphere necessary for a fresh start and a new beginning. It is the lifting of a burden or the canceling of a debt."[95] That King encouraged the state to practice this type of forgiveness is evident in his affirmation of India during his trip there in 1959. King praised India for what he perceived to be its ability to forgive Great Britain for its grave injustice of colonialism. "Today," King stated, "a mutual friendship based on complete equality exists between India and the British people within the commonwealth."[96] King was especially pleased with the ways in which India's nonviolent campaign led to reconciliation, but his implied point, consistent with his emphasis on love, is that India performed admirably by canceling Great Britain's debt.

Indeed, King believed that reconciliation is the proper end of all state action. In a sermon on humanity, King even portrayed Yahweh as saying that the United States, among other states, is "made for something high and something noble and something good," by which he meant reconciliation, the antithesis of segregation, discrimination, and colonialism.[97]

King's theological appeal to reconciliation as the proper end of state action is especially evident, in this first period, in his various citations of Abraham Lincoln. When discussing the redemptive power of love, for example, King claimed that Lincoln "tried love and left for all history a magnificent drama of reconciliation."[98] What King had in mind was Lincoln's decision to hire Stanton, who had mercilessly derided Lincoln during the campaign for the presidency, as secretary of war. Lincoln had plenty of reasons to hate Stanton, King believed, but instead chose to seek reconciliation—a choice that resulted in Stanton's becoming not only a trusted secretary but also a true friend.

This example is too interpersonal to draw a conclusion about King's understanding of the state's responsibility to reconcile, but King also went on to discuss Lincoln's efforts to reconcile with the Confederacy,

---

[95] Ibid., 48–49.
[96] King, Jr., "My Trip to the Land of Gandhi," in *A Testament of Hope*, 25.
[97] King, Jr., "What Is Man?," in *The Measure of Man*, 30.
[98] King, Jr., *Strength to Love*, 52.

noting that when feelings between the Union and the Confederacy were terribly bitter, Lincoln spoke a "kind word" about the South. "Asked by a shocked bystander how he could do this Lincoln said, 'Madam, do I not destroy my enemies when I make them my friends?'" King's point was that Lincoln's kind word, and his justification for speaking it, revealed "the power of redemptive love."[99] But, on another level, King's political example shows his belief that the state's proper business is to mold reconciliation out of a divided world. The state's proper business is not to foster division, as Lincoln might have done had he anathematized Stanton and the Confederacy, but to seek to overcome division so that friendship between peoples and between states may result.

King also maintained, in this first period, that the state should develop a universal perspective in its reconciling actions. King made this point relatively early in the first part of his career when he offered his recommendations for "the birth of a new age": "The first thing is this, that we must rise above the narrow confines of our individualistic concerns, with a broader concern for all humanity." In this new world of "geographical togetherness," no state can live alone. King's point here is theological. As he stated so many times, and as he stated again in this sermon, God has linked humanity together in "a great chain," so that "whatever affects one directly affects all indirectly." "We are all," King said, "involved in a single process."[100]

King believed the domestic responsibility of the state, in light of human togetherness, is to acknowledge the political universalism that was expressed so well in the Declaration of Independence, and to enact this universalism through domestic policies that prohibit segregation as well as other obstructions of universalism. As King put it negatively: "The universalism at the center of the Declaration of Independence has been shamefully neglected by America's appalling tendency to substitute 'some' for 'all.'"[101]

King held that, on the international front, the responsibility of the state is to recognize its abiding connection with other states and to seek to live peacefully with them. He made this point most explicitly after the

---

[99] Ibid., 53. Miller, *Voice of Deliverance*, 101–102, demonstrates that King borrowed the Lincoln story, without acknowledgement, from J. Wallace Hamilton, *Horns and Halos in Human Nature* (Westwood NJ: Revell, 1954).

[100] King, Jr., "The Birth of a New Age," *Papers*, 3:342.

[101] King, Jr., *Strength to Love*, 28.

Cuban missile crisis, when he stated that the time had come to affirm the United Nations in its efforts to secure an accord on nuclear testing and disarmament. "This is what foreign policy is all about anyway: Seeking out a formula by which we may create a community of nations in the world mutually interdependent upon each other."[102]

King's theological account of humanity and love led him to argue against the state's willingness to resort to total nuclear war. Such war, he felt, countered the God-given right to survive, as well as Jesus' example of nonviolence on the cross. King believed that the state should be nonviolently loving in its international relations. However, the language of nonviolent love dropped out of King's speech when he spoke of the need for federal power in resisting violent racists who threatened his marches. As noted above, King distinguished between war making and keeping law and order through the intelligent use of police power. When he called for the use of police power to establish law and order, he invoked the mandates of justice but not love.

Love, Justice, and the Beloved Community

King did not admit to the presence of a fracture between love and justice, primarily because he understood God (and the good state) to be a union of the two. In one of his famous sermons of this first period, King described God as "a creative synthesis of love and justice," a description consistent with what he had proclaimed at the first meeting of the MIA at Holt Street Baptist.[103] Both at Holt Street and in this sermon, King understood the nature of God as both "tough" and "tender," as revealed in the Bible. "On the one hand God is a God of justice who punished Israel for its wayward deeds, and on the other hand, he is a forgiving father whose heart was filled with unutterable joy when the prodigal returned home."[104] Nevertheless, an easy synthesis of King's understanding of the relationship between love and justice is not possible, primarily because of the numerous meanings that he had in mind when he spoke of love and justice. Considering just two of the various relationships,

---

[102] Martin Luther King, Jr., "New Year Hopes," 5 January 1963, MLKJP, GAMK, 1–2.

[103] King, Jr., *Strength to Love*, 16.

[104] Ibid., 15.

however, will help clarify King's understanding of the different ways in which the state is related to love and justice.[105]

Consider first the relationship between love as nonviolent persuasion and justice as enforced compliance. King believed that this type of love and justice complement, rather than contradict, each other. The existence of sin within society means that the tool of love, nonviolent persuasion, will not always succeed in moving people to keep order and experience moral growth. Thus, the use of the tools of justice (for example, legislation, arrests, armed forces) is sometimes necessary to establish freedom for humanity. Justice complements love, in this case, by doing what love does not do—force sinners to behave as if they believe the mandates of love. Conversely, King believed that love complements justice. Humanity is not wholly depraved, in King's thought, and so the tool of love can assist the tools of justice.

Positing a relationship of complementarity between love as nonviolent persuasion and justice as enforced compliance, King argued that the state has a responsibility to be both loving and just in its domestic affairs. On the one hand, the state has a responsibility to use its means of coercion in the pursuit of freedom for all—hence, King's call for federal marshals at voting polls. On the other hand, the state has a responsibility to adopt the tools of nonviolent persuasion—hence, King's appeal to President Kennedy to use the moral power of his office to persuade the American people that segregation is immoral.[106]

All this is not to say, however, that King did not prefer love as nonviolent persuasion to justice as enforced compliance, or vice versa. King's preference switched according to his social location. If he was in a situation in which hostile segregationists threatened the lives of him and his followers, King preferred the God of the Hebrew Bible and the ways in which Yahweh used power to cut down enemies. So King called for the presence of federal troops. But if the situation was not critical, King

---

[105] Problems in King scholarship arise when authors do not attend to the many meanings King attributed to these two terms. For example, Greg Moses, *Revolution of Conscience: Martin Luther King, Jr. and the Philosophy of Nonviolence* (New York: The Guilford Press, 1997) 185–226, offers an entire chapter on love and justice without attending to the nuances in King's thought.

[106] King, Jr., "An Appeal to the Honorable John F. Kennedy, President of the United States, for National Rededication to the Principles of the Emancipation Proclamation and for an Executive Order Prohibiting Segregation in the United States," 17 May 1962, MLKJP, GAMK, 25–34.

seemed to prefer the God revealed in the unflinching Jesus. Thus, in a 1959 speech to religious leaders, King stated that he and his fellow believers, though recognizing the need for the tools of justice, really "prefer that men would voluntarily comply" with the mandates of justice and love.[107]

Another of King's conceptions of the relationship between love and justice posits justice as desegregation and love as reconciliation. Justice is the means, in this case, and love is the end. With this conception, King held that desegregation is "eliminative and negative": it eliminates and negates a sinful system that denies blacks equal access to schools, housing, transportation, and more. Integration, however, is "creative" and "positive": it is "the positive acceptance of desegregation and the welcomed participation of Negroes into the total range of human activities."[108] Unlike desegregation, integration is true reconciliation. For integration to exist, all members of society must express an attitude of acceptance—an attitude which holds that each person is a worthy member of society and that all people are united as equal members of a family. Lacking the proper attitudinal dimension, desegregation is not the same as integration, but is the "necessary step" for achieving integration. "Desegregation," King wrote, "will not change attitudes but it will provide the contact and confrontation necessary by which integration is made possible and attainable."[109]

Understanding justice as desegregation and love as integration, and claiming that the former is the means for effecting the latter, King held that the state can assure justice but not love, that the state can desegregate but not integrate society. The demands of desegregation can be "regulated by the codes of society and the vigorous implementation of law-enforcement agencies," but the demands of integration "concern inner attitudes, genuine person-to-person relations, and expressions of compassion which law books cannot regulate and jails cannot rectify." In King's view, the state can establish justice, but only "a higher law produces love"—an "inner law, written on the heart."[110]

---

[107] King, Jr., Address at Conference of Religious Leaders Under the Sponsorship of the President's Committee on Government Contracts, MLKJP, GAMK, 6.

[108] King, Jr., "The Ethical Demands for Integration," *A Testament of Hope*, 118.

[109] Ibid., 123.

[110] Ibid.

Given this understanding of the relationship between love and justice, then, the state has only indirect responsibilities regarding the emergence of love in society. The state's direct responsibility is to establish justice, but, by doing so, the state serves love; that is, it provides the material conditions and boundaries required for the flourishing of love.

The State and the Beloved Community

This brief discussion of just two of the various relationships between love and justice in King's thought leads directly to his notion of the beloved community and of the state's role in creating the community. The beloved community, for King, is a dream, and nowhere in this period did he recount the dream more eloquently than he had at the 1963 March on Washington. But King began to speak about his dream of the beloved community years earlier. For example, on the eve of 11 August 1956, he gave a speech in Buffalo, New York, which sketched the end that he hoped the Montgomery boycott would serve. Speaking of a transition from an "old age" to a "new age," King argued that the transition would sometimes require that "we will have to rise up in protest." With Montgomery on his mind, King noted that sometimes boycotts would be necessary, but only as a means "to awaken a sense of shame in the oppressor." Boycotts are means, King stated, "but the end is reconciliation. The end is the creation of a beloved community."[111] Near the end of the speech, King sketched his vision of this community, a new world in which "men will live together as brothers; a world in which men will no longer take from the masses to give luxuries to the classes. A world in which men will throw down the sword and live by the higher principle of love."[112] This brief statement, the contents of which remained consistent in his reflections through the years, reveals three dimensions of King's vision of the beloved community: reconciliation, economic justice, and nonviolent love.

The role of the state in creating the beloved community, as King conceived it, varies according to the elements. As detailed above, the state cannot assure reconciliation but it can certainly establish the physical conditions required for its presence, namely, desegregated conditions. In this sense, the state's role in creating the beloved community is indirect:

[111] Martin Luther King, Jr., "The Birth of a New Age," *Papers*, 3:344.
[112] Ibid., 346.

the state cannot create the beloved community, which includes an attitude of the love known through God in Christ, but it can create the conditions required for the flourishing of reconciliation. Further, as detailed above, the role of the state is not to throw down its sword when dealing, on the domestic front, with those who dissent from just laws, but to judge and punish them, sometimes with forcible means that use violence. But the state should use its forcible means of justice if and only if it intends for them to establish love as reconciliation. In this sense, too, the state has an indirect role in creating the beloved com-munity: the state can use its forcible tools of justice in the short term so that the beloved community, which mirrors the nonviolence of God in Christ, may occur in the long term. Regarding the establishment of economic justice, however, King believed, even in this first period, that the state can play a direct role in creating the beloved community: the state can and should redistribute the wealth so that poverty is eliminated and so that all have the basic goods required for the flourishing of the human personality.

The state, then, has both a direct and an indirect role to play in establishing the beloved community.[113] In King's theological perspective, the state is made for the beloved community—a community of loving reconciliation that God in Christ intends for all of humanity.

Grounding the State in Human Sociality: A Theological View of the Origin of the State

King could conceive such a high purpose for the state in part because of his theology of the origin of the state. Preston Williams has argued that King located the state's origin in the social dimension of the human. According to Williams, King believed that humanity is social in nature

---

[113] John Cartwright, "The Social Eschatology of Martin Luther King, Jr.," in *Essays in Honor of Martin Luther King, Jr.*, ed. John Cartwright (Evanston: Garrett Evangelical Theological Seminary, 1971) 11, argues that King emphasized not a specific plan for the beloved community but "the specific attributes and qualities which persons must acquire in order to hasten the coming of the 'Beloved Community' and insure its survival." The problem with this statement, as the following chapters will demonstrate, is that it completely dismisses the numerous ways in which King specified a state role in the creation of the beloved community.

and so "destined to live in communities and states."[114] Williams offers no textual evidence to support his description of King's view, but if he is right, King understood the state as an institution that has its roots in the natural inclination of the human person to depend upon and relate to other people.

As noted above, throughout the first period of his public career, indeed throughout his life, King understood people to be deeply social, naturally in kinship, and inextricably bound to and dependent upon all others. King's untiring reiteration that the human person is by nature a societal creature has important implications regarding his understanding of the state, some of which he drew out in "The Ethical Demands for Integration," his famous 1962 speech on the philosophy of integration:

> Not only are all men alike (generically speaking), but man is by nature a societal creature. Aside from the strength and weakness found in Homo sapiens, man has been working from the beginning at the greatest adventure of "community." Whenever Cro-magnon man, under whatever strange impulse, put aside his stone ax and decided to mutually cooperate with his caveman neighbor, it marked the most creative turn of events in his existence. That seemingly elementary decision set in motion what we now know as civilization. At the heart of all that civilization has meant and developed is "community"—the mutually cooperative and voluntary venture of man to assemble a semblance of responsibility for his brother. What began as the closest answer to a desperate need for survival from the beasts of prey and the danger of the jungle was the basis of present day cities and nations.[115]

Implied in this important passage is King's belief that the state arose out of the natural human inclination to form community. The base human instinct to survive the beasts of the jungle, whatever they might have been, is the earliest foundation of the state, but it is also much more than the need to survive that drove humanity together. People simply needed to be together in order to realize their potential, and thus they

---

114 Preston N. Williams, "An Analysis of the Conception of Love and Its Influence on Justice in the Thought of Martin Luther King, Jr." *Journal of Religious Ethics* 18 (Fall 1990): 18.

115 King, Jr., "The Ethical Demands for Integration," in *A Testament of Hope*, 122.

formed the state so that it would lead to a more perfect community, a place where no person would be solely responsible for every dimension of his or her existence and where every human personality could fully develop. For King, then, the state originated in the social dimension of the human personality, with its quest for a fulfillment not available in the life of the jungle.

Interestingly, King separated himself, on the issue of the origin of the state, from Martin Luther, who had located the origin in the fall of humanity from a life of perfect grace and in divine need to rectify that fall. Luther held that the state arose because wicked people, especially non-Christians, would otherwise murder one another and plunge the world into a chaos where no one could serve God.[116] There is nothing in King's writings to suggest that he intentionally tried to be at odds with Luther on the subject of the origin of the state, but his separation from Luther allowed him to refrain from stressing only the coercive dimension of the state. As part of a family subjected to political repression, as one who felt he suffered at the hands of a police state, and as a leader of those who suffered state-sanctioned brutalities, King was wary of granting too much of a role to state violence. Of course, King always wanted the state to use its police powers in situations in which the lives of activists were threatened. Still, King wanted to call the state to concern itself primarily with more positive functions—for example, the provision of medical care for the elderly and livable housing for the poor—and this required offering a different ontological grounding of the state from the one Luther provided. More exactly, as King knew, it called for an ontological grounding of the state in human sociality, in the relatedness between human persons, or in something similarly positive.

Like his teachers at Boston University, then, King understood the state to be grounded in human sociality. King's Bostonian ontological grounding of the state allowed him, on the one hand, to refrain from stressing only the coercive dimension of the state, and, on the other hand, to posit the state as properly concerned with issues related to the fulfillment of human personality.

---

[116] Martin Luther, "Secular Authority," in *Luther and Calvin on Secular Authority*, trans. and ed. Harro Hopfl (Cambridge: Cambridge University Press, 1991) 30.

The Good State and Voluntary Associations

It is necessary but insufficient, then, to argue that King emphasized, in this first period, his notion that the state is a force for evil. More than a force for evil, the state is also God's minister for human freedom. On the one hand, this is King's normative view of the state: the state should be God's minister for human freedom within the beloved community. On the other hand, King believed that he saw glimpses of the just and loving state within human history. He publicly acknowledged the federal courts working for justice as desegregation, federal troops acting for justice as enforced compliance, the Indian government realizing love as forgiveness, Lincoln striving for love as reconciliation, and more. In other words, King realized that the state within history was not only a force for evil but also God's minister for human freedom. Thus, King not only heavily criticized the state; he also praised it and even appealed to its goodness when seeking to counter the state's sinful manifestations. Interestingly, even in "What Is Man?," in which he preached that he could see nothing but evil in collective institutions, King also went on to grant that collective institutions, as well as individuals, are never beyond the redeeming grace of a loving God. Both individuals and the state are made for a higher purpose—reconciliation—and both always have the capacity to return to their purpose. They always have that capacity because their characters are never wholly depraved; there is always an element of good in human nature.

Nevertheless, King believed that the state, even as the minister of God, cannot, by itself, bring about human freedom within the beloved community. Regarding the problem of race alone, King recognized that the state cannot provide the whole solution. As King put it: "I am convinced, as I have said many times, that the salvation of the Negro is not in Washington."[117] Thus, King stated that the racial problem "cannot be solved on a purely political level,"[118] and that government action, though necessary, "is not the whole answer to the present crisis."[119]

In this view, the state is necessary but insufficient for bringing about the beloved community. King thus concluded that voluntary associations

---

[117] Martin Luther King, Jr., "Virginia's Black Belt,"14 April 1962, MLKJP, GAMK, 9.

[118] King, Jr., "We Are Still Walking," *Papers*, 3:450.

[119] King, Jr., *Stride Toward Freedom*, 198.

are necessary to complement the work of the state and to prompt the state to stop its sinful ways. King especially embraced two voluntary associations: the church and the SCLC.

Consider just the church. Regarding the race problem, King believed, the presence of the church is necessary for touching the hearts and transforming the souls of individuals so that they would support and move towards love as integration. King held that the state can and should change external behavior, and that the church can and should change internal feelings. As he put it, the church "should try to get to the ideational roots of race hate, something that the law cannot accomplish."[120] The state needs the church, in this sense, because the proper end of the state—reconciliation—can exist only if the church accomplishes its task of changing human feelings.

But King believed that the state needs the church for another reason, too. Like all sinners, the state is in need of a catalyst that will help point it towards its proper end. Deeply sinful, the state is in need not of a wholly supportive institution but of an active conscience. It is exactly the church, in King's view, that should play the role of the conscience of the state. As the agent of divine reconciliation on earth, "The church must be reminded that it is not the master or the servant of the state, but rather the conscience of the state. It must be the guide and critic of the state, and never its tool."[121]

But churches often act as if they were "ready lackeys of the state."[122] King was especially disappointed with the church's unreserved blessing of the two world wars and, of course, its failure to call the state to end its support for segregation. On this latter point, King faulted both black and white churches—the former for its apathy and the latter for its sheer silence. As this first period progressed, King grew increasingly frustrated with the white church in particular for the obstructionist stance it was beginning to assume in protesting the civil rights movement. Nowhere is this more evident than in King's famous "Letter from Birmingham Jail." King granted that there were "notable exceptions,"[123] and in these he put his hope that the "church within the church" would continue to be

---

[120] Ibid., 205.

[121] King, Jr., *Strength to Love*, 62.

[122] Ibid., 61.

[123] King, Jr., *Why We Can't Wait*, 89.

strong. But he registered his major disappointment in the white church for becoming "an arch-defender of the status quo."[124]

Made for Humanity

Theologically speaking, King understood his criticisms of and praises for the state as the work of God. Politically speaking, however, King portrayed the work of guiding and critiquing the state, of saying "yes" and "no" to the state, as the political practice of "democratization." Following in the footsteps of Benjamin Mays, King felt that he was doing the work of God by affirming democracy and by being critical of the form it assumed in the United States.

At the first mass meeting of the MIA, King spoke of his "deep-seated belief that democracy transformed from thin paper to thick action is the greatest form of government on earth."[125] That night, King extolled the virtue of US democracy because of its establishment of "the right to protest for right."[126] In the period that followed, however, the civic republican King expanded his appreciation of democracy to include its creedal beliefs that all are created equal and that all possess inalienable rights to life, liberty, and the pursuit of happiness.

Like his former teacher, Kenneth Smith, King often compared democracy to totalitarianism, finding the latter to be fatally flawed. King argued that democracy, as opposed to totalitarianism, "says that each individual has certain basic rights that are neither conferred by nor derived from the state. To discover where they came from it is necessary to move back behind the mist of eternity, for they are God-given."[127] Totalitarianism, unlike democracy, refuses to admit the existence of such God-given human rights, and thus treats individuals as if they are merely means to an end. In totalitarian systems, "the individual ends up in subjection to the state,"[128] and the state itself is understood to be the end of life. "And if any man's so-called rights or liberties stand in the way of that end they are simply swept aside."[129]

---

[124] Ibid., 92.
[125] King, Jr., "MIA Mass Meeting at Holt Street Baptist Church," *Papers*, 3:71.
[126] Ibid., 73.
[127] Martin Luther King, Jr., "The American Dream," in *A Testament of Hope*, 208.
[128] King, Jr., *Stride Toward Freedom*, 92.
[129] Ibid., 93.

King presented his critique of totalitarianism as part of his critical analysis of communism.[130] Echoing Williams and Maritain, King understood communism as a "protest against unfair treatment of the poor," and thus as a challenge for any disciple of Jesus Christ, who was anointed to preach the gospel to the poor.[131] But King also preached that "communism is based on an ethical relativism and a metaphysical materialism that no Christian can accept."[132] King was especially appalled by the ways in which an ethically relativist communism justified almost any means, including murder and lying, as necessary to achieve the end of a communist society. In King's view, a good end cannot justify just any means, "because in the final analysis the end is preexistent in the means." As one who believed in a personal God active in history, King was equally disturbed by the absence of God in communism's materialistic views on history. More important for this study's purposes, however, King "opposed communism's political totalitarianism," arguing that it subjected the individual to the state.[133] "True," King wrote, "the Marxist would argue that the state is an 'interim' reality...but the state is the end while it lasts, and man only a means to that end."[134] In communism, the state tramples liberties of expression, the right to vote, and the freedom to read and hear what one chooses. "Man hardly becomes more, in communism, than a depersonalized cog in the turning wheel of the state." The subjection of the individual is so problematic, because individuals are children of God, ends in themselves. Thus, echoing Maritain, King wrote: "Man is not made for the state; the state is made for man." The state, in his view, must never treat the individual as "a means to the end of the state."[135]

Disturbed by communism's political totalitarianism, King continued to turn to and embrace democracy, finding its creed to converge nicely with his theology. As democracy holds that the human person possesses rights conferred by God, so does Christianity; as democracy believes that

---

[130] Miller, *Voice of Deliverance*, 101–104, traces King's critical analysis of communism to Robert McCracken, *Questions People Ask* (New York: Harper & Brothers, 1951) 163–72. King's two-sided interpretation, however, is also rooted in the analyses offered by Maritain and Williams.

[131] King, Jr., *Stride Toward Freedom*, 94.

[132] King, Jr., "Paul's Letter to American Christians," *Papers*, 3:416.

[133] King, Jr., *Stride Toward Freedom*, 92.

[134] Ibid., 92–93.

[135] Ibid., 93.

all are created equal, so does Christianity; as democracy views individuals as ends, so does Christianity; and as democracy sees all of humanity as united together, so does Christianity. Democracy expresses Christian beliefs, in King's view, and Christianity embraces the democratic creed.

The problem is the historical manifestation of democracy—the "anemic democracy" of history.[136] As King saw it, US democracy in particular practiced "the antithesis of democracy," namely, segregation.[137] Harking back to "The Negro and the Constitution," King claimed that "segregation and discrimination are strange paradoxes in a nation founded on the principle that all men are created equal."[138] On a related note, US democracy also disgusted King because of its willingness to allow states' rights to run roughshod over God-given human rights. US democracy, as expressed through the founding documents, was the best form of government because of its recognition of God-given rights; but, in its earthly form, US democracy was problematic because states' rights were often used as "an excuse for insurrection."[139]

But nowhere did King ever suggest that his followers should outright reject the democratic form of state as it appeared in the United States. On the contrary, King encouraged his followers to use the tools of democracy, especially the right to protest, to transform democracy from "thin paper to thick action," or, as he put it in "I Have a Dream," "to make real the promises of democracy."[140] Further, King also stressed the importance of "the sacred right" of democracy—the right to vote.[141] Like Mays and his family, then, King was far from being a rabid revolutionary committed to overthrowing the democratic state.[142] Rather, the reformist

---

[136] King, Jr., "The Ethical Demands for Integration," in *A Testament of Hope*, 117.

[137] King, Jr., *Stride Toward Freedom*, 190.

[138] Ibid., 191.

[139] Martin Luther King, Jr., Remarks to the NAACP Sponsored Mass Rally for Civil Rights, Los Angeles, 10 July 1960, MLKJP, GAMK, 1.

[140] Martin Luther King, Jr., "I Have a Dream," in *A Testament of Hope*, 218.

[141] King, Jr., "Give Us the Ballot," in *A Testament of Hope*, 197.

[142] This is not to say that King saw his movement as anything less than revolutionary. In fact, King spoke of his movement as a different type of revolution. "In this situation," he stated, "there is no attempt to overthrow the government." Rather, the civil rights movement "is a revolution to get in, and not to destroy the existing government or to destroy property." Transcript of "March on Washington," Metropolitan Broadcast Television, 28 August 1963, MLKJP, GAMK, 6.

King recommended democratization, "our most powerful weapon for world respect and emulation."[143]

Clearly, King expressed no thin understanding of democracy. Like the democracy favored by Mays and Rauschenbusch, the democracy favored by King was not a thin one that would give individuals the right to vote, as well as minimal physical protection, and then leave them to exist as they will. Rather, King affirmed a social democracy that seeks to bind all individuals together as free and equal citizens who enjoy the basic necessities of life. Thus, democratization meant not only opposing segregation but also creating the economic and physical conditions under which all human personalities can flourish.

In King's view, democratization also meant counteracting the demand for states' rights that troubled him so much in his fight against segregation. Such counteracting, in King's mind, did not require forming a "centralized government" but a "Jeffersonian democracy" with a federal government that respects both states' rights and God-given human rights, allowing the latter to trump the former when the two conflict. As King put it: "But 'states' rights' are valid only as long as they serve to protect larger human rights. I have no opposition to state government. I believe firmly in Jeffersonian democracy and would not advocate a strong centralized government with absolute sovereign powers. But I do feel that the doctrine of states' rights must not be an excuse for insurrection."[144]

King was ever wary of a centralized government that would wield unchecked power, but he was equally wary of a government so decentralized that wrong carried out by more localized political authorities would remain unchecked. Although he was a proponent of Jeffersonian democracy, which stood opposed to the centralized power of monarchies, King also desired state power to be centralized enough to be able to correct the injustices of more localized political authorities.

---

[143] King, Jr., *Stride Toward Freedom*, 196–97.

[144] King, Jr., Remarks to the NAACP Sponsored Mass Rally for Civil Rights, MLKJP, GAMK, 1. For more on Jefferson's idea of republican government, see David N. Mayer, *The Constitutional Thought of Thomas Jefferson* (Charlottesville: University Press of Virginia, 1994) 101–107.

Summary

The first part of King's public career shows that he refused to think of the state in merely secular terms but insisted on offering a distinctively theological interpretation. His views on the state were inextricably connected with his theological beliefs about God, Jesus Christ, humanity, and the moral order. It is therefore impossible to understand King's political thought, in this first part of his career, without attending to his theology.

Following Boston personalists, King located the origin of the state in the divinely created sociality of the human personality. Understanding the state partly as an "order of creation" allowed him to avoid Luther's emphasis on order over justice. Still, Luther's realism, particularly as expressed through Niebuhr, found a home in King's political ethics. Like Niebuhr, King offered a deeply realistic interpretation of the character of the state: he found the state to be racist, classist, and militaristic. King's realism deepened so much during this period that he even began to refer to the state as "evil."

Finding the state to be evil, King counseled his followers, on a contextual basis, to disobey the state. Refusing an unqualified Pauline ethic of subordination as his only option, King insisted that the state is not a final, wholly authoritative entity that properly requires unreserved obedience from its citizens. Believing the state to exist under God, King encouraged his followers to break the state's unjust laws—ones in discord with the eternal law, natural law, and the Constitution, all of which serve and uplift the human personality. Yet King never gave up on the state. Even though his realism deepened, King continued to understand the state as partially good and praised the goodness he experienced. With this goodness in mind, King also refused an unqualified ethic of resistance as his only option. King therefore continued, in this first part of his career, to embrace the dialectical response to the state that he had expressed since his days in high school, college, seminary, and graduate school.

Regarding the internal functions of the state, King argued that the state should actively serve human freedom, as well as the beloved community, by mirroring divine justice and love. In accord with Mays, Niebuhr, Rauschenbusch, and the Boston personalists, King claimed that the state must assume an active role in establishing economic justice for all its citizens, but this was not his major emphasis. King primarily emphasized his belief that the state must legislate justice as desegregation, as well as enforce compliance with desegregation by prosecuting and punishing those who break just laws and by providing physical protection, even through forcible means, for citizens brutalized by those who break just laws. Like Niebuhr, King began to argue that justice, in domestic politics, is a more important value than peace.

Regarding the external life of the state, King focused primarily on the mandates of cruciform love, moving away from his earlier realistic interpretation of war and calling instead for the state to assume a pacifist stance in light of the possibility of total nuclear war. Further, with reconciling love as his political goal, King also began to focus his attention on the field of international relations, suggesting, among other things, that the state work cooperatively with the United Nations, especially on world peace.

King's insistence on applying the mandates of cruciform love to the life of the state suggests that his interpretation of the state is deeply christocentric. Indeed, the fundamental purpose of the state, in King's view, is to serve the reconciling work of Christ by providing the conditions that would allow for the emergence of the beloved community. King's understanding of the state's purpose, then, begins and ends in his belief that God in Christ wills the formation of a community of reconciliation.

On the question of the form of the state, King followed the theological path of his liberal Protestant professors. In King's view, democracy expresses Christian beliefs, and Christianity embraces the democratic creed. In addition, Mays and Rauschenbusch, King affirmed a social democracy that seeks to bind all individuals together as free and equal citizens who enjoy the basic necessities of life within the beloved community. Further, like the republican Thomas Jefferson, King embraced a democracy that eschews a centralized government that one might see in a monarchy. But King did favor a state with enough centralized power that would permit it to direct the public good in the face of opposition from more localized political authorities.

Still, however much praise King bestowed upon the democratic state, he never argued that the state is the ultimate solution to the sins of life. Because he saw the work of the state as extremely limited in effecting the transformation of individual hearts required by the beloved community, King began an earnest effort to activate voluntary associations that would guide and criticize the state while also seeking to implant the ideals of the beloved community within the hearts of individual citizens.

6

AGAINST A MINIMALIST STATE,

BUT FOR A SOCIAL-DEMOCRATIC STATE

1964–1965

"Throughout the New Testament," King stated in September 1964, "there runs the theme of reconciliation." Paul's letters to the churches of Corinth and Ephesus, as well as the Gospels, read of God's plan for reconciliation in the world and "of a ministry [of] reconciliation which has been given to us in Christ." By "us," King meant those who follow Jesus Christ, but, more particularly, he also had in mind blacks involved with the civil rights movement. From King's distinctively theological perspective, blacks in the movement were nothing less than "agents" of the reconciliation that God established through the crucified Christ. As agents of reconciliation, blacks properly acted as the conscience of the state and so pushed the state "to fulfill its particular role in history under God."[1]

As the previous chapter noted, King argued that the role of the state is to provide the physical and material conditions required for full reconciliation—the beloved community—to become a reality within society.

---

[1] Martin Luther King, Jr., "East or West—God's Children," Berlin, Germany, 13 September 1964, MLKJP, GAMK, 3.

From 1955 to 1963, King focused his efforts on the need for the state to act as an agent of reconciliation by sanctioning desegregation in the various forms of public accommodations. In the two years that followed, King focused his work on calling the state to effect reconciliation between its citizens and the economic and political systems that alienated them.

A Theological Understanding of the State and Poverty

On 17 January 1964, King and other black leaders met in the White House with President Johnson to hear of the administration's plans for the War on Poverty.[2] King was pleased to hear of the plans, which were in concert with his own belief, publicized a year earlier in *Why We Can't Wait*, that blacks were in desperate need of a state-sponsored compensatory package that would finally lift them out of the poverty created by years of slavery and discrimination.

For King, the issue of state compensation was theological at root. The state had committed a great sin by sanctioning slavery, segregation, and discrimination, and so needed to atone for its sins. King came across the idea of connecting atonement with state compensation most directly on a trip to India, where he experienced state compensation for the untouchables of Indian society. "The Indian government," King wrote approvingly, "spends millions of rupees annually developing housing and job opportunities in villages heavily inhabited by the untouchables." King also noted that India practiced affirmative action in its college admission practices, giving greater weight to the applications of untouchables than to those of high caste. Such compensatory practices, King reported the prime minister as saying, constitute "our way of atoning" for state-sanctioned sins against the untouchables.

Atonement struck King as divinely just, and he recommended the same practice for the United States. "I suggest atonement," he wrote, "as the moral and practical way to bring the Negro's standards up to a realistic level."[3] Atonement in the form of state compensation was such a

---

[2] David J. Garrow, *Bearing the Cross: Martin Luther King, Jr., and the Southern Christian Leadership Conference* (New York: Vintage Books, 1986) 310.

[3] Martin Luther King, Jr., *Why We Can't Wait* (New York: Harper, 1963) 135. King started mentioning atonement shortly after his trip to India, but his practical application of atonement reached a culmination during this period.

good idea in King's mind because the practice would support the freedom of the human personality and lead to a just society. Atonement would make "freedom real and substantial for our colored citizens."[4] King never believed that the mere absence of desegregated public accommodations would fully free the human personality and establish a just society.

King thus began, in this period, to emphasize his belief that "real and substantial" freedom, as well as the mandates of the just society, require not only desegregated public facilities but also the economic goods that would allow blacks to use such facilities. What good is freedom to eat at an integrated restaurant, King wondered, if blacks have no money to dine there? "Giving a pair of shoes to a man who has not learned to walk," King stated, "is a cruel jest." His point, of course, was that freedom from desegregation requires the material goods to enjoy freedom for integration. Or, as he otherwise stated the point, "with equal opportunity must come the practical, realistic aid which will equip blacks to seize it."[5]

King's own response to the Johnson administration's War on Poverty was to push for state atonement in the form of "a broad-based and gigantic Bill of Rights for the Disadvantaged." King hinted at the idea in the last chapter of his book on the Birmingham story, and presented the idea publicly at the 1964 meeting of the Platform Committee of the Republican National Convention. The inspiration for the proposal was the GI Bill of Rights of 1944, which assisted soldiers in financing their education, acquiring home mortgages, starting businesses, receiving adequate medical care, and winning civil service jobs, among other things. In King's view, just as the state properly compensated World War II veterans for the time they spent away from their homes and jobs, so too should it compensate blacks for their years of enslavement. "Few people," King claimed, "consider the fact that, in addition to being enslaved for two centuries, the Negro was, during all those years, robbed of the wages of his toil." King believed that "no amount of gold could provide adequate compensation" for the psychological turmoil caused by slavery,

---

[4] Ibid.

[5] Martin Luther King, Jr., Statement before the Platform Committee of the Republican National Convention, San Francisco, 7 July 1964, MLKJP, GAMK, 9.

but that "a price can be placed on unpaid wages," a price that the Bill of Rights for the Disadvantaged would begin to repay.[6]

Shortly after meeting with the Republicans, King appeared before the Platform Committee of the Democratic National Convention and, perhaps because he felt the Democrats would be more receptive than the Republicans to his calls for bigger government, further unpacked the specifics of his proposal. He announced to the Democrats that the proposed bill's target would be "the disadvantaged of the nation, our 9.3 million families who are earning less than three thousand dollars per annum."[7] The bill, that is, would target not merely blacks but any and all who lived in poverty. King proposed that the state compensate the poor in part by providing direct payments of cash to families earning less than the said figure, with the payments being determined by subtracting the family's actual income from the figure. In effect, the bill would seek to eliminate poverty by having the state provide the poor with a guaranteed annual income that would lift them out of poverty.[8]

Moreover, King argued that "there must be a full program of free quality education and training plus broad health services, so that the limited family income would not be expended for these essential needs."[9] Eliminating poverty, then, required not only direct state payments to the poor but also education and health care freely provided by the state. Expounding on this point, King cited five major areas that the proposed bill would address: employment, education, health and welfare, housing, and the rural poor. Consider the first four.

Regarding employment, the proposed bill's fundamental goal was to "assure employment," in the private and public domains and at skilled and unskilled levels, to those physically able to work.[10] The goal, in short, was "full employment." King declared that those fit to work should work and that the state should assist them in securing employment, even by

---

[6] Ibid., 10.

[7] Martin Luther King, Jr., Statement before the Platform Committee of the Democratic National Convention, Atlantic City, August 1964, MLKJP, GAMK, 9.

[8] King did not use the words "guaranteed annual income" in either of his reports, though he would use them at a later point. The guaranteed annual income debate loomed large in the public sphere during and after King's comments before the platform committees.

[9] King, Jr., Statement before the Platform Committee of the Democratic National Convention, MLKJP, GAMK, 9.

[10] Ibid.

creating jobs for them. But he also desired a safety net for the "unemployed and those lacking the ability to be self-supporting, such as the aged, widowed heads of families, or broken families with children, [and] the disabled." These people, King insisted, "must receive the subsistence minimum without stigma."[11]

The education dimension of the proposed bill "would provide schooling to establish the missing skills to qualify the disadvantaged for employment at remunerative levels above the lowest rung of the ladder." King wanted the state to provide free schooling so that the poor could move into the professional world of teachers, lawyers, and doctors. In his view, state-sponsored temporary training programs for low-level positions were not enough to establish justice. "For the youth and adults of all ages," he testified, "the emphasis must be on intensive and quality vocational, professional or academic training."[12] Further, King proposed that the state cover the costs of tuition, books, and supplies, as well as provide a stipend that would guarantee the student's earnings to equal the subsistence floor income. He called, too, for an increase in the number of "programs for special or remedial instruction of our younger children who are culturally lagging or retarded."[13]

King suggested that the Bill of Rights for the Disadvantaged should also provide the poor with "free medical, hospital, dental and related health care." Beyond medical care, King's proposal addressed, both positively and negatively, the issue of housing for the poor. Negatively, his bill would ensure the elimination of slums, ghettos, and all other inadequate housing conditions. Foreshadowing his later commitments in Chicago, King stated: "All urban racial ghettos and slums, like Harlem, and all shacks and shanties blighting rural America, must be bulldozed into a rubble wherein will be buried all the rats, vermin, and slumlords that have infested these wastelands." Positively, the bill would provide for the construction of integrated, well-maintained, affordable housing for the poor. "Like the symbols of the era of good will and peace on earth," King argued, "soaring, integrated dwellings, rent controlled at the lowest levels, must rise from the rubble of greed, ignorance and selfishness."[14]

---

[11] Ibid., 10. King did not explain how stigma could be avoided when the state would make direct payments to the poor.

[12] Ibid.

[13] Ibid., 11. Read: Head Start.

[14] Ibid.

King presented not just a negative theological case for the proposed bill, that is, a case based upon the practice of atonement, but also a positive one. The proposed bill, he believed, would make real the Christian belief in the equality of humanity. "If we are all really God's children," King argued in the same month he addressed the Democratic Platform Committee, "then all of us are entitled to the same opportunities, pleasures, and responsibilities."[15] Further, underlying King's proposal was his belief that state resources belong not to the state itself but to the sovereign God and that the state should act as a faithful steward of its material resources. Faithful stewardship, King preached to a gathering of European Baptists, requires the state to provide basic necessities to all of its citizens. "Christians must encourage, yea demand, that their governments act as though the financial and technical resources entrusted to them belong to God, and that these resources are used to the Glory of God for the care of God's children wherever they may be in need."[16] This theological point was simply another way of saying what he had earlier stated in "Paul's Letter to American Christians"—that "God intends for all his children to have the basic necessities of life, and he has left in this universe 'enough and spare' for that purpose."

Politically speaking, King presented the bill by using the language of human rights and justice. Speaking before the NAACP Legal Defense Fund, a group unlike the European Baptists, King argued that "human rights involves two basic elements—recognition and opportunity." Desegregation, he contended, expanded the recognition dimension of human rights in the United States, "but opportunity has stagnated or even receded."[17] By addressing opportunity, the proposed bill would begin to make human rights a reality in the United States. "If we are to talk of human rights in the US," King said, "we must face the necessity for a program of aid to the disadvantaged which raises the poor white and Negro from poverty and failure."[18] Such a program would manifest "the essence

---

[15] Martin Luther King, Jr., "Revolution and Redemption," Closing Address, European Baptist Assembly, Amsterdam, Holland, 16 August 1964, MLKJP, GAMK, 3.

[16] Ibid., 9.

[17] Martin Luther King, Jr., Remarks by King at the Convocation on Equal Justice under Law of the NAACP Legal Defense Fund, 28 May 1964, MLKJP, GAMK, 3.

[18] Ibid., 4.

of justice and Christian morality," a concern to liberate the human personality.[19]

Becoming more global in outlook, an evolution effected in part because of trips abroad, King also began to claim that the state must attend to the issue of global poverty. In fact, in the NAACP speech cited above, King stated that "we must assume responsibility for an international program of aid to those nations whose progress was forcibly inhibited."[20] Writing specifically about Johnson's War on Poverty in March of 1965, King offered: "Cannot we agree that the time has come for an all-out war on poverty—not merely in President Johnson's 'Great Society,' but in every town and village of the world where this nagging evil exists?"[21] In a 1965 address to Massachusetts legislators, King stated: "Everybody must join the war against poverty so that all of God's children will be able to have the basic necessities of life."[22]

Again, as chapter 5 suggested, underlying King's global perspective in general and his comments on world poverty in particular was nothing less than his deeply-held theology. From King's perspective, in a world where divine law establishes that the action of one state affects the actions of all other states, there is a natural and theological imperative for wealthy states to work to eliminate poverty in poor states. Each state is bound together in a social fabric sewn together by God, and so any isolationist tendencies of a state rip at the fabric and thereby begin to destroy the holistic creation of God.

[19] Martin Luther King, Jr., Draft Copy of Remarks by King at the Convocation on Equal Justice under Law of the NAACP Legal Defense Fund, 28 May 1964, MLKJP, GAMK, 11.

[20] Ibid., 5. King had in mind India and the emerging new states in Africa, all of which, he believed, should receive assistance from the United States.

[21] Martin Luther King, Jr., "Brighter Day," Copy of Article for *Ebony* Magazine, March 1965, MLKJP, GAMK, 4.

[22] Martin Luther King, Jr., Address of Reverend Doctor Martin Luther King, Jr. Delivered to a Joint Convention of the Two Houses of the General Court of Massachusetts, Boston, 22 April 1965, MLKJP, GAMK, 11.

Against Goldwater:
A Theological Affirmation of Sweden's
Social-Democratic State

Senator Barry Goldwater, a presidential candidate the time, disagreed with almost everything in King's vision of the good state. Also appearing before the Platform Committee of the Republican National Convention, Goldwater presented a vision of freedom, and of the state, that differed greatly from King's. "The prerequisite of a free society," Goldwater stated, "is the widespread diversion of powers. It means a minimum of government, limited and balanced,"[23] by which he partly meant a state that would refuse to advance anything even remotely like King's proposed Bill of Rights for the Disadvantaged, let alone a program of international aid.

Goldwater despised what he called "centralized government," the type of government the War on Poverty and King's proposed bill would seem to require, primarily because he saw the state in general as "the chief instrument for thwarting man's liberty."[24] Goldwater found the state of the 1950s and 1960s to be much too big for its own good and much too removed from the American people. The state was "a Leviathan, a vast national authority out of touch with the people, and out of their control."[25] Goldwater was especially irritated with the welfare state for subordinating the individual to the state and for seeking to impose socialism on the American people.[26]

For Goldwater, the welfare state would reintroduce a slavery of sorts. The recipient of welfarism "mortgages himself," conceding to the state "the ultimate in political power—the power to grant or withhold from him the necessities of life as government sees fit."[27] The predictable results of the welfare state, then, are (1) increased power for the state and (2) the elimination of individual responsibility, both of which undermine, rather than support, individual liberty. "Let welfare," Goldwater wrote, "be a private concern."[28]

---

[23] Barry Goldwater, *Where I Stand* (New York: McGraw-Hill Book Company, 1964) 121.

[24] Ibid., 16.

[25] Ibid., 20.

[26] Ibid., 69.

[27] Ibid., 73.

[28] Ibid., 74.

Goldwater's minimalist state would simply exercise two "inherent responsibilities": (1) maintaining "a free and competitive economy" and (2) enforcing law and order at home and abroad. Any functions that would go beyond these basic responsibilities—for example, implementation of a Bill of Rights for the Disadvantaged, establishing Medicare, offering economic assistance to most foreign nations, or seeking the unilateral disarmament of our nuclear weapons—were anathema in his vision of the limited state.[29] "If you cherish your freedom," he would often say, "don't leave it all up to BIG GOVERNMENT."[30]

On 16 August 1964, King responded to Goldwater's vision of the minimalist state, a version of which he had encountered in college when reading Thoreau's "Resistance to Civil Government," with a resounding "no." Speaking before the European Baptists in Amsterdam, King drew a connection between Goldwater and the corruption of life in the United States. Troubled by Goldwater's vision of a minimalist state, King spoke of "the corruption of our national life as evidenced by the popularity of a presidential candidate who promises to return the nation to a world of the past, where there will be no taxes, no foreign aid, no social security, and no problems that can't be solved by nuclear power."[31]

The summer of 1964 saw King actively campaigning against Goldwater's presidential candidacy. In 1956 and 1960, King had chosen not to support particular candidates, but, with the emergence of Goldwater's candidacy, King felt that he had "no alternative but to urge every Negro and every white person of good will to vote against Mr. Goldwater" and to withdraw their support for Republican candidates who identified with him.[32] King felt that he had no alternative partly because of Goldwater's embrace of states' rights, which impelled him to accuse Goldwater of giving "aid and comfort to the racist."[33] If Goldwater were to be elected,

---

[29] The US Constitution, Goldwater believed, allowed for nothing other than a limited state. The Constitution is "an instrument, above all, for limiting" the state and its functions. Thus, whereas King appealed to the US Constitution to expand the role of the state in establishing human freedom, Goldwater appealed to the Constitution to limit the role of the state so that human freedom would be guaranteed. See Barry Goldwater, *The Conscience of a Conservative* (Shepherdsville KY: Victor Publishing Company, 1960) 16.

[30] Ibid., 185.

[31] King, Jr., "Revolution and Redemption," MLKJP, GAMK, 6.

[32] Martin Luther King, Jr., "Statement on Goldwater," St. Augustine, 16 July 1964, MLKJP, GAMK, 1–2.

[33] Ibid., 1.

King declared, everything that he and the civil rights movement had fought for would be endangered: Goldwater's candidacy "threatens the health, morality and survival of our nation."[34]

But it was more than just Goldwater's embrace of states' rights that led King to fight his candidacy—it was also the other elements of Goldwater's vision of the minimalist state. Goldwater's state, on the one hand, would not support the War on Poverty, let alone the Bill of Rights for the Disadvantaged and a global war on poverty. Thus, King's own vision of the domestic role of the state would have no chance for recognition and implementation. On the other hand, Goldwater's foreign policy proposals would both pull resources from social programs that King favored and commit the resources to preparing for the possibility of nuclear war. Thus, King's own pacifist vision of the international role of the state would have no chance for recognition and implementation.

But King's expressed disappointment with Goldwater's candidacy was more than a political matter; it was a deeply spiritual matter. Regarding the internal functions of the state, King (unlike Goldwater) believed that the state, as a trustee of God's creation, has a responsibility to redistribute God's resources so that poverty would be eliminated; and that the state, as accountable to a God of unity, has a responsibility to eliminate segregation. Regarding the external functions, King (unlike Goldwater) believed that the divinely created network of mutuality requires the state to offer economic aid to struggling states, especially those in Africa; and that the divine love revealed on the cross requires the state to turn away from militaristic stances. In short, there were theological reasons that led King to call Goldwater "the most dangerous man in America"[35] and to fight hard against the vision of the minimalist state that he embraced.

King's vision of justice as the elimination of poverty, especially as outlined in his proposal for a Bill of Rights for the Disadvantaged, more than implied that he had little patience for Goldwater's vision of the state—a state devoted primarily to supporting as free a capitalist system as possible, trusting all the while that wealth would trickle down from the rich to the poor. On the contrary, the type of state that underpinned King's vision of justice as the elimination of poverty was more in line

---

[34] Ibid., 2.

[35] "*Playboy* Interview: Martin Luther King, Jr.," in James M. Washington, ed., *A Testament of Hope* (San Francisco: Harper & Row, 1986) 373.

with the social-democratic state that he experienced on his 1964 trip to Scandinavia.

Shortly after his appearances before the platform committees, and shortly after campaigning against Goldwater, King traveled to Scandinavia to accept the Nobel Peace Prize, the awarding of which celebrated the nonviolent spirit with which King had led the civil rights movement.[36] At a press conference held in Norway on the day before he accepted the prize, King expressed his belief that Scandinavia's social democracy was a commendable and invaluable source of wisdom for the United States and other countries. "We feel," King stated, "we have much to learn from Scandinavia's democratic socialist tradition and from the manner in which you have overcome many of the social and economic problems that still plague far more powerful and affluent nations."[37] A few days later, at yet another press conference, this one in Sweden, King reiterated his belief that the United States and other countries could learn from Sweden especially, but this time he specified which problems he had in mind, namely, "the problems of poverty, housing, employment, and medical care for your people which problems still plague far more affluent nations."[38] Significantly, these problems were the same ones that King had focused on in his statements to the Republican and Democratic policy makers—a focus he reiterated yet again upon his return to New York City.

King's affirmation of Sweden's handling of such problems as poverty, housing, unemployment, and medical care signaled his embrace

---

[36] I intend for this section, as well as a similar one in the following chapter, to provide backing for the thesis—set forth by Cartwright, Colaiaco, Fairclough, Franklin, and Sturm, among others—that King was supportive of democratic socialism. See John H. Cartwright, "The Social Eschatology of Martin Luther King, Jr.," in *Essays in Honor of Martin Luther King, Jr.*, ed. John Cartwright (Evanston: Garrett Evangelical Theological Seminary, 1971) 4; James A. Colaiaco, *Martin Luther King, Jr.: Apostle of Militant Nonviolence* (New York: St. Martin's Press, 1988) 187; Adam Fairclough, *Martin Luther King, Jr.* (Athens: University of Georgia Press, 1990) 119; Robert Michael Franklin, "An Ethic of Hope: The Moral Thought of Martin Luther King, Jr." *Union Seminary Quarterly Review* 40 (January 1986): 43; and Douglas Sturm, "Martin Luther King, Jr., as Democratic Socialist." *Journal of Religious Ethics* 18 (Fall 1990): 79–105. Only Sturm, however, presents a full case for the thesis.

[37] Martin Luther King, Jr., Press Conference and Statement on Nobel Peace Prize, Forneby, Norway, 9 December 1964, MLKJP, GAMK, 3.

[38] Martin Luther King, Jr., Press Statement on Arrival in Sweden, Stockholm, 12 December 1964, MLKJP, GAMK, 1.

of the country's many, and varied, social welfare institutions. Beginning in the 1930s, Sweden's Social Democrats had sought to construct social welfare institutions designed to yield a social democracy, a democracy of class. According to Tilton, a scholar of Sweden's Social Democrats, this intense struggle for social democracy culminated after World War II, when the Social Democrats "achieved full employment, established a generous new basic retirement system, child benefit, universal health insurance, a more democratic single-track educational system, longer statutory holidays, more progressive taxes, an active labor market policy, and housing subsidies."[39] The Social Democrats added to these massive social welfare policies, backed by state institutions, even further in the 1950s and 1960s, shortly before King's arrival in Sweden, when the party established an income-related supplementary pension.

King's general sense and knowledge of these social welfare institutions, all of them designed to effect a more equitable distribution of economic goods, was at the foreground of his affirmation of the means and ends of the Swedish state. Sweden's social welfare institutions, in King's mind, provided exactly what his own just state would provide—the basic necessities required for the flourishing of the free human personality within the beloved community.

King's affirmation of Sweden's methods was also a commendation of the state's extremely limited nationalization policies. King would have known, at least on a general level, that the Social Democrats in Sweden did not (and still do not) heavily favor nationalization of industries and businesses. Tilton argues that both the troubles the Swedish Social Democrats have had with developing successful means for nationalization and the different strands of the Social Democratic tradition—one that is skeptical of "the amalgamation of economic and political power in the state," and another that favors only gradual socialization—have limited the nationalization of public business to "about 10 percent of the means of production." Sweden controls some utilities, banks, and industries, but has largely relied throughout its history on means other than state ownership to create the society favored by its social democracy.[40]

---

[39] Tim Tilton, *The Political Theory of Swedish Social Democracy: Through the Welfare State to Socialism* (Oxford: Clarendon Press, 1990) 4.

[40] Ibid.

This limited state ownership of the means of production is certainly part of what King had in mind when he commended the methods of Sweden. Given his realistic understanding of the character of the state, King, like some of the Swedish Social Democrats (and like his former professor, Benjamin Mays), was skeptical of economic power centralized within the state and so would have stood against state socialism, that is, control of at least most of the means of production and distribution by a centralized state bureaucracy. But with his realistic perspective, as well as with an intense dissatisfaction with capitalism as he knew it, King opted instead, in his affirmation of Sweden's methods, for the country's participatory socialism, that is, control of the means of production and distribution by a mix of public and cooperative ventures.

What is more, Sweden's political democracy is also part of what King had in mind when he commended the methods of Sweden. Contrary to the totalitarian ways of the former Soviet Union, the Social Democrats of Sweden have always insisted on the presence of political democracy. Tilton reports that the very first stage of democratic socialism in Sweden actually focused not on social democracy but on political democracy. Until 1918, the Social Democrats "engineered a reform establishing equal and universal suffrage."[41] For the Social Democrats of Sweden, then, democracy is the political system that is most consistent with the goals of socialism—goals that would provide for, not detract from, human freedom in community.

Clearly, King's expressed appreciation of Sweden's democratic socialism, and its methods, further reveal his deep opposition to Goldwater's political and economic conservatism. Correlatively, King's appreciation left no doubt that he preferred Sweden's social-democratic state over Goldwater's minimalist state. The reasons behind these preferences were, once again, deeply theological.

King's theological view of human nature was in line with the implicit view of humanity in Sweden's democratic socialism. Underlying the formation of the welfare state by the Social Democrats is an implied belief that what affects one affects all—that the individual must always be placed within the context of the community. Further, the Social Democrats held a substantive notion of human freedom within community. Unlike Goldwater, who understood human freedom primarily as an

---

[41] Ibid.

individual's freedom from encroachment by the state, the Social Democrats held that freedom is freedom for material well-being, even as supported and sanctioned by the state. Unlike Goldwater, the Social Democrats held an affirmative doctrine of economic rights—rights to such things as food, housing, employment, education, and medical care, among other things.

Finding humanity to be deeply social, the Social Democrats eschewed a state that would simply support and enhance individual liberty, as Goldwater envisioned the state, in favor of a state whose overriding responsibility would be to serve the individual in community—the public good. With an affirmative doctrine of economic rights, the Social Democrats refused a state that would simply guarantee a free and competitive economy, as Goldwater envisioned the relationship between the state and the market, in favor of a state that would actively safeguard and serve the economic rights of all the citizenry, even to the point of nationalizing some private industry.

King favored Sweden's social-democratic state over Goldwater's minimalist state partly because his view of human nature was consistent with the Social Democrats' understanding. Unlike Goldwater, King never identified the individual alone as the most important moral and political value. As noted in previous chapters, King had learned from his family and his earlier teachers, especially Benjamin Mays and the Boston personalists, to develop a solidaristic and relational view of human nature. Moreover, unlike Goldwater, King held an affirmative doctrine of rights that included economic rights. Again, King had learned from his family and his teachers, especially Mays and the Boston personalists, that all individuals had God-given rights to food, housing, employment, education, medical care, and more.

King's realistic view of human nature also supported his affirmation of the democratic dimension of Sweden's state. Armed with a realistic perspective on the sinfulness of collective behavior, as well as a belief that the individual is an end, King rejected totalitarian socialism in favor of Sweden's democratic state.

Beyond this, however, King's doctrine of God also led him to embrace the Swedish state. On the one hand, with its understanding of divine justice, King's doctrine of God affirmed the social-democratic state as a faithful response to the divine mandate to provide all people with the basic necessities required for the flourishing of the human personality.

Sweden's active attempt to eliminate poverty, in King's mind, is the proper enactment of the mandates of divine justice. On the other hand, with its understanding of divine love, King's doctrine of God commended the social-democratic state as a faithful response to the divine mandate to seek reconciliation in all action. Sweden's attempts to create a democracy of class, in King's view, is the proper enactment of the mandates of a divine love that seeks to establish the beloved community.

The issue of reconciliation is an important key to understanding King's embrace of Sweden's social-democratic state. If the social telos of democratic socialism is, as Sturm describes, "directed toward the overcoming of alienation, toward the reconciliation of estranged groups, toward the formation of a new society of genuine mutuality permeating all its political and economic processes," it is wholly understandable that King would have affirmed Sweden's social-democratic state.[42] As seen in the previous chapter, King believed that the proper end of all state action is reconciliation among a divided humanity. With this theological belief in mind, King affirmed Sweden's social-democratic state as an agent of reconciliation that sought equality, mutuality, and unity through the elimination of poverty.[43]

---

[42] Douglas Sturm, "Martin Luther King, Jr., as Democratic Socialist," 83.

[43] Additional evidence that King leaned towards a social-democratic perspective exists in the 1964–1965 period. David Garrow reports that in a May 1965 speech to A. Philip Randolph's Negro-American Labor Council, King stated: "Call it what you will, call it democracy, or call it democratic socialism, but there must be a better distribution of wealth within this country for all of God's children." *Bearing the Cross*, 427. Before making this statement, however, King embraced socialism, in a backhanded way, in a copy of an article describing the movement's prospects for 1965. King wrote:

> In a society where commerce proceeds on roads, via airlines, and railroads subsidized up to 90% by federal funds; and where most men of higher learning have been educated in institutions built by government loans and paid their tuition via such programs as the G.I. Bill; and where government is the largest single purchaser, talk of creeping socialism in relation to a war on poverty or Medicare bill is far fetched indeed. As one astute young Negro puts it, "what we have in this country is socialism for the rich and free enterprise for the poor."

Martin Luther King, Jr., "The Movement: Prospects for '65," Manuscript for *IUD Agenda*, MLKJP, GAMK, 13. Further, Charles Fager, an SCLC staff member, claims that while imprisoned with King during this second period of his career, King stated: "If we are going to achieve real equality, the United States will have to adopt a modified form of socialism." Quoted in Garrow, *Bearing the Cross*, 382.

Evolving Criticism:
On War and World Government

Upon his return to the United States, King expounded on the political implications of his trip abroad, including a brief visit he enjoyed with Pope Paul VI before traveling on to Sweden. More particularly, King expressed his deep appreciation for the Pope's plea for a "'peaceful battle'" in which states would "cease the armament race and devote their resources and energies to assisting those throughout the world who lack food, clothing, shelter, and medical care." With this papal statement in mind, King critiqued Johnson's War on Poverty, claiming that it did not go far enough in its efforts to eliminate poverty. "We must," King said, "implement this [papal] plea here in the United States where the budget for the war on poverty is less than one percent of the military budget."[44]

King's criticism was part of an evolving, intensified focus on the problem of poverty and the state. Having been in Scandinavia, where there is "free medical care" and "quality education" but "no unemployment and no slums," and having heard the Pope's message, King felt a "greater sense of urgency" to devote time and energy to the problem of poverty. The "limited, halting steps" of the United States "deeply troubled" him, and so he would "press even more vigorously for a broad alliance" of political forces interested in eliminating poverty. "We must," he said, "escalate the slow, cautious reconnaissance to a broad, sweeping offensive against poverty."[45]

This "broad, sweeping offensive against poverty" meant that the United States would have to change its strategy in dealing with poverty and its related issues. King's personal strategy favored not only the adoption of the Bill of Rights for the Disadvantaged, but also a redistribution of resources away from the military budget.

As he posited an inextricable relation between racial and economic justice, so too did he see a similar relationship between the state sins of militarism and the neglect of poverty. The vast resources that the state poured into maintaining its nuclear military, in King's view, siphoned off the resources that could and should address the elimination of poverty: the arms race slowed the race to economic justice. Just so, the arms race is

---

[44] Martin Luther King, Jr., "Speech Upon Acceptance of NYC Medallion Award," New York City, 17 December 1964, MLKJP, GAMK, 4.

[45] Ibid., 4–5.

theologically problematic. Because it detracts from the divine work of providing basic necessities to all people, the arms race is deeply sinful.

This point marked a new emphasis in King's thought. In the earlier part of his career, King had generally dealt with war, and its preparation, as if it was an issue largely separated from the issue of poverty, but, upon hearing the Pope's message, King began to emphasize his belief that states should shift from "the arms race into a 'peace race,'" more particularly, a race for economic justice.[46]

In the second part of his career, King also continued to condemn war on practical and theological grounds. Remaining consistent with his statements in the first stage of his public career, King argued that "no nation can really win a war if it becomes a world war, and in this sense it is no longer a choice between violence and nonviolence, but ultimately it will be nonviolence and non-existence." World war, in this sense, would be "futile." More than futile, however, a world war would be deeply sinful. Again, remaining consistent with the position he stated in the first part of his career, King stated:

> ...there was a period when I felt that war could serve a negative good.... I never felt that war could be a positive good but I did think that it could be a negative good in that it could prevent the flowering of a negative force in history. But now I have come to the conclusion that because of the potential annihilation of the whole human race, there can be no justification for any large scale war. And, I think that the sooner men come to see that, the better off we will all be, and the better the future will be. In short, if man assumes that he has a right to survive, then he must find some substitute for war...[47]

Because a world war would lead to annihilation, and because annihilation would take away the God-given right to life, a world war would be sinful.

In this second period of his life, King also offered an explicitly christological argument against world war. Speaking to the European Baptists, King argued, on christological grounds, that the church must concern itself with the question of world peace: "This is the world for

---

[46] King, Jr., "Brighter Day," MLKJP, GAMK, 5.

[47] *Redbook* transcript of interview with Martin Luther King, Jr., 5 November 1964, MLKJP, GAMK, question 1.

which Christ died."[48] King's point here is that because Christ gave his life to save the world, thereby proving his love and concern for the world, Christians should fight for world peace. In this sense, world war is sinful not only because it counters the God-given right to life but also because it makes a mockery of the deep and abiding love that Christ showed for the world.

Ever realistic, King continued to believe that world war was a possibility. On the one hand, King stressed that war was possible because states are "genocidal and suicidal in character."[49] Spoken during his trip to Oslo, this new characterization of the character of states highlights the Niebuhrian realism that King had learned so well in his studies and in his experiences. King personalized this realism, too, in the speech he offered a few months later to the European Baptists. "We cannot sit idly by and watch [the world] destroyed by a group of insecure and ambitious egoists who can't see beyond their own designs for power."[50] War arises, in other words, because individual world leaders are sinful egoists who fail to recognize that Christ gave his own life for the world. King offered a similar point, minus the christology, a few months later in an interview in which he stated that the greatest danger to peace is "the existence of individuals often in power positions who have not recognized the danger of warfare. They have a sort of chip-on-the-shoulder diplomacy, always inviting somebody to knock it off."[51]

Ever optimistic, however, King expressed his ongoing belief in the possibility of eliminating war. In his Nobel prize acceptance speech, King declared his refusal "to accept the cynical notion that nation after nation must spiral down a militaristic stairway into the hell of thermonuclear destruction." Eschewing cynicism, King chose to believe that "unarmed truth and unconditional love will have the final word in reality." Rather than ending in thermonuclear hell, humanity will eventually "bow before the altars of God and be crowned triumphant over war and bloodshed, and nonviolent redemptive goodwill will proclaim the rule of the land."[52] King grounded this optimism in his reading of scripture and the vision it

---

[48] King, Jr., "Revolution and Redemption," MLKJP, GAMK, 10.

[49] Martin Luther King, Jr., "The Quest for Peace and Justice," Oslo, Norway, 11 December 1964, MLKJP, GAMK, 21.

[50] King, Jr., "Revolution and Redemption," MLKJP, GAMK, 10.

[51] Redbook transcript, MLKJP, GAMK, question 1.

[52] Martin Luther King, Jr., "Nobel Prize Acceptance Speech," MLKJP, GAMK, 226.

presents to its readers. "'And the lion and the lamb,'" King quoted, "'shall lie down together and every man shall sit under his own vine and fig tree and none shall be afraid.'"[53]

Interestingly, King claimed to have become even more optimistic in this part of his career. In March 1965, he stated: "The Nobel Peace Prize has given me deeper personal faith that man will indeed soon rise to the occasion and give new direction" to the rage of humanity against humanity.[54] The world's recognition of the method of nonviolence, then, actually deepened King's personal faith that humanity, with the help of God, would create a world of peace.

King's deepening faith also resulted in general suggestions for world peace, some of which he did not offer in the first part of his career, and all of which reveal his opposition to Goldwater's vision of the ideal state. One suggestion called for moving away from the "chip-on-the-shoulder diplomacy" to diplomacy centered in the United Nations, "the best instrument we have at this time to bring about the dream of peace." The United Nations, he believed, would offer opportunities for real dialogue between nations, rather than the usual monologue delivered by one nation to another. As King put it, "the greatest channel to peace...is through dialogue—nations sitting down at the peace table talking together about problems that must continue to arise." King acknowledged that "as long as we have men, we are going to have differences," but he also believed that "we can disagree without being disagreeable."[55]

A second suggestion called for "a greater suspension of nuclear tests."[56] King was never President Kennedy's biggest supporter, but after the president's death, he extolled Kennedy's commitment to the test ban treaty. Under "the threat of total destruction of mankind," King stated, Kennedy "guided to reality the historic treaty banning atmospheric nuclear testing."[57] The ban somehow lessened the "ultimate horror" of a

---

[53] Ibid.

[54] King, Jr., "Brighter Day," MLKJP, GAMK, 5.

[55] *Redbook* transcript, MLKJP, GAMK, question 2.

[56] King, Jr., Address of Reverend Doctor Martin Luther King, Jr., Delivered to a Joint Convention of the Two Houses of the General Court of Massachusetts, MLKJP, GAMK, 12.

[57] Martin Luther King, Jr., Comments on John F. Kennedy, Berlin, Germany, 13 September 1964, MLKJP, GAMK, 3.

pending nuclear war, and King hoped for a "permanent test ban treaty all over the world."[58]

A third suggestion, which King offered when asked in an interview what he would do if he possessed "omnipotent powers," commended universal disarmament and the establishment of a world police force under the auspices of the United Nations. With omnipotent powers, King stated: "I would work to bring about universal disarmament and set up a world police force through the UN that could handle any problems that arise. I am not at all an anarchist, I believe in the intelligent use of police power, and I don't think men will ever come to the point where we will not need some checks."[59] Universal disarmament would begin to take away the choice between nonviolence and nonexistence, thereby reestablishing the divine right to life, and a world police force would provide the check on state behavior that the nuclear weapons had earlier provided. The check was necessary because humanity would always be sinful and in need of order; without order, the result would be a demonic chaos. But the check should not be greater than that provided by a police force because humanity is also capable of redemption.

A fourth suggestion called for the establishment of a world government. If in possession of omnipotent powers, King stated, he "would consider some form of world government."[60] Thus, he separated himself even further from Goldwater, who dismissed the possibility of a world government. Unfortunately, King did not provide any explanation of what he meant by "world government," but he did provide a theological rationale for his position. For King, the interconnectedness of humanity—the inescapable fact that what affects one state affects all states—requires nothing less than a world government.

A fifth suggestion, which King alluded to during his trip to receive the Nobel Peace Prize, centered on the practice of nonviolence in the field of international relations. During his stay in Oslo, King suggested that "the philosophy and practice of nonviolence become immediately a subject for study and for serious experimentation in every field of human conflict, by no means excluding the relations between nations."[61] In King's perspective, not only concerned individuals but also (and

---

[58] *Redbook* transcript, question 6.
[59] Ibid.
[60] Ibid., question 7.
[61] King, Jr., "The Quest for Peace and Justice," MLKJP, GAMK, 21.

especially) states should practice nonviolence. Unfortunately, King did not expound on this evolution in his thoughts.

All these suggestions, which he set forth as means by which states and citizens could achieve world peace, point to King's belief that the state as he experienced it in history is sinfully flawed and limited. Sinful and limited, the state regularly fails to consider the needs and desires of other states—hence, the need for the United Nations to encourage the state to stop its monologues and to sit down at "the peace table" to begin dialogues with other states. Sinful and limited, the state is obsessed with its own power, even to the point of demonstrating a complete willingness to sacrifice human existence—hence, the need for universal disarmament. Sinful and limited, the state will seek to gain territory and material from other states—hence, the need for a police power under the auspices of the United Nations. Sinful and limited, the state cannot achieve on its own everything that it needs to achieve for the flourishing of human personalities in a modern world—hence, the need for a world government.

Nevertheless, King's suggestions also reveal his optimistic belief that the state can respond to collective ventures intended to establish world peace. King actually believed that the state could move away from chip-on-the-shoulder diplomacy, obsessive concern with demonstrating its own power, the constant search for more territory and material, and a false belief in itself as the perfect society. Exactly because King believed in the possible redemption of the state, he offered constructive suggestions regarding the elimination of nuclear war and the establishment of world peace.

In this part of his career, King also began to comment sporadically on the US military involvement in Vietnam. On more than a few occasions, he called for a "negotiated settlement" to the conflict, arguing that the United States should put its energies into stopping the conflict rather than into continuing it. Likewise, American activists should consider holding "peace rallies just like we have freedom rallies."[62] Still, King did not grant Vietnam a lot of attention in this period, and even stated publicly, when criticized for making statements about Vietnam, that his primary target was not US foreign policy but the injustices suffered by blacks.[63] But King did bristle at the suggestion that he should

---

[62] Quoted in Garrow, *Bearing the Cross*, 429.
[63] Ibid., 430.

not comment on foreign policy. Indeed, he reserved some of his harshest words, as well as his harshest characterization of the state, for his response to critics who told him to stay out of foreign policy issues:

> ...behind the criticism of my role in international affairs is the assumption that foreign policy is a white man's business. But when I look around and see the mess that the white man is making of this business, I must encourage men of goodwill and sound judgment, whatever their color may be, to call our nation to her senses and not allow us to be driven down the road to international disaster by allowing the decisions in regard to human life and destiny to be made by military men in the Pentagon and under-cover politicians in the Central Intelligence Agency.[64]

Vietnam would, indeed, become a focus in the third part of King's career, and at that point King would fully explain his reasons for opposing US military involvement.

A Realist View of Limited Democracy

Upon his return to New York City from Sweden, King expressed his intense desire to devote more of his time and energy to the problem of poverty in both the United States and the world, but, in spite of this desire, most of King's time and energy became focused on yet another problem—taxation without representation. At the launching of the Crusade for Citizenship six years earlier, in 1958, King had described the problem as he saw it: "To Negro Americans, it is ironic to be governed, to be taxed, to be given orders, but to have no representation in a nation that would defend the right to vote abroad." It was ironic, given the inability of blacks to vote throughout the South, that Secretary of State Dulles devoted "tireless and indefatigable effort...to obtain free elections

---

[64] Martin Luther King, Jr., "A Christian Movement in a Revolutionary Age," Fall 1965, MLKJP, GAMK, 8.

in Germany."[65] The irony was more than an intellectual point in King's mind: it was a real problem in need of a concrete solution—a task to which he devoted himself in the second part of his career.

For King, Selma, Alabama posed the problem of undemocratic disfranchisement most vividly.[66] Indeed, he proclaimed that disfranchisement in Selma was nothing less than slavery itself and that there were numerous "links in the chain of slavery" in Selma. The first link was "the Gestapo-like control of county and local government" by Sheriff Jim Clark. This "High Sheriff," as blacks referred to him, used the gun, the club, and the cattle prod to transform the local courthouse, where blacks attempted to register to vote, into "an image of fear."[67] The second link included city ordinances "contrived to make it difficult for Negroes to move in concert." Prohibiting mass meetings, the type of which King had held in Montgomery, the local ordinances kept "Negroes from working out a group plan of action against injustice." The third link was "the slow pace of the registrar and the limited number of days and hours during which the office is open." When tens of blacks lined up to register to vote, the registrar would process only two or three. A fourth link was the literacy test—a test with detailed questions about US history that few blacks were educationally equipped to answer.[68]

Selma, in King's view, had constructed all sorts of racial barriers to and within the courthouse, with the result that blacks saw the courthouse as anything but an institution of justice. "To the Negro the courthouse is a place where he pays his taxes and gets nothing in return, a place where he is often sentenced to jail for inconsequential violations of that law and

---

[65] Martin Luther King, Jr., Section of Speech Given by Dr. Martin Luther King, Jr., President of Southern Christian Leadership Conference, at a Meeting Launching the Crusade for Citizenship, Miami, 12 February 1958, MLKJP, GAMK, 2.

[66] This is not to say, of course, that King did not see the problem of taxation without representation in other areas. In fact, King fought, albeit weakly, for the seating of the Mississippi Freedom Democratic Party at the 1964 Democratic National Convention. See King, Jr., Statement before the Credentials Committee of the Democratic National Convention, Atlantic City, 22 August 1964, MLKJP, GAMK. The black members of the MFDP waged a losing battle to be seated against the all-white Mississippi delegation. King's efforts on behalf of MFDP proved to be ineffective as well as half-hearted. See Taylor Branch, *Pillar of Fire: America in the King Years, 1963–65* (New York: Simon & Schuster, 1998) 441ff.

[67] Martin Luther King, Jr., "Selma—the Shame and the Promise," *IUD Agenda* 1/2 (March 1965): 19.

[68] Ibid., 20.

a place where civil rights murderers are acquitted with speedy regularity. To the Negro, the courthouse is the concrete manifestation of the system of oppression under which he lives."[69] King argued that disfranchisement was not an atomistic problem. Rather, it was related to many of the social and economic problems that blacks faced since the time of slavery. Because blacks were denied the right to vote in Selma and in other places, they were also denied equal protection under the law, educational opportunities, fair wages, the right to collective bargaining, and the right to govern themselves.[70] Therefore, in King's view, the education of children, the provision of adequate jobs and shelter, and the physical protection of blacks required exercising the right to vote within the black community. By exercising the right to vote, blacks would be able to place in power those who were committed to eliminating economic and social injustices. As King put it, voting

> is the foundation stone for political action which will eventually vote out of office the public officials who stand barring the doorway to decent housing, public safety, jobs and decent integrated education. It is now obvious that each of these basic elements so vital to our advancement can only be achieved by redress principally from governments at local, state, and federal levels. To make this redress a reality, the vote is mandatory.[71]

Although he perceived the vote as mandatory for achieving the type of redress that he outlined in the Bill of Rights for the Disadvantaged, King did not, when making the case against disfranchisement, point merely to the possibility of redress. Moving to a different level, King made the case by offering an internal criticism of US democracy. Politically speaking, he saw disfranchisement of blacks in the South as a contradiction within a democratic political system. Harking back to themes he expressed in "The Negro and the Constitution," and continuing to embrace civic republicanism, King stated that blacks have

---

[69] Martin Luther King, Jr., Report to the Administrative Committee Re: Voter Registration Since the 1965 Voting Rights Act, November 1965, MLKJP, GAMK, 3–4.

[70] King, Jr., "The Movement: Prospects for '65,'" MLKJP, GAMK, 3.

[71] Martin Luther King, Jr., Untitled Speech on 1965 and the Civil Rights Movement, MLKJP, GAMK, 13.

been "inculcated with the rituals of democracy," and have been taught that

> we are a nation of the people, for the people, and above all by the people; that in the words of Lincoln there is a constitutional right to choose and change the government dramatically at the ballot box—whether it be the President, or Congress, or Governor, or the Town or Village Supervisor, or Sheriff, and that the public servant must answer to the electorate.[72]

The disfranchisement of blacks in the South contradicted the democratic creed that government is of the people, by the people, and for the people. Disfranchisement contradicted the democratic creed that those of voting age may use the ballot to effect change within the government. Disfranchisement contradicted the democratic belief that public office holders must be accountable to all of the electorate. Disfranchisement, in short, contradicted democracy.

Disfranchisement also contradicted King's theology. King's demand for the ballot at Selma was a natural result of his theological view of human nature. The denial of the right to vote, as he saw it, is an assault on God-given human freedom. God has made human individuals with the capacity to participate freely in the selection of those who would occupy positions of the state. God, that is, has made us to be citizens in a full democracy—citizens who can and should participate in the democratic practice of voting for leaders of the state. Beyond the issue of freedom, though, King also held that individuals, especially as they form together in groups, are incredibly sinful and in need of the checks and balances that truly democratic systems establish. "Our democracy," a Niebuhrian King wrote, "depends on checks and balances to power, and whenever one group is deprived of power another group concomitantly gains inordinate power."[73] Given the tendency of the group in power to abuse its power, a true democracy with full enfranchisement is not only helpful—it is necessary.

King's demand for the ballot was also a natural result of his doctrine of God. The previous chapter noted that the justice of God, in King's view, requires fair and equitable treatment for all, especially for those

---

[72] Ibid.
[73] King, Jr., "The Movement: Prospects for '65,'" MLKJP, GAMK, 5.

who, like the poor in the prophecy of Amos, are often taken advantage of at "the gate," where the claims and counterclaims of society are weighed and decided. The justice of God stands over against any political system that excludes certain people, like the poor, from participating fairly in the leadership of society and so from receiving what is their due. What is more, the love of God requires reconciliation among humanity to be the goal of all state action. Thus, the love of God stands firmly against any political system that would seek to divide people according to race. In this sense, the disfranchisement of blacks, which separates voting whites from non-voting blacks, is nothing less than a mockery of divine love as reconciliation.

King held that this theological truth evidenced itself within world history as a divine law that prohibits colonialism and other forms of political systems in which one group of people attempts to govern another type. "If there is one fact that history has confirmed, it is the fact that no one can govern and represent people as adequately as they can represent and govern themselves."[74] In King's view, divine law, as evidenced through history, mandates the existence of representative government—government of the people, by the people, and for the people.

With these intertwined democratic and theological beliefs, King led thousands of activists in fighting the registration politics practiced in Selma, Alabama. Again, King held a realistic perspective on the extent to which the political leaders would fight to maintain their own political power. Governor Wallace and Sheriff Clark, King observed, "are determined to perpetuate their reign of terror and oppression. These men control the registration procedure and will go to the most bestial extremes to maintain their own political empires." Wallace and Clark had more interest in preserving their "citadel of racism" than in creating a fully democratic state, and would use any means possible to preserve their political empires.[75] The "racist oligarchy," as King put it, would not willingly become democratic.[76]

These strong words are not a mere repetition of the realism that King expressed in the beginnings of the Montgomery campaign in the first part of his career. Although it sounds similar, the realism expressed

---

[74] Ibid., 9.
[75] Ibid.
[76] Garrow, *Bearing the Cross*, 418.

here, in this second part of his career, has greater depth in the sense that it is a product of many additional experiences with a belligerent state. By this point, King experienced and understood the belligerence of the state more fully, and he expressed an ever-deepening realism when he claimed: "One of the difficult lessons that we have learned in the movement is that you cannot depend upon American institutions to function without pressure."[77] This lesson—that the state, as a bastion of the privileged classes, would not volunteer to redistribute power—was Niebuhrian in nature, and, again, King cited Niebuhr to explain the realist's perspective. "As Reinhold Niebuhr has written, individuals may see the moral light and voluntarily abandon their unjust posture, but groups tend to be more immoral, and more intransigent, than individuals."[78]

King had learned, through experience after experience, that it was absolutely necessary to push, pull, and prod the sinful state—and in a particular way. "Any real change in the status quo is dependent upon continued creative action which will sharpen the conscience of a nation."[79] It is not sufficient, in King's mind, to fight the state by praying that it will change its ways, or by trying to sit down and negotiate with it, or by organizing regional skirmishes against it. The state is so belligerent that nothing less than a sharpened conscience of an entire nation is required to transform the attitude and actions of the state.

Therefore, King began to emphasize the need for blacks to form alliances in the fight against the state. The fight, he believed, must be fully democratic: it must be of the people, by the people, and for the people. It is not sufficient for the battle to engage only blacks or only civil rights activists: the people—not just some of the people—must participate. With this evolving sense of the need for a more democratic approach, King argued that the civil rights movement would need to deepen its alliances with national groups, for example, organized labor.

On the one hand, King's evolving embrace of political alliances was practical. Greater numbers of people, of course, meant greater resources, as well as greater political power, for the movement towards democracy. But, on the other hand, the embrace was profoundly theological. For King, the laws of God's universe require people to act together with the confidence that what affects one individual affects all people.

---

[77] Ibid., 14.

[78] "*Playboy* Interview," in *A Testament of Hope*, 374.

[79] Ibid.

King's call for the formation of alliances culminated, in the second part of his career, in the march from Selma to Montgomery. In this march, King and the world witnessed a new level of commitment against the state—a commitment that included greater numbers of people and a greater diversity of people than King had experienced before. The strength of the numbers and diversity of the march, of course, was due not only to King's call but especially to the horror with which the nation watched Sheriff Jim Clark brutalize Selma's black men, women, and children. With its own deepening realism, the nation largely turned its back on Wallace and Clark and embraced the cause of the protestors in Selma.

The size and length of the march also reflected King's evolving belief in the need for "creative action" that would activate the conscience of the nation. The march from Selma to Montgomery was something new and dramatic: it was different from, and more dramatic than, a walk from a church to a courthouse two blocks down the street. The march creatively captured the interest and involvement of the coalitions King dreamed of, and by doing so the movement shifted "from protest to politics," a shift King hoped for and mentioned to his fellow SCLC workers in 1964.[80] As it played itself out in the second part of his career, the shift came to mean not leaving behind the politics of protest—the March from Selma to Montgomery, after all, protested the disfranchisement of blacks—but the creation of a political movement which, consisting of both whites and blacks, would accrue enough power to influence decision-making in the corridors of political power. The march from Selma to Montgomery was just such a creation.

During the march from Selma to Montgomery, as well as during other Selma marches, King continued to embrace nonviolence as the proper method for establishing justice as political participation. "The goal of the demonstrations in Selma, as elsewhere, is to dramatize the existence of injustice and to bring about the presence of justice by

---

[80] Garrow, *Bearing the Cross*, 354. The context of King's statement suggests that, in his view, successful passage of something like the Bill of Rights for the Disadvantaged would require such a shift. Speaking of the political fight to gain the billions of dollars required to establish full employment, just one of the requirements of the proposed bill, King said: "This is more than a demonstration. This is a question of creating political power to induce Congress to appropriate such a sum of money." Martin Luther King, Jr., Annual Report of Martin Luther King, Jr., Eighth Annual Convention of the SCLC, Savannah, 2 October 1964, MLKJP, GAMK, 13.

methods of nonviolence."[81] But, as he had in the first part of his career, King backed the nonviolent methods with calls for the state, in this case, the US federal government, to assume its role as physical protector.

Before moving into Selma, a realist King described the "police state" in which the Southern black had to live: "A ruling state apparatus, accustomed for generations to act with impunity against him, is able to employ every element of unchecked power." Southern blacks, King wrote, are forced to rely on "their own resources to face a massively equipped army." No friend, this massively equipped army is not seeking out blacks as potential recruits. Rather, the army—the police state—is arrayed against blacks, intent on limiting, if not eliminating, their civil and human rights. The only possible check blacks possess is the federal government, with its armed marshals and troops. But the federal government, King argued, "has been able to muster only the minimum courage and determination to aid them."[82]

King felt he and others faced the "police state" especially in Wallace, Clark, and other Southern politicians. Turning the law-and-order argument of the segregationists on its head, King stated at a night vigil in Selma that

> law and order in Alabama no longer exist. I think in the black belt countries we experience a reign of terror and a breakdown of law and order and I am absolutely convinced that the federal government needs to do something to protect persons who are engaged in a quest for basic constitutional rights and basic God-given rights. Now whether this protection comes in the form of troops or in the form of federal marshals is another matter. But I do think that there must be some form of federal protection. If not, I'm afraid that we'll have some of the same things developing as we face now, with the death of Reverend Reeb.[83]

Seven months earlier, when he appeared before the Platform Committee of the Democratic National Convention, King was more specific, calling for the presence of federal marshals in the South. The

---

[81] Martin Luther King, Jr., "Behind the Selma March," in *A Testament of Hope*, 127.

[82] King, Jr., "Hammer on Civil Rights," in *A Testament of Hope*, 173.

[83] Martin Luther King, Jr., Statement during Night Vigil, Selma, 13 March 1965, MLKJP, GAMK, 1.

federal government, he argued, has a responsibility "to assure to its citizens protection against vigilantes, the Ku Klux Klan, the White Citizens Council and other hate groups seeking to terrorize and intimidate [black citizens] in the exercise of their constitutional rights."[84] Without the presence of federal marshals, blacks would continue to live in a police state that failed to police white segregationists.

As he had in the first part of his career, King never ruled out the possibility that federal troops would be required in the South to establish law and order. In fact, while caught in a wave of violence in St. Augustine, King called upon President Johnson to offer federal protection, possibly in the form of federal troops, to the civil rights workers.[85] Interestingly, King called for the United States to use its forcible means to establish law and order in the South, but he refused to call the international community to use the same means to establish law and order in a similar situation in South Africa.

King described South Africa's apartheid supporters in much the same way that he described Southern segregationists—as little more than fascists. Those who occupied state positions in South Africa were "savages, "brutes," and "barbarians"[86] who brutally imposed "a sophisticated form of slavery" upon black South Africans. The state consisted of Nazis: "The South African government to make the white supreme has had to reach into the past and revive the nightmarish ideology and practices of Nazism." Arrogantly defying world opinion, the fascist ideology and practices of the South African government keep the majority of South African citizens—the blacks—in "grinding poverty," in conditions "in which the dignity of the human personality is defiled," and in a general state of war.[87]

Faced with such "a monstrous government," King argued, states across the globe have a fundamental responsibility to fight against it.[88] Like segregation in the United States, apartheid in South Africa is morally wrong and theologically sinful. As with American citizens who face

---

[84] King, Jr., Statement before the Platform Committee of the Democratic National Convention, MLKJP, GAMK, 5.

[85] Branch, *Pillar of Fire*, 379.

[86] Martin Luther King, Jr., Address of Dr. Martin Luther King, Jr., to the South Africa Benefit of the American Committee on Africa, Hunter College, New York City, 10 December 1965, MLKJP, GAMK, 1.

[87] Ibid., 2.

[88] Ibid., 3.

segregation, states that face South African apartheid cannot be neutral: non-cooperation with evil is a fundamental moral obligation.

King did not suggest that the international community should use all the means at its disposal to establish justice in South Africa. Rather, he proposed "a potent nonviolent path." King noted that the United States, as well as other states, sanctioned apartheid by supporting South Africa through investments, loans, trades, and economic assistance. With this in mind, he argued that South Africa's apartheid would collapse under the weight of "nonviolence through a massive international boycott."[89] (The implication of this proposal, of course, is that the market drives the state. Economics, in King's view, forms and transforms politics.)

But King doubted that the international community would undertake a massive international boycott against South Africa. King simply argued that "the great nations of this world will not sacrifice trade and profit" for the sake of doing the right thing, that is, seeking to eliminate apartheid.[90] King continued to believe that the state is classist: the state serves the interests of the monied classes rather than those of the poor.

Important to note here, though, is that King refused to call the international community to adopt arms in a quest to establish justice in South Africa, even though blacks in South Africa had perhaps even less physical protection from the state than had blacks in the South. King, that is, refused to apply to the field of international relations the argument he used to support the physical protection of blacks in the South. Conversely, he refused to apply to domestic relations in United States the argument he used to support a boycott against South Africa. In other words, King did not call upon the federal government to carry out a domestic boycott against Selma or Alabama—even though the practice of segregation would, in his mind, warrant an "economic withdrawal campaign."[91]

---

[89] Ibid.

[90] Ibid., 3.

[91] The quoted words come from King's general call to US society for "an economic withdrawal against the state of Mississippi and its products." "The Movement: Prospects for '65," MLKJP, GAMK, 6. King's advisers [sic] counseled against the call for the boycott, suggesting that it was not politically sagacious. Eventually, the idea, which King never directed to the federal government, disappeared from his public rhetoric.

A Born-Again State and the Christian Church

Throughout this period of his life, King remained a reformist, even though he faced violence from the ruling "racist oligarchy." Nowhere did King even suggest a revolution that would seek to overthrow the undemocratic and sinful state. On the contrary, he argued: "The demand is for a new order to be born within the institutions of our democracy. It is much more akin to the Christian notion of being 'born again,' that is, this old body politic of ours will be transformed by a new spirit of concern and justice for all of humanity."[92]

The reformer King also commended the state when it showed signs of conversion. In 1964, at the time of the passage of the 1964 Civil Rights Act, lavish praise poured from a grateful King. The bill's passage, he stated, was a perfect time for "thanksgiving," especially in light of "the blood, sweat, toil and tears of countless Congressmen of both major parties, legions of amateur lobbyists, and great volumes of grass roots sentiment."[93] King was so optimistic at this point that he even dared to declare: "The slope of the road now curves downhill."[94]

King's willingness to praise the state would never falter during this part of his career. Even in spite of the reluctance of the federal government to come to the physical aid of civil rights workers in Florida, Alabama, and Mississippi, and even in spite of the horrors that his followers faced when they went head-to-head with Sheriff Clark and others, King offered high praise for the state at the time of the passage of the 1965 Voting Rights Act, describing the act as nothing less than "a strong, legislative plank of democracy"—a reason for "renewed hope" among all democratic citizens.[95]

Perhaps the most interesting example of King's willingness to praise the state in this part of his public life concerns the work of the Federal Bureau of Investigation. Throughout his public career, the FBI practiced "surveillance politics" against King, even to the point of bugging his hotel rooms and attempting to use the bugged material as blackmail against

---

[92] Martin Luther King, Jr., Untitled Speech on 1965 and the Civil Rights Movement, MLKJP, GAMK, 15.

[93] Martin Luther King, Jr., Statement Regarding Passage of the 1964 Civil Rights Act, June 1964, MLKJP, GAMK, 3.

[94] Ibid., 4.

[95] Martin Luther King, Jr., Draft of Speech on Passage of 1965 Voting Rights Act, August 1965, MLKJP, GAMK, 1.

King.[96] In 1964, for example, the FBI assembled a "suicide package," in which they placed a recording of King's personal indiscretions and a letter implying that suicide would be King's best option in light of pending publicity of the indiscretions, and sent the package to King's home, where it landed in the hands of Coretta, King, and a few others.[97] At that point, King experienced the state, in the form of the FBI, as a personal enemy intent on destroying his public career, and yet he actually praised the FBI shortly after receiving the package, after he had met personally with Hoover and after the FBI had taken action to arrest some violent segregationists in Mississippi.[98]

King also remained consistent in his recognition that salvation, including political salvation, does not lie solely in the hands of political institutions, even those of a more democratic state. On the one hand, King offered great praise for the state when it supported blacks in their quest to achieve the right to vote. On the other hand, however, he cautioned against the belief that the right to vote in a more democratic state would automatically yield improved conditions for blacks.

In King's view, the real, and final, power for improving the conditions of humanity—for leading to a society of reconciliation—lies with the people who exercise the right to vote. The real engine that would pull a beloved community into existence consists of the society of people who vote for their representative government. The state, in this sense, is and does only what the people tell it to be and do.

King therefore stressed, shortly after the passage of the 1965 Voting Rights Act, that the movement towards the beloved community ultimately depends upon the citizens and the votes they cast. For King, it is not sufficient to have the right to vote; it is also necessary to know how to vote the right way: "For free men must not only have the right to vote, they must also know how to use the vote to eliminate evils that existed before they could vote."[99]

Because of his view that power lies not only within but also beyond political institutions, King embraced not only political lobbying, as the

---

[96] The phrase belongs to Branch, *Pillar of Fire*, 530. The account in the body of the text is indebted to Branch's narrative.

[97] Ibid., 528–29.

[98] Ibid., 536.

[99] King, Jr., Draft of Speech on Passage of 1965 Voting Rights Act, MLKJP, GAMK, 1.

previous chapter noted, but also voter education—a cause that became urgent with the passage of the 1965 Voting Rights Act.[100] For his own part, King emphasized that black people must learn how to vote not along racial lines but according to the policies espoused by the candidate. Blacks "must vote only for men whose leadership is concerned with organizing forces so that there will be power to eliminate the ills that centuries of segregation have left us." Further, King warned against voting for politicians who would merely work on superficial needs and problems faced by individual citizens. "We should not be content to vote for a man merely because he can get a traffic ticket fixed, get a job for our sons and daughters, see to it that the welfare check comes on time, or gives out food baskets at Christmas. We must ask our representatives to work for the death of those things which create these social ills."[101] The implication here is that political officials would not work to eliminate the root problems of social ills unless the people pushed the officials to do so. King's realism, hardened in battle after battle with politicians, led him to put less faith in the politicians and more faith in the people who would elect them.

King's instructions to the people also moved to the exact issues he had in mind—unemployment, poverty, housing, education, and peace. The good politician, King argued, would create policies that would establish full employment, the training of workers displaced and replaced by automation, integrated and high-quality housing for all, integrated and high-quality public education, and a world free from the possibility of nuclear death. But King believed that the good politician would not just arise within and from existing political institutions; the people would have to seek or create such a politician.

Ever since the boycott in Montgomery, King maintained that the power to convert the state does not lie within the state itself, and ever since his early calls for increased voter registration among blacks, King demonstrated his belief that the power to convert the state rests with

---

[100] The task of voter education had been important to King ever since his first days at Dexter, when he formed the social and political action committee. But voter education became all the more pressing, at least in King's mind, when the Voting Rights Act of 1965 became a reality. Interestingly, however, King's actions did not focus so much on voter education after the passage of the bill: Chicago was just around the corner.

[101] King, Jr., Draft of Speech on Passage of 1965 Voting Rights Act, MLKJP, GAMK, 1.

enfranchised people. But, in this part of his life, King stressed his belief that the real power to transform the soul of the state—to bring about born-again political institutions—is held, more particularly, by the people who knew how to vote the right way. The state would not and could not convert itself, and uninformed voters would not and could not convert the state. Only those who have a vision of the good politician, and who vote for the good politician, could and would convert the state to the ways of divine love and justice.

With this belief in mind, King continued to critique the church for its failure to act as the conscience of the state. Speaking to the European Baptists in 1964, King stated that the church must begin "to accept responsibility for the governments which we elect, or allow to be elected through our indifference."[102] Problems with the state, in King's view, often directly point to a church that has reneged on its responsibility to act as the public conscience. State-sponsored segregation in the South, according to King, can be traced in part to a church that preached unity but remained largely quiet when confronted with discrimination.

In King's understanding of church-state relations, as he expressed it to the European Baptists, the church has two options—either escape or engage the world. The option of escape means that the political world would go unattended and that the church would fail in its divine call to be the conscience of the state. The second option is the faithful one.

> The alternative to escape is a creative and courageous attempt to enter the world in revolution and there struggle with principalities and powers of this age as though we really believed that Christ has overcome the world, not just our little private world of salvation for my own soul, but the world of rockets, steel mills, and hungry over-populated nations.[103]

Rather than a self-contained entity, the state needs the church, primarily because the state continues to fail to recognize the lordship of Christ. The state, in other words, is in need of redemption, and the church, as an agent of redemption, can supply what the state needs—opposing views and actions that embody the belief that Christ has overcome the world.

---

[102] King, Jr., "Revolution and Redemption," MLKJP, GAMK, 9.
[103] Ibid., 7.

King's theology of the world grounded his unwavering belief that the church must begin to address the limitations and sinfulness of the state. He expressed this theology of the world at the beginning of his address: "There are two aspects of the world which we must never forget. One is that this is God's world, and He is active in the forces of history and the affairs of men. The second is, Jesus Christ gave his life for the redemption of this world, and as his followers, we are called to give our lives continuing the reconciling work of Christ in this world."[104] In this view, the world, including the political world, is not lost to demonic principalities and powers but always exists as the handiwork of God the Creator and Christ the Reconciler. As an agent of God in Christ, the church must not escape from the world, primarily because God in Christ is in the world, reconciling the world unto God's own self. Given the work of Christ, the church must join the act of divine reconciliation by going to the world and fighting for the reconciliation begun in Christ.

In his speech to the European Baptists, King did not fully explain what he meant by the work of reconciliation in the affairs of the state. But he did suggest that the mandates of reconciliation require the church to work towards a wider distribution of the world's resources. Financial and technical resources, King preached, belong to God and must be used to the glory of God for the physical care of all of the children of God.[105] Further, the church must begin to work for "world peace." "Now is the time," he preached, "for Christians to develop a creative approach to this problem and break the stalemate on disarmament and bring about a thaw in the cold war before it becomes a hot war."[106]

By stating all this, of course, King was expressing his frustration with the church for failing to engage the principalities and powers of this world. King directed his deepest frustration to the American white church in particular. In a 1965 interview with *Playboy*, King stated that he was "greatly disappointed" with the leadership of the "white church," with its "pious irrelevancies" and "sanctimonious trivialities," its timidity and ineffectuality, and its "defense of bigotry and prejudice."[107] At the beginning of the Montgomery campaign, he was optimistic that the white churches and synagogues "would prove strong allies in our just cause."

---

[104] Ibid., 3.

[105] Ibid., 9.

[106] Ibid., 10.

[107] "*Playboy* Interview: Martin Luther King, Jr.," in *A Testament of Hope*, 345–46.

But such optimism, "was shattered; and on too many occasions since, my hopes for the white church have been dashed." This increasing realism about the church's failure to act as a conscience of the state led him to claim: "There are many signs that the judgment of God is upon the church as never before."[108]

King did not mean to offer an unnuanced view of the white church. During the interview, he noted, albeit in passing, "some outstanding exceptions" within the white church.[109] Further, in April 1965, King conceded that the religious leadership of some states had organized themselves to fight for a fuller democracy for blacks.[110] Nor did King mean to offer an unnuanced view of the black church. He noted, again in the interview, that he had experienced similar frustration with some of the black churches in the communities in which he and others organized the civil rights movement. Still, King held that "the role of the Negro church today, by and large, is a glorious example in the history of Christendom."[111]

Summary

In the second part of his career, King continued to express, in word and deed, a deeply theological understanding of the state. Especially prominent in this period was King's application of his theology of atonement, which led him to call upon the state, as a trustee of God's earthly creation, to mirror divine justice and love by offering material compensation to blacks so that all citizens might move towards the beloved community. Indeed, this period saw King begin to emphasize his belief that the state should assume an active role in establishing economic justice—a belief that extended back to his high-school speech on blacks and the US Constitution. King's hope, as revealed through his proposal of the Bill of Rights for the Disadvantaged, was for a massive welfare state. Following Mays, Williams, Rauschenbusch, the early Niebuhr, and Boston personalists, among others, King even expressed an inclination for democratic socialism by extolling the virtues of the social-democratic

---

[108] Ibid., 346.

[109] Ibid., 345.

[110] Martin Luther King, Jr., Statement to SCLC Board re Alabama Movement, 2 April 1965, MLKJP, GAMK, 1.

[111] Ibid., 346–47.

state of Sweden over the minimalist state of Barry Goldwater's campaign rhetoric.

Embracing Sweden's democratic socialism, King revealed his distaste for, among other things, totalitarianism, which Smith had taught him to dislike, and a thin democracy that would give individuals the right to vote, as well as minimal physical protection, and then leave them to exist as they will. When King pointed to Sweden as the good state, he affirmed a social democracy that seeks to bind all citizens together as free and equal citizens who enjoy the basic necessities of life—a social democracy that provides the material conditions required by the beloved community willed by God in Christ.

Yet another new emphasis arose in King's take on the internal functions of the state. King began to emphasize, in a way that he had not done before, that justice means the elimination of not only poverty but also disfranchisement. Following Daddy King, George Davis, and, before them, the republican Thomas Jefferson, King began to stress his theological belief that eternal law and natural law reveal God's desire for representative government—government of the people, by the people, and for the people.

Remaining constant in King's views on the internal functions of the state was his conviction that the just state must enforce compliance with its just laws by prosecuting and punishing the disobedient and by providing physical protection, even through the use of force, for citizens unjustly brutalized. King as realist continued to value justice more than peace—and not only on the domestic front. Interestingly, King moved beyond a simple pacifism and towards a deeper realism by calling for the presence of a world police force. Still, he continued to preach against war on theological and practical grounds, and his commitment to the United Nations, the idea of a world government, universal disarmament, international aid, and a proposed boycott against South Africa, demonstrated his ongoing commitment to nonviolent principles of applied love.

Also constant was King's dialectical attitude towards the state. He certainly continued to envision the state as a force for evil. The intensity of his public rhetoric against the state increased considerably during this period, but his accusation that the state is racist and classist remained the same. With a deepened realism, King continued to refuse an unqualified ethic of subordination, choosing instead to call citizen alliances to a new level of civil disobedience, the type found at Selma.

Although his realism deepened, King never once placed the state beyond the power of divine redemption; nor did he ever call for the overthrow of existing political institutions. Rather, he continued to envision the state as an active, and unique, agent within the divine plan of reconciliation. Adopting the optimism of Boston personalism, King believed that political institutions can be "born again," and noted his experiences with the good side of the state—with India, Sweden, and US politicians who fought for civil rights. With these experiences in mind, King continued to refuse an unqualified ethic of resistance, choosing instead to be resistant only when the context demanded it. What is more, during this period, King claimed to have become even more optimistic in his faith that states across the world can establish the conditions for reconciliation.

Even with this increased optimism, however, King continued to believe that true salvation for humanity rests not with the state alone but primarily with the people, especially voters and those who fill political society's voluntary associations. During this period, King grew increasingly frustrated with the white church in particular, but expressed his pleasure with some white churches and the black church in general for being the conscience of the state—a constant critic that points the state towards human freedom within the beloved community.

7

AGAINST A SEPARATE BLACK STATE,

BUT FOR A REVOLUTIONIZED STATE

1966–1968

For all of his victories, from the desegregation of buses to the integration of schools to the removal of literacy tests, King remained convinced, from 1966 to 1968, that the battle for America's soul had only just begun. He conceded that the struggles of the civil rights movement had achieved substantial accomplishments during the period from 1955 to 1965, but he insisted that they were far too limited. "We made some strides toward the ending of racism," he stated, "but we did not stride into freedom."[1] Freedom, he believed, would continue to be an elusive goal until its three interrelated obstructions—racial discrimination, economic exploitation, and militarism—were defeated in total.[2] In the last three years of his life, King sought to overcome these barriers to human freedom by demanding that the state institutionalize nothing less than a revolution of values.

---

[1] Martin Luther King, Jr., "Why We Must Go to Washington," Atlanta, 15 January 1968, MLKJP, GAMK, 3.

[2] Martin Luther King, Jr., "To Charter Our Course," Frogmore, South Carolina, May 1967, MLKJP, GAMK, 9.

The Black State and Black Politics:
The Separatist Vision of Malcolm X and
Stokely Carmichael

The years 1966 to 1968 witnessed a strong surge of opposition to King from within the ranks of civil rights activists, and nowhere was the surge more visible than in the Student Nonviolent Coordinating Committee, whose mantle of leadership had passed from the nonviolent John Lewis to the militant Stokely Carmichael, the young activist who popularized the phrase "Black Power" during the 1966 Meredith March. Under the leadership of Carmichael, who was elected as chairman in May 1966, SNCC began to embrace ideological foci and practices that were different from those accepted during Lewis's tenure. In particular, SNCC began to embrace the philosophy of black nationalism, the formation of black-controlled institutions, and the use of violence as a means of establishing justice.[3]

Popularized by Carmichael, SNCC's call for racial separatism, including separation from white-controlled political institutions, had part of its roots in the political thought of Malcolm X. Malcolm, especially in his early years, expressed nothing but contempt for the state as he experienced it in the United States. Expressing this contempt through a vocabulary of opposition, the early Malcolm derisively referred to the US government, especially in front of white audiences, as "your Christian government."[4] The US government was not his government—it was the white folks'.

Indeed, the early Malcolm envisioned himself, as well as all other blacks, as victims of a racist and undemocratic state, rather than as beneficiaries of a democracy, and the later Malcolm continued this sharply critical portrayal of the state. For example, just after his separation from Elijah Muhammed in 1964, Malcolm spoke of the US government as being involved in a "segregationist conspiracy." The government, he proclaimed, is involved in a massive conspiracy to deprive blacks of voting rights, adequate economic opportunities, and decent education. As he put it, "it is the government itself, the

---

[3] See Clayborne Carson, *In Struggle: SNCC and the Black Awakening of the 1960s* (Cambridge: Harvard University Press, 1981).

[4] *Malcolm X: Speeches at Harvard,* ed. Archie Epps (New York: Paragon House, 1991) 126.

government of America, that is responsible for the oppression and exploitation and degradation of black people in this country."[5] Moreover, Malcolm often characterized the state under which blacks lived as a police state so corrupt that those in political positions actually control such things as drugs and prostitution.[6]

The early Malcolm argued that, given racism and a racist state, only complete separation of the white and black races could solve the race problem in the United States. More particularly, Malcolm called for the state to atone for its sins by providing land on which blacks could create their own homeland, with their own political and economic institutions. The territory, as he envisioned it, would be a second-best option; the best option would be the return of blacks to Africa, an unlikely happening, he thought, given the recalcitrance of the United States. Speaking at Harvard in 1961, Malcolm criticized the US government for not allowing the twenty million "ex-slaves" to leave, and then called for a "portion of this country that we can call our own," along with "everything we need to start our own civilization."[7]

The early Malcolm, then, clearly favored a separate black nation-state. "Give us some land of our own," he said, "some separate states, so we can separate ourselves from you."[8] Racism was so deep, he felt, that nothing less than black separatism, including a separate black state, could eliminate the oppression of blacks. Integration, in his view, was certainly not a viable option, especially the token integration promised by political leaders.[9]

Carmichael and other SNCC workers in the late 1960s agreed with Malcolm's call for racial separatism. Driving Carmichael's rallying call for the separation of the races was his belief that blacks are nothing less than

---

[5] Malcolm X, "The Ballot or the Bullet," in *Malcolm X Speaks*, ed. George Breitman (New York: Grove Weidenfeld, 1965) 31.

[6] Malcolm X, "Speech at Founding of Organization of Afro-American Unity," in *By Any Means Necessary: Speeches, Interviews, and a Letter by Malcolm X*, ed. George Breitman (New York: Pathfinder, 1970) 52.

[7] *Malcolm X: Speeches at Harvard*, 126.

[8] Ibid., 130.

[9] In his later years, Malcolm softened his critical stance towards the US government. The softening is especially evident in the evolution of his political methods. Rather than calling for an immediate revolution that would establish a black state, the later Malcolm began to strategize about working within the state. Thus, voter registration and political education became driving topics in his final years.

victims of colonialism—political, economic, and social colonialism. "Politically," Carmichael and Hamilton wrote, "decisions which affect black
lives have always been made by white people—the 'white power
structure.'"[10] In response to the white corridors of power, Carmichael
and Hamilton called for a new type of power—Black Power.

"The concept of Black Power," they wrote, "rests on a fundamental
premise: *Before a group can enter the open society, it must first close
ranks.*"[11] By this, the Black Power activists meant, at least in part, that
"black people must lead and run their own organizations."[12] Political
institutions were no exception: "If political institutions do not meet the
needs of the people…then those institutions must be discarded."

Discarding the white political institutions did not necessarily mean
overthrowing them by violent revolution, but, in the view of the Black
Power activists, discarding should at least entail forming "independent
party groups"[13] and establishing an entirely new "independent
politics."[14] As Carson points out, the Black Power activists did not
outline in helpful detail what they meant by independent party groups
and new forms of political parties, but it is without doubt that
Carmichael had in mind the creation of political parties not unlike the
Lowndes County Freedom Organization (LCFO), an all-black political
party that espoused as one of its goals the political empowerment of
blacks in local government.

Nevertheless, there is also no denying that Carmichael at times
sounded like a revolutionary intent on using any means possible, including violence, to overthrow the state. For example, during the Mississippi
March, he publicly advocated burning down all state courthouses.[15] And
during a trip to Cleveland after a volatile situation there, he openly
embraced the physical destruction of all things Western, presumably the
state among them.[16] Carmichael's justification of violence was itself
purely practical. "Nothing," he and Hamilton wrote, "more quickly
repels someone bent on destroying you than the unequivocal message:

---

[10] Stokely Carmichael and Charles V. Hamilton, *Black Power: The Politics of
Liberation in America* (New York: Random House, 1967) 7.

[11] Ibid., 44.

[12] Ibid., 46.

[13] Ibid., 173.

[14] Ibid., 176.

[15] Ibid, 211.

[16] Ibid., 221.

'O.K., you fool, make your move, and run the same risk I run—of dying.'"[17] This practical need to adopt forcible means becomes even more compelling when the state fails to restrain unjust violence. "If a nation fails to protect its citizens, then the nation cannot condemn those who take up the task themselves."[18]

Against the Black State:
King's Criticism of Black Power

King disagreed with calls for a separate black state and for permanently separate black political institutions, and he adamantly opposed rallying cries to incite crowds to take up arms against state institutions.[19] Regarding separation from the state, King offered three arguments to support his opposition to separation: the first is based on self-interest and self-identity, the second on his theological view of human nature, and the third on the promises of democracy.

King countered the notion of separating from the state by claiming that he had a vested and historical interest in the creation of the wealth of the nation. In a sermon on Jesus and the fool, King stated that, because blacks had contributed to the success of America, he had no plans to go elsewhere. "My grandfather and my great-grandfather did too much to build this nation for me and you to be talking about getting away from it."[20] In this view, blacks had sacrificed to make the country a better place, and so to create a separate black state would be to leave behind all

---

[17] Ibid., 52.

[18] Ibid., 53.

[19] I intend for this part of my study to demonstrate, among other things, that Paul Garber overstates his point when he describes King as "a Black Power devotee without the slogan." See Garber, "Black Theology: The Latter Day Legacy of Martin Luther King, Jr.," *The Journal of the Interdenominational Theological Center* 2 (Spring 1976): 113.

[20] Martin Luther King, Jr., "Why Jesus Called a Man a Fool," in *A Knock at Midnight: Inspiration from the Great Sermons of Reverend Martin Luther King, Jr.,* ed. Clayborne Carson and Peter Holloran (New York: Warner Books, 1998) 154. Interestingly, the nature of the argument revolves, at least in part, around self-interest: leaving the United States, in King's mind, would counter the self-interests of the blacks. With this argument in mind, I disagree with Fairclough's unqualified statement that "King appealed to reason, not passion, to ethics, not self-interest, to consensus and reconciliation, not racial and class animosities." See Adam Fairclough, *Martin Luther King, Jr.* (Athens: University of Georgia Press, 1990) 138. On more than a few occasions, King appealed to the self-interests of individuals and states when arguing his viewpoint.

the contributions of his family and of all other blacks who had sacrificed themselves in the pursuit of a better life. Indeed, King held that the United States belonged in part to blacks and that American blacks were exactly that—Americans. "Since we are Americans, the solution to our problem will not come through seeking to build a separate black nation within a nation."[21]

Predictably, King thought similarly about white participation in the political struggle of blacks: because whites had suffered and sacrificed for the cause of civil rights, they should in no way be excluded from any civil rights institution or action. In this view, a separate black state and separate black political structures would be a repudiation of sacrifices that whites made on behalf of blacks.[22]

On a practical level, King argued against a separate black state as well as separate black politics because of his belief that the foe of civil rights was so large and so powerful that blacks needed all the help that they could get, even from whites, to counter the foe. The mandate, as he saw it, was not to exclude whites, or any other racial group, but to enlist consciences.

More fundamentally, though, the idea of a separate black state and permanently separate black politics could find no room at all in King's theological understanding of humanity. As previous chapters have noted, King believed that God had created people to be in relation with one another. But underlying the idea of a separate black state was an opposing view. To be sure, the Black Power movement had a deep sense of brotherhood and sisterhood, but that sense was limited to the black population. King found this limitation theologically wrongheaded: God had created all of humanity to be in relation with one another.

The idea of a separate black state and permanently separate black politics also stood against King's optimistic belief that people and their institutions are always capable of redemption, that no person or institution is wholly corrupt and totally sinful. In King's view, the white political structure, and those who fill it, should never be surrendered to death, primarily because each person and each institution has within it the ability to be and do good. For King, the problem with Black Power, as

[21] Martin Luther King, Jr., *Where Do We Go from Here: Chaos or Community?* (Boston: Beacon Press, 1967) 54.

[22] Martin Luther King, Jr., *The Autobiography of Martin Luther King, Jr.*, ed. Clayborne Carson (New York: Warner Books, 1998) 319.

well as its calls for black separation, is its failure to recognize the potential goodness in people and their institutions. Offering this criticism, King stated: "It is, at bottom, the view that American society is so hopelessly corrupt and enmeshed with evil that there is no possibility of salvation from within."[23]

Just as the call for black separatism expresses no hope in the possibility of divine salvation, so too does it fail to express hope in democracy. Speaking of Black Power activists, King argued that their "fantasy of a separate black state" is "cynical" and "nihilistic" because of its complete "loss of faith in the possibilities of American democracy."[24] Unlike the Black Power activists, the republican King never completely lost faith in the promises of democracy—in the promises he read in America's founding documents—even though he experienced the totalitarian dimensions of American democracy, and even though he came to know that the founding documents were themselves the products of slave owners.[25]

Although King never gave up on the political system he loved, he did recognize that there were times when "temporary segregation" might be required. Having observed the South's integration of schools and its teachers' associations, King noted that sometimes blacks can be "integrated without power." Deeply troubled by a loss of power, he declared: "We don't want to be integrated *out* of power; we want to be integrated *into* power."[26] Until full integration is a possibility, he claimed, temporary segregation—including, presumably, temporary segregation in political structures—should be an option for blacks. What should not be an option, however, is a separate black state that Black Power activists intend to be permanent, or any other permanently separate political structure.

---

[23] King, Jr., *Where Do We Go from Here?*, 44.

[24] Ibid., 122.

[25] With King's critique of Black Power in mind, I disagree with Richard Lischer, who contends that, in the last three years of his life, King gave up any reliance he had on the democratic ideals of American democracy. See Richard Lischer, *The Preacher King: Martin Luther King, Jr. and the Word That Moved America* (New York: Oxford University Press, 1995) 108.

[26] King, Jr., *Autobiography*, 325. I agree with James H. Cone's contention, in *Martin & Malcolm & America* (Maryknoll: Orbis Books, 1991) 226–27, that King made advances towards the black separatist position near the end of his career.

It was not only the call for a black state and black political structures that irked King; it was also, and perhaps especially, the occasional suggestion that blacks should use any means possible, including violence, to destroy white-controlled political institutions. In addition to offering a theological justification for the use of peaceful means, King emphasized a very practical case against the Black Power call to arms against the state. Black Power activists, he argued, simply failed to recognize the historical truth that no violent revolution has ever succeeded in a country in which the armed forces have not switched allegiance from the government in power. Without the support of the armed forces, any and all Black Power revolutionaries would be doomed to fail. Further, King noted that no violent revolution has ever succeeded without a coalition between the violent minority and the non-resisting majority. Until that coalition is unwaveringly in place, any and all Black Power revolutionaries would, once again, be doomed to fail. Without the support of the armed forces and the non-resisting majority, the Black Power call to arms against the state remained fanciful at best and suicidal at worst.[27]

But for a State Revolutionized by Empowered Blacks: King's Affirmation of Black Power

All this is not to say that King merely condemned Carmichael and his colleagues in the Black Power movement. King certainly did not favor the Black Power call for separate political institutions, but he also felt that there were convergences between his position and the one advocated by Carmichael and others.

King appreciated the voice—the "cry of disappointment"—that the Black Power movement gave to blacks discouraged by the state's failure to implement civil rights legislation. The cry of disappointment, in King's view, is understandable in light of the deep, and ongoing, resistance of the white power structure. The anger of the young people shouting

---

[27] King, Jr., *Where Do We Go from Here?*, 58–59. With King's comments in mind, it is understandable why Rosemary Radford Ruether, "The Relevance of Martin Luther for Today," in *Essays in Honor of Martin Luther King, Jr.*, ed. John H. Cartwright (Evanston: Garrett Evangelical Theological Seminary, 1977), contends that "the nonviolent aspect of direct action rested on a realistic appraisal of the overwhelming balance of legal force available to those in power" (5). But, of course, King's nonviolence rested on other bases as well, including his biblical belief in the pacifist ways of cruciform love.

"Black Power," King wrote, is not congenital: "It is a response to the feeling that a real solution is hopelessly distant because of the inconsistencies, resistance, and faintheartedness of those in power."[28] Although he never felt that the solution was hopelessly distant, King did share the Black Power movement's realistic belief that the state had failed time and again to execute its proper responsibilities.

Indeed, with their incessant and penetrating criticisms, Black Power activists encouraged King to go further than ever before in criticizing the state for its failure to serve black interests. That King's realism deepened in this period is evident, among other places, in his adoption of the Black Power theme of white dominance in black politics. King adopted this theme especially in a 1967 article in which he depicted black politicians as "still selected by white leadership, elevated to position, supplied the resources, and inevitably subjected to white control."[29] King had stated before his disappointment with black politicians, especially Adam Clayton Powell, but what was new was his adoption of the Black Power language that described black politicians as mere puppets of white society. In King's Black Power view, it was not only the white political structure that played the role of foe; it was also the white-dominated black political structure.

King's deepening realism, prompted in part by Black Power, is also visible in his increasingly emphatic claim that state action can never fully establish the freedom sought by him and his followers. He had stated in earlier years that salvation for the blacks does not lie solely with state action. But, from 1966 to 1968, King began to emphasize the Black Power belief that salvation for blacks is largely dependent upon the action of blacks themselves.

King appreciated the Black Power movement as a psychological call for "somebodyness" to take root within each black. For years, he noted, the white power structure had been teaching blacks that they were nobody—a condition in need of reversal if blacks were to be fully free. King appreciated Black Power as a catalyst in effecting the psychological reversal required for full human freedom. Indeed, Black Power's call for psychological strength in the face of the failure of the state became King's own mantra in the late 1960s. Time and again, King stated:

---

[28] King, Jr., *Autobiography*, 323.

[29] Martin Luther King, Jr., "Black Power Defined," in James M. Washington, ed., *A Testament of Hope* (San Francisco: Harper & Row, 1986) 308.

"Psychological freedom, a firm sense of self-esteem, is the most powerful weapon against the long night of physical slavery." Nothing within the power of state action, in his view, could ever establish this type of precious freedom. [30]

King's deepening realism is also evident in the very basic fact that he talked about power more during the last period of his life than during any other period. King had addressed power in his first public speech in Montgomery, and had dealt with the topic throughout his life, but not until the emergence of the Black Power movement did he devote considerable time and energy to the theme and language of power. King affirmed the basic Black Power premise regarding the distribution of power within American society. Like Carmichael and others, King held that the problem blacks face is that there is a radically unequal distribution of power: whites have power and blacks do not. "This [problem] has led Negro Americans in the past to seek their goals through love and moral suasion devoid of power and white Americans to seek their goals through power devoid of love and conscience."[31] But all that must change, King believed, because the right use of power is necessary to achieve the mandates of love and justice.

King adapted Black Power's use of the language of power for his own use, giving it a definition that did not perfectly match Black Power's. Unlike Carmichael and others, King refused to admit violence as a necessary element of power. For King, "Power, properly understood, is the ability to achieve purpose. It is the strength required to bring about social, political, or economic changes."[32] King simply refused to say that power is the will and ability to use, as well as the actual use of, any means necessary to achieve one's rights.

On a related note, King continued to refuse to contrast love with power. As he had in earlier years, King borrowed heavily from Paul Tillich, a subject of his dissertation, when explicating the meaning of power.

One of the greatest problems of history is that the concepts of love and power are usually contrasted as polar opposites. Love is identified with a resignation of power and power with a denial of

---

[30] King, Jr., *Where Do We Go from Here?*, 43.
[31] King Jr., *Autobiography*, 325.
[32] King, Jr., *Where Do We Go from Here?*, 37.

love. What is needed is a realization that power without love is reckless and abusive and that love without power is sentimental and anemic. Power at its best is love implementing the demands of justice. Justice at its best is love correcting everything that stands against love.[33]

This Tillichian definition, when placed within the context of the Black Power movement, helps us understand that King stood apart from and yet also with his Black Power colleagues in SNCC and elsewhere. On the one hand, the definition implies his opposition to power as violence and thus to the Black Power embrace of violence. On the other hand, the definition implies King's support of Black Power's efforts to amass strength through such hard-hitting political action as bloc voting for black-friendly public policies and for certain black politicians. Placed in context, the Tillichian definition is King's nod to the Black Power activists who held that loving moral suasion is not good enough—a conviction King held since even before his first public speech in Montgomery.

Clarifying his understanding of power, King also joined the Black Power activists in claiming that power has political and economic dimensions. Power is not simply about feeling powerful; it is about having political and economic strength in society. Power is about having and exercising political representation, and about having the material goods required to live freely. Holding this definition, King certainly appreciated Black Power's efforts to strengthen the political clout and the economic security of blacks. More particularly, King affirmed Black Power's insistence on pooling black political and economic resources in the struggle for political and economic security.

Nevertheless, King thought it too limiting for blacks to pool their own economic and political resources in the quest for power. Self-help, in his view, would never be sufficient for blacks to achieve the power available through the white-controlled political and economic institutions. Further, King envisioned political and economic power as an ingredient of the beloved community, not as a wedge to drive between whites and blacks. Political and economic power is not a tool that blacks should use to pull themselves away from white society, but a tool for becoming first-class citizens in the beloved community of all colors.

---

[33] King, Jr., *Autobiography*, 325.

With these differences in mind, King separated himself from Black Power in two other areas regarding power: the role of the state and the goal of integration. Because he thought it too limiting merely to call upon blacks to pool their resources, King continued to devote most of his time and energy to calling upon the state to redistribute political and economic power. And because he envisioned political and economic power as an ingredient of the beloved community, King called for the state to redistribute power to blacks by integrating white-controlled political and economic institutions.

But this is not to say that the influence of Black Power disappeared in his political thought at this point. Prompted by the radicality of Black Power, King also began to emphasize the language of revolution. Only a revolution, he began to stress, could result in the empowerment of blacks. King was not referring to a violent revolution that would entail, say, the burning of government and personal property. To the end of his life, King believed that the revolution must remain nonviolent. And so, in 1966, a pragmatic King stated: "The American racial revolution has been a revolution to 'get in' rather than to overthrow. We want a share in the American economy, the housing market, the educational system and the social opportunities. This goal itself indicates that a social change in America must be nonviolent."[34] To be sure, in the last period of his life, King did not understand "getting in" as reformist integration into white-controlled social, political, and economic institutions. Rather, "getting in" meant the sharing of power in fully integrated social, political, and economic institutions operating with an entirely new ethic. In the last period of his life, King began to emphasize the need for a revolution of values and institutions as part of a redistribution of power. Dissatisfied with reform, King called upon his SCLC staff to seek not only the good work of charity but especially "a radical redistribution of economic and political power."[35]

For King, the Black Power language of revolution was helpful, not because of its connotations of violence, but because of its connotations of the need for new values to revolutionize old institutions. So, like the Black Power activists, King began to emphasize his belief in the power of revolution. The time had come, he began to declare, for citizens of all

---

[34] Martin Luther King, Jr., "Nonviolence: The Only Road to Freedom," in *A Testament of Hope*, 58.
[35] King, Jr., "To Charter Our Course," MLKJP, GAMK, 9.

colors to rise up against the state and to demand the institutionalization of an entirely new ethic—an ethic that embraced economic justice over economic colonialism and pacifism over militarism. King stated the challenge most directly in a 1967 speech to his SCLC staff: "Our economy must become more person-centered than property-centered and profit-centered. Our government must depend more on its moral power than on its military power."[36]

The State and Economic Exploitation: From Economic Colonialism to a Person-centered Economy

During the last three years of his life, King moved away from focusing on desegregation and voting rights—traditional concerns of the civil rights movement in its efforts to eradicate racism. Instead, he moved into the area of what he liked to call "human rights," particularly the rights to the basic economic goods required for human existence, emphasizing his belief that the state should mirror divine justice by eliminating poverty.[37] As the previous chapter showed, the theme of economic justice was not at all new in King's work. Nevertheless, the theme became prominent in the last three years of King's life to a degree that was not present even in the second part of his career.[38] In this last part of his life, King called for a revolution of economic values by demanding that the state move from its ethic of economic colonialism to a new ethic of economic justice.

King demanded a state-sponsored end to economic exploitation most vividly in 1966, when he moved to Lawndale, a slum located in Mayor Daley's Chicago, to bring attention to the plight of Northern slum dwellers. "The slum of Lawndale," King wrote, "was truly an island of poverty in the midst of an ocean of plenty."[39] More pointedly, King

---

[36] Martin Luther King, Jr., "The State of the Movement," The Staff Retreat of the SCLC, Frogmore, South Carolina, 28 November 1967, MLKJP, GAMK, 9.

[37] Ibid., 1.

[38] James Cone, *Martin & Malcolm & America*, 222, suggests that King began to shift his focus to economics especially after the riots in Watts. According to Bayard Rustin, Cone reports, King was deeply moved by the poor blacks in Watts, who had the right to eat hamburgers in a once-desegregated restaurant, but no money to buy them.

[39] King, Jr., *Autobiography*, 300.

described Lawndale as a colony in which its dwellers were condemned to live a life of hardship, sickness, and poverty.

Even though Lawndale was a substandard slum, the cost of rent, consumer goods, and basic human services exceeded the cost found in Chicago's well-kept suburbs. The slum residents found themselves having to pay such high costs partly because they had no personal means of transportation to go elsewhere. "It was a vicious cycle," King wrote. Without education, slum dwellers could not find a decent job, and without a decent job they had to turn to welfare. But once on welfare, the state prohibited them from owning property, including cars. Confined to jobs and shops closest to the slums, then, the slum dwellers became victims of price gouging, about which the state did nothing. As a result of this and other problems, slum dwellers became essentially powerless individuals in a colony whose important decisions were dictated from outside the slum. "Many of its inhabitants even had their daily lives dominated by the welfare worker and the policeman. The profits of landlord and merchant were removed and seldom if ever reinvested."[40]

King blamed the state for the existence of slums and for the violence within them. As a colonizing power, the state had sanctioned the construction of the slums, and continued to possess the power to eliminate slum life and construct better living conditions, but simply (and stupidly) chose not to do so. This belief is quite evident in King's reaction to the riots that erupted during his work in Chicago. The responsibility for the riots, he declared, rested with "elected officials whose myopic social vision had been further blurred by political expedience rather than commitment to the betterment of living conditions and dedication to the eradication of slums and the forces which create and maintain slum communities."[41]

King believed that the best way to stop riots from erupting again was to call upon the state to eradicate the slums. His call for state action included much more than fixing up dilapidated housing, for, like Chivers, he saw the existence of slums as interrelated with problems in education, unemployment, underemployment, welfare dependency, and more. The problems of slum life were huge, and, in King's view, no single program could adequately address the problems. If King could have had everything he wanted in Chicago, he would have directed political leaders

---

[40] Ibid., 301.
[41] Ibid., 303.

to create public jobs for the poor, tear down all the slums, create entirely new housing, integrate new schools, and more.

But King the realist scaled back his own ideals and focused on just a few goals, especially when he confronted the belligerent Daley machine. On one front, King and his thousands of marchers called upon political leaders to create an open housing market in Chicago, and were more than pleased when an agreement actually found its way to paper. (Enforcing the agreement was an entirely different issue, and King fully predicted the heavy resistance he and others received from Chicago's bureaucracy.) On another front, King's workers successfully formed various tenant unions in the city's slum areas, with the intention of increasing the bargaining ability of the slum dwellers. Community-based housing cooperatives also came into existence, allowing local residents a voice in decision-making about local properties. Further, King's workers established Operation Breadbasket, a successful campaign which sought job opportunities for poor blacks from major industries that sold goods to slum dwellers without reinvesting in the slum community.[42]

But the Chicago campaign, despite King's positive spin on it, was a failure: slums, inadequate education, discriminatory housing practices, and discriminatory hiring remained.[43] Still, the campaign is so important here because it shows King's unwavering belief that the state is an active creator of domestic colonies. In the second part of his career, King had begun to attend quite seriously to the issue of economic justice, but he did not focus on the state as a colonizing power on the domestic front. That all changed in the last period of his life, when King allowed the language of Black Power to infiltrate his own.

But the Chicago campaign is also important because it shows King's belief that the state is a potential force for good that can bring together different classes in a beloved community where the American dream is available to all. King truly believed that the state has the responsibility as well as the ability to eradicate the very slums that it sustains. He recognized that, in Chicago alone, the Housing Authority, the Department of Urban Renewal, and the Commission on Human Relations could have done significant work in eliminating the slum, and so he

---

[42] Ibid., 307–309.

[43] Adam Fairclough, *To Redeem the Soul of America: The Southern Christian Leadership Conference and Martin Luther King, Jr.* (Athens: University of Georgia Press, 1987) 279–308, provides a helpful account on the defeat in Chicago.

called not for their overthrow but for their active cooperation in establishing economic justice in Lawndale and other places.

In Chicago, then, King revealed his deep-seated belief that the state can and should play a key role in creating a beloved community where class is no longer an obstruction—a belief that complements his earlier emphasis on the state as a key player in creating a beloved community where race is no longer an obstruction. King was well aware that a program to eliminate the slums, as well as other programs designed to bring about the beloved community, would create a state whose domestic functions would grow considerably, but that was acceptable to him in light of his conviction that the state, and only the state, possesses the power required to wrong the evil of slum life and other economic injustices.

Finally, the Chicago campaign is important also because it witnessed an evolution in King's understanding of the ways in which the state should liberate humanity from economic injustice. Within the Chicago movement, King developed a strategy that called upon the state to undertake various ways to eliminate the slums—for example, through open housing, quality education, and more. At the same time, however, King began to emphasize a new strategy that he believed the state should assume in the war on poverty.

Meeting with the United Neighborhood Houses of New York during the Chicago campaign, King argued that "dislocations in the market operation of our economy and the prevalence of discrimination have thrust people into idleness and bind them in constant or frequent unemployment against their will."[44] Poverty is "less the failure of the poor and more the failure of a system that perpetuates poverty. We also know now that no matter how dynamically the economy develops and expands it does not eliminate all poverty."[45] The market, in King's view, lacks the mechanisms required to direct distribution and redistribution so that the poor can move from their stations of poverty to a life enjoyed by the middle and upper classes. In light of the market's failures and limitations, King argued that it is the responsibility of the state to eliminate poverty. Unlike the market, the state can make and implement

---

[44] Martin Luther King, Jr., Address to the United Neighborhood Houses of New York, Biltmore Hotel, New York City, 6 December 1966, MLKJP, GAMK, 5.

[45] Ibid., 6.

decisions that will directly benefit the poor in their attempts to move out of poverty.

In this address, King had in mind a specific tool that the state could use to eliminate poverty—the guaranteed annual income. He had indirectly mentioned the guaranteed annual income in earlier years, but had approached the problem of poverty largely by calling upon the state to increase educational opportunities for the poor, to provide them with high quality jobs, to eradicate their inadequate housing, and more. But now, King held that all these means, though helpful and necessary in their own right, were too indirect in the goal of eliminating poverty and often resulted in fragmentary programs that failed to meet the immediate needs of the poor.[46] A more revolutionary way of eliminating poverty, King argued, is by shifting the state's attention away from production and towards distribution. "We have so energetically mastered production that we must now give attention to distribution."[47] What King wanted the state to distribute was nothing less than cash—an annual income to all of the poor in society. He provided no details of the formula that the state would use to provide guaranteed annual incomes to the poor, but firmly suggested that the income should be sufficient to raise the poor out of their station of poverty.

Ever optimistic, King further claimed that, if the state abolishes poverty by first guaranteeing an annual income, improvements in housing and education would naturally follow. Transformed into purchasers, the poor themselves would seek to change their housing and educational opportunities. Furthermore, the assurance of a stable income would result in the flourishing of the "dignity of the individual" as well as in the diminishment of "personal conflicts" among the poor.[48] In this sense, the state could become an agent of psychological and moral change. By guaranteeing an annual income, the state could affect not only the behavior of the poor but also their hearts—the affection they hold for one another and for those beyond their community. This particular point marked yet another evolution in King's understanding of the state. In earlier years, King had maintained that the state could change behavior but not the hearts of its citizens. But in this case for the guaranteed annual income,

---

[46] Ibid., 1–3.
[47] Ibid., 6–7.
[48] Ibid., 10.

King began to suggest that the state could affect the hearts of the citizenry by providing them with cash.[49]

Nine days later, during an appearance before the Senate Subcommittee on Urban Reorganization, King further explained his belief that the state needs to assume an active role in eliminating poverty, particularly by guaranteeing an annual income, but this time he also added a call for public jobs.

Skipping the pleasantries, King began his statement by faulting the US government for being more concerned with size, power, and wealth, than with creating a more just society. While engaging in a space race and arms race, the government foolishly misses opportunities to stop the increase in wage inequality, the rise of unemployment, and the decline of personal income. As King put it: "The sorry record of income, public service, and education indicates that the federal government's not doing enough."[50]

King told the senators that the state itself—local, state, and federal governments—was a major cause of the anger that the senators witnessed on the streets of their cities in 1966. "The anger in the streets results from the discriminated's powerlessness at city hall, and a sense that those in power are passive and uncaring."[51] Being poor and black means being powerless—to be governed, without the right to redress, by police, housing authorities, and welfare departments, all of them under control of the state. Sensing their concern over urban riots, King then told the senators that their failure to establish economic justice would result in the growth of urban tensions and turbulence in the streets.

King testified that the sure way for the state to avoid rioting is by refusing to place responsibility for poverty on the shoulders of poor individuals and by assuring jobs and income for all. "If the society changes its concepts by placing the responsibility on its system, not on the individual, and guarantees secure employment or guaranteed income,

---

[49] It is therefore insufficient to argue, as John Rathbun does, that King acknowledged "that the state should not, indeed cannot, legislate morality." See John W. Rathbun, "Martin Luther King: The Theology of Social Action." *American Quarterly* 20 (Spring 1968): 49.

[50] Martin Luther King, Jr., Statement by Dr. Martin Luther King, Jr., before the Senate Committee on Urban Reorganization, Washington, DC, 15 December 1966, MLKJP, GAMK, 5.

[51] Ibid., 30.

dignity will come within the reach of all."[52] Adequate jobs and income, provided by the state, would raise the morale, spirit, and dignity of the poor, and help them lead fruitful lives. Again, King suggested that state policy could change not only behavior but also the hearts and minds of the citizenry.

By meeting with the senators, King confirmed his earlier belief that the state has the potential to be both a force for evil and a force for good. On the one hand, King implied that the senators were forces for evil for having allowed the riots to continue in an environment of economic justice. But as he noted that, King also challenged them to be forces for good by guaranteeing income or jobs for all.

Deeply affected by realism, however, King did not present the senators with a vision of the good state without any checks and balances. King understood well that he was calling for a significant expansion of the state and that this expansion was reason for deep concern. Ever realistic, he recognized that a bigger state could leave bigger footprints on the backs of the poor, and so he fully embraced two additional actions: the creation of the role of a local ombudsman who would address grievances filed by the poor against the state, and the establishment of the "maximum feasible participation" provision of the Equal Opportunity Act. Regarding the importance of a liaison, King stated: "In the ghettos the bureaucracies are becoming as oppressive as sweat shop employers or absentee landlords."[53] In light of bureaucratic abuse, then, the poor should have the right to file grievances against the state as well as the right to appear before a liaison who would address and respond to the grievances. More fundamentally, however, King also supported the direct involvement of the poor in decision-making processes about the social welfare, employment, education, and training systems in which they found themselves and from which they benefited.[54]

Perhaps the most telling part of his appearance before the Senate in 1966, however, is his closing reflection on the will of the state to seek a more just society:

I am under no illusions that the mere detailing of defaults and the listing of some solutions will lead to swift remedial action.

---

[52] Ibid., 31.
[53] Ibid., 32.
[54] Ibid., 33.

Administrations under Democratic and Republican leadership both have inconsistent records. Whether the causes for delays and retreats are attributable to war diversions or the threats of white backlash, the attainment of society and equality for Negroes has not yet become a serious and irrevocable national purpose. I doubt that there ever was a sincere and unshakable commitment to this end.

Negroes therefore have a responsibility to act with greater vigor and frequency than during the past decade. They will have to act on various fronts and in a variety of ways.[55]

This closing statement is not at all devoid of hope in the state, primarily because King had just spent time and energy asking the state to back his efforts to create a more just society. Nevertheless, the statement reveals King's ever-deepening sense that blacks and the poor can in no way rely on the good will of the state to effect change for the good of society. The state, in this realistic view, is a bastion of middle and upper classes devoted to their own good and resistant to the ceding of any power to the poor. For change to happen, blacks and the poor must continue to seize power, in even more creative ways than before, and thereby force the state to establish justice for all. This realistic view is not new in King's thought, but the bluntness with which he described it to senators in a public hearing, including those who had offered assistance to the civil rights movement in earlier years, clearly represents a deepening of realism.

King's embrace of the guaranteed annual income did not stop him from pushing the state to develop a holistic program to counter the various ill effects of poverty. Favoring expansive and comprehensive state action, King once again pointed to Sweden as a concrete example of a just state, praising its lack of poverty and slums as well as its abundance of human services. King brought up Sweden again during an SCLC staff retreat in 1966, during which he expressed his frustration with the preceding periods of the civil rights movement, noting in particular that the victories of the movement had failed to address "the lot of millions of Negroes in the teeming ghettos of the North." The changes in the preceding period were merely "surface changes," ones that undermined

---

[55] Ibid., 41–42.

white supremacy but not "the monster of racism itself."[56] So the result of the preceding years was the same result that blacks experienced at the end of the Civil War—abstract freedom. "It was freedom without roofs to cover their heads, without bread to eat, without land to cultivate."[57]

The continued presence of merely abstract freedom led King "to ask the question of whether something is not wrong with the very structure of society."[58] King concluded, in this 1966 speech, that nothing other than the faulty economic system of capitalism had created more than forty million poor people in the United States, and that Sweden's democratic socialism offered a better systemic response to poverty than capitalism ever could. Sweden is the good state, he argued, because it has addressed the pressing economic need for a "more equitable distribution of wealth." With these words, King acknowledged that he was saying that "something is wrong with capitalism" and that something is right with the more equitable distribution of wealth favored by democratic socialism.[59]

King further explained his preference for Sweden by invoking the theological image of the kingdom of God in opposition to both capitalism and communism. Like Crozer professor George Davis, among others, King stood opposed to "the rugged individualism of capitalism and the impersonal collectivism of communism." Adopting the synthesizing economics of Knudson, King claimed: "The kingdom of God is found in a synthesis that combines the truths of these two opposites."[60] On the one hand, then, capitalism is faulty because it has consistently failed to address poverty systemically, and communism is faulty because it runs roughshod over individual rights and dignity in its attempts to eliminate poverty. On the other hand, capitalism is right in the sense that it acknowledges individual liberties, and communism is right in the sense that it acknowledges the need for systemic measures to combat the systemic problem of poverty. Because both systems— capitalism and communism—are partly wrong, neither is to be affirmed wholeheartedly, and because both are partly right, neither is to be condemned un-

---

[56] Martin Luther King, Jr., Speech to Staff Retreat at Frogmore, South Carolina, 14 November 1966, MLKJP, GAMK, 6.

[57] Ibid., 15.

[58] Ibid., 18.

[59] Ibid., 19.

[60] Ibid., 20.

reservedly. The best response to both capitalism and communism is to leave behind their weaknesses and to use their strengths in the creation of a new system that both preserves individual liberty and allows for the collective action required to solve systemic problems. Indeed, such a system would be a reflection of the kingdom of God.

In King's view, the democratic socialism of Sweden reflects the kingdom of God. On the one hand, Sweden's democracy, unlike Soviet Union's totalitarianism, ensures the preservation of individual liberties. On the other hand, Sweden's socialism, unlike an unfettered capitalism, allows for collective means designed to eliminate poverty—for example, the nationalization of some private industries and the establishment of state welfare agencies. Sweden's socialism, that is, allows for state intervention in the market so that wealth would be more equitably distributed throughout society.

King continued on, in this 1966 speech, to lay additional theological foundation for his belief in the need for a more equitable distribution of wealth. Not only did he invoke his theological account of human freedom and the reign of God; he also, once again, portrayed the earth's material resources as belonging to God, who has "left enough and to spare in this world for all of his children to have the basic necessities of life." In King's theological view, "God never intended for some of his children to live in abject, deadening poverty."[61] As King saw it, the more equitable distribution of wealth effected through Sweden's democratic socialism is faithful stewardship of God's creation.

King wanted the state to act as a trustee because he believed that individuals or groups alone, no matter how rich they might be, could never achieve the elimination of poverty: poverty is a systemic issue, not a personal issue. For King, no group or individual in isolation can come close to achieving what the state, with its massive machinery and resources, can achieve in the realm of economic justice. Thus, King stood against not only permanent political separatism but also permanent economic separatism. With the Black Power movement in mind, King argued in his 1967 book that blacks cannot attain economic power through separatism. Later, as previously noted, he granted that blacks may need to separate temporarily from mainstream institutions, but King never stopped believing "the fact that the larger economic problems

---

[61] Ibid., 21.

confronting the Negro community will only be solved by federal programs involving billions of dollars."[62]

At the end of the staff retreat in 1967, King and other SCLC members agreed that they would demand federal economic programs involving billions of dollars by organizing a massive poor people's march on Washington. The purpose of the march, in King's words, was "to demand redress of their grievances by the United States government and to secure at least jobs or income for all."[63] King did not publicly say that the intent of the march was to move the United States closer to the model of government found in Sweden, but the implication of that move is clear. King believed that, as Sweden adopted a democratic socialism that supplied jobs or income for all, the United States should move towards doing the same.

The appendix of King's 1967 book, in addition to his positive evaluation of Sweden's democratic socialism, indicates much of what King was hoping for in the Poor People's Campaign. The themes are familiar by now. Regarding employment, King favored direct employment over training, and he saw an activist role of the state in guaranteeing direct employment. "Instead of training for uncertain jobs, the policy of the government should be to subsidize American business to employ individuals whose education is limited."[64] King envisioned massive subsidies to support businesses that would train unskilled workers on the job and even move them into professional fields. Moreover, King believed that the state should move beyond providing subsidies to private industry to creating public jobs in the field of human services. The state should begin a massive public works program that would employ large numbers of blacks and the poor.

If jobs with good incomes would not be forthcoming to those able to work, King favored the distribution of a guaranteed annual income. He also hoped that the Poor People's Campaign would result in a much greater distribution of funds to the field of education, with grants going directly to teacher support, the construction of new facilities, educational parks, integrated schools, and more. Regarding housing, King hoped that the state would subsidize the elimination of slums and the construction of integrated housing. "We need the equivalent of Medicare for

---

[62] King, Jr., *Where Do We Go from Here?*, 49.

[63] King, Jr., *Autobiography*, 346.

[64] King, Jr., *Where Do We Go from Here?*, 197.

housing."[65] Further, King hoped that the march would result in adequate medical care for the poor, as well as in their participation in governing bodies that decide on issues of community education and urban planning.

King saw the march as an evolution in his political ethics. In the preceding years of protest, it was more often than not the federal government that came to the aid of the civil rights workers as they confronted the policies and powers of local and state governments. But the Poor People's Campaign would put him and his followers into a largely new relationship with the federal government. "In this instance, we will be confronting the very government and the very federal machinery that has often come in as our aid."[66]

The "we" that King referred to in this statement points to another evolution in his political praxis. Although he largely relied on alliances between clergy, students, and other middle-class citizens for his previous marches, King intended for the Poor People's Campaign to consist largely of the nation's utterly poor and dispossessed. King came to believe, as did Morehouse professor Walter Chivers, that this group consisted of "the real revolutionaries." King held that, if organized in the right way, people who have "nothing to lose" would protest with "a freedom and power that will be a new and unsettling force in our complacent national life."[67] Like Chivers, who put his hopes for a better democracy in the masses of poor blacks in particular, King began to hope that the masses of the dispossessed poor of the United States—white and black—would rise against the political structure with an intensity and endurance unknown to people with material stakes in the status quo of society.

But King did not mean for the confrontation with the state to be merely adversarial, even though he planned for the nonviolent tactics of the marchers to disrupt the governing process in Washington. He did not mean for the march to be merely adversarial exactly because he wanted—and needed—the federal government to come to the aid of the protestors by expanding the War on Poverty that it had begun (and allowed to languish) under Johnson's direction. Though he did not want the march to be merely adversarial, King did expect that it would effect a

---

[65] Ibid., 202.

[66] King, Jr., "Why We Must Go to Washington," MLKJP, GAMK, 17.

[67] Martin Luther King, Jr., *The Trumpet of Conscience* (New York: Harper & Row, 1967) 60.

revolution, not in the sense of overthrowing the existing government, but in the sense of overthrowing the values that supported economic colonialism. The march, as he envisioned it, would demand a revolution of economic values that would shift the economy from being property- and profit-centered to person-centered. On the one hand, then, the march would decry a federal government that failed to attend to the material needs of the poor by sanctioning a slightly fettered capitalism that sought profit at the expense of most other things. On the other hand, the march would affirm the state as having the power required to do good for the poor of society.

It was King's thirst for justice that drove him to plan for the Poor People's Campaign. At this point, King described justice in the Aristotelian language of receiving what is due. "There is nothing abstract about this. It is as concrete as having a good job, a good education, a decent house, and a share of power."[68]

Coupled with this thirst for concrete justice as an underpinning of the march was King's understanding of human nature. Citing the US Constitution, as he had in his high school years, the republican King stated that the Poor People's Campaign was necessary to establish life, liberty, and the pursuit of happiness—the inalienable rights that the Creator has bestowed upon humanity. "And if one does not have a job or income, he's deprived of life; he's deprived of liberty; and he's deprived of the pursuit of happiness."[69] In King's ongoing perspective, the people have natural rights—inalienable rights, God-given rights—to the basic goods of life, and the state has a divinely-ordained responsibility to provide the goods to which the people are already entitled. The campaign was not about asking for handouts; it was a matter of demanding what was already due the poor.[70]

But more than his republican heritage, King's Christian heritage drove him to organize the Poor People's Campaign. "And as I said the other day, it may be true that Jesus said, 'Man cannot live by bread alone.' But the mere fact that he added 'alone' means that he cannot live without bread."[71] People, in King's theology, are not disembodied souls; they are

---

[68] King, Jr., *Where Do We Go from Here?*, 90.

[69] King, Jr., "Why We Must Go to Washington," MLKJP, GAMK, 11.

[70] Ibid., 18.

[71] Martin Luther King, Jr., "Why a Movement," 11 November 1967, MLKJP, GAMK, 1.

ensouled bodies, hungry for food and thirsty for water, and entitled to both. King went on to identify Jesus of Nazareth as the inspiration he and others felt as they moved toward the march on Washington. "I didn't get my inspiration from Karl Marx; I got it from a man named Jesus, a Galilean saint who said he was anointed to heal the broken-hearted."[72]

As King saw it, the problem was not that the United States was wealthy but that it did not share the wealth with the poor. While in Memphis in the last year of his life, King offered this point, as he had done many times before, by pointing to the biblical story of Dives and Lazarus. Every day, King preached, Lazarus visited the gate of Dives, hoping to receive the basic necessities of life, but Dives never did anything about Lazarus. So Dives went to hell, not because he was rich, but because he ignored the poor. "Dives went to hell because he sought to be a conscientious objector in the war against poverty."

As the God of justice condemned Dives, so too would God condemn the United States. "If America does not use her vast resources of wealth to end poverty and make it possible for all of God's children to have the basic necessities of life, she too will go to hell." God faults the United States for not feeding the hungry, clothing the naked, and providing economic security for those in need. "And so," God judges, "you cannot enter the kingdom of greatness."

These were King's words to the political structure of the United States. But as he stood there in Memphis, he also meant them to be divine words to the local political structure. As King put it, "And that same voice says in Memphis to the mayor, to the power structure, 'If you do it unto the least of these my children you do it unto me.'"[73]

For King, in Memphis and in Washington, economic justice was a theological issue, as was the required revolutionary move from a profit-centered economy to a person-centered economy. The God of justice demands an economic revolution.

Moreover, King held that God wanted the United States to engage in economic justice not only within its own borders but also throughout the world. As domestic economic policies of the United States greatly disturbed King, so too did US global economic policies.

King believed that US global economic policies wreaked havoc around the world. For example, he contended that US economic policies

---

[72] King, Jr., *Autobiography*, 351.
[73] Ibid., 354.

towards South Africa propped up a government that supported apartheid and the physical and spiritual oppression of South African blacks.[74] King also was convinced that US economic policies robbed Latin American countries of their material resources and established the United States as a colonial power that dictated policy decisions to local government puppets. "We in the west must bear in mind that the poor countries are poor primarily because we have exploited them through political and economic colonialism."[75]

King called upon the United States to leave behind profit-centered global economic policies and to execute person-centered ones by developing a world war against poverty. Expounding on what he began to describe in earlier years, King recommended the formation of a Marshall Plan of sorts to eliminate poverty throughout the world, particularly in Asia, Africa, and South America. King added that the plan must not be short-lived but must extend through many years. In addition, he recommended that each wealthy state should allocate 2 percent of its annual gross national product towards the funding of this plan, and that the funds should support programs designed to improve education, health, and the elimination of poverty.[76]

Underlying this vision of global economic health was King's familiar theological belief that God created life to be interrelated. Divinely created natural law, King claimed, rewarded those who sought to preserve their neighbors. Regarding the preservation of others, he stated: "It is the first law of life precisely because we cannot preserve self without being concerned about preserving other selves." Natural law, then, demanded international aid to states struggling for survival. "But the real reason that we must use our resources to outlaw poverty goes beyond material concerns to the quality of our mind and spirit." The real reason for establishing international aid is the religious conviction that all of humanity is created in the image of God and that each person is of infinite value. "If we accept this as a profound moral fact, we cannot be

---

[74] For a helpful analysis of King's views on Africa, see Lewis V. Baldwin, *To Make the Wounded Whole: The Cultural Legacy of Martin Luther King, Jr.* (Minneapolis: Fortress Press, 1992) 163–244.

[75] King, Jr., *Trumpet of Conscience*, 62.

[76] King, Jr., *Where Do We Go from Here?*, chapter 6.

content to see men hungry, to see men victimized with ill-health, when we have the means to help them."[77]

In the last period of his life, King did not favor a separate black state, but he did favor a state that integrated the poor, blacks among them, into a system of economic justice. King did not favor integration into the existing capitalist system. Rather, he desired integration into a massive welfare state that ensured jobs and income, among other things, for all the citizenry. That new system would be revolutionary, not in the sense that it toppled political structures, but in the sense that it institutionalized a new economic ethic—one that affirmed all people as entitled to the basic goods of life that their Creator intended for them to have. By breaking down the walls of class, the institutionalization of this new ethic would provide the material conditions required for full reconciliation—the beloved community—to become a reality within society.

The State Among States: Moving from Military Power to Moral Power

King's mature plan for the state included a revolution of values not only in the state's economic policies, on both the domestic and international levels, but also in its policies on war and peace.

In January 1966, Georgia State Senator-elect Julian Bond faced a crisis: his fellow legislators did not want to seat him because of his dissent on the issue of US military involvement in Vietnam, a controversial subject on which King had offered little commentary. On 14 January 1966, however, King offered his full public support for Bond's right to dissent and for his anti-war views.

Appearing at the state capital in defense of Bond, King argued that one of the fundamental rights within the United States is the right to dissent. "That right to dissent even means the right to criticize the policy of one's government in a time of war."[78] King did not offer a constitutional defense of the right to dissent, but he did appeal to the example of Abraham Lincoln, who had condemned his generation's war with Mexico. King also implied that Bond had the right to dissent

[77] Ibid., 180.
[78] Martin Luther King, Jr., SCLC Press Release: Address by Dr. Martin Luther King, Jr., at the State Capital, Atlanta, Georgia, 14 January 1966, MLKJP, GAMK, 2.

because he owed his ultimate allegiance to God rather than to any human authority.

> Somewhere, Julian Bond read and believed, 'Thou shalt not kill.' Somewhere, Julian Bond read, 'There must be a day when men will beat their swords into plowshares and their spears into pruning hooks, and nations will not rise up against nations, neither will they study war anymore....' Somewhere, Julian Bond read, 'Blessed are the peacemakers, for they shall be called children of God.'[79]

With these words, King suggested that US military involvement in Vietnam conflicted with the peaceful ways of God, and that when there is a conflict between the state and God, the disciple must follow the Lord. Bond, King suggested, was right to obey God rather than the state when the two conflict, and to believe that God calls disciples to support a life of peace, not one of military involvement in Vietnam.

As the previous chapter noted, King had already supported negotiations to end US military action in Vietnam. Still, in the second part of his career, King did not grant Vietnam a lot of attention. This lack of attention, however, wholly subsided in the last part of his career, when he claimed, in the face of strong opposition within the civil rights movement, to be anointed by God to speak out against US involvement in the Vietnam War.[80]

In earlier years, King had posited an inextricable relation between the state sins of militarism and the neglect of poverty. The vast resources that the state poured into maintaining its nuclear military, in King's view, siphoned off the resources that the state could and should use to eliminate poverty. In the last part of his career, King adapted this argument as he built a case against the Vietnam War. When he appeared before the Senate Subcommittee on Urban Reorganization, for example,

---

[79] Ibid., 4.

[80] Henry E. Darby and Margaret N. Rowley, "King on Vietnam and Beyond," *Phylon*, 47 (Spring 1986): 49, report that James Farmer, Roy Wilkins, Whitney Young, and Ralph Bunche were among those who questioned King's public stance on the Vietnam War.

King argued that the state expenditures on the Vietnam War diverted huge resources away from the War on Poverty.[81]

King made the same argument in his first full public statement on the Vietnam War. Speaking at Riverside Church in New York City, he stated without qualification that the Vietnam War was an enemy of the poor. This time, however, King added a dimension that he had excluded in his previous public statements. The war was an enemy of the poor not only because it diverted money away from the War on Poverty. In addition, "It was sending their sons and their brothers and their husbands to fight and to die in extraordinarily high proportions relative to the rest of the population."[82] The war was classist in the way it was sending so many poor men to fight and die on the fields in Vietnam. Further, because he saw the issues of classism and racism as inextricably related, King also labeled the war as deeply racist and bemoaned the disproportionate deaths of not only the poor but also the many poor blacks.

The Vietnam War was especially problematic, King also argued, because the United States, while proclaiming its desire to liberate Vietnam, had actually been a colonial power over the country. After Vietnam had declared independence in 1945, King argued, the United States failed to recognize it, choosing instead to ally itself first with France (as it attempted to recolonize Vietnam) and later with a series of vicious dictators who denied land reform for the peasants. Rather than liberating Vietnam, the United States had done everything in its power to prevent the independence of Vietnam and the type of policies that would establish freedom among the Vietnamese, especially policies that would redistribute land from wealthy landlords to the peasants. In Vietnam, King preached, the United States fought on the side of the wealthy to ensure that the peasants would remain in their stations of poverty. In this sense, the Vietnam War was a classist and racist war executed by a colonial power.[83]

Arguments familiar in the history of King's thought came to the foreground as he continued in the ensuing months to offer statements on the Vietnam War. At a 1967 SCLC staff retreat, King remarked that he stood against the war not only because it diverted resources from the civil

---

[81] King, Jr., Statement by Dr. Martin Luther King, Jr., before the Senate Subcommittee on Urban Reorganization, MLKJP, GAMK, 10–11.

[82] Martin Luther King, Jr., "A Time to Break Silence," in *A Testament of Hope*, 233.

[83] Ibid., 235.

rights fight, but also because it was yet another step towards nuclear annihilation. "I'm afraid," King declared, "that if we continue the way we are going as a nation, we are going to end up in World War III."[84] This argument was merely a version of King's earlier claim that war in general is wrong because the nuclear weapons of mass destruction would lead to total annihilation.

The SCLC staff also heard King call upon the state to love its enemies, a familiar message throughout his life. King did not offer a rigorous explanation of what it would mean for the United States to love Vietnam, but simply suggested that love would entail halting the war. His comments on love, though, dealt more with his own resistance to the Vietnam War, which he understood as the path of cruciform love. "Love," he stated, "means going to any length to restore the broken community." It means going the second mile and turning the other cheek so that the community might be restored to wholeness. In King's case, love meant fighting against the Vietnam War so that the broken communities within Vietnam and the United States might be restored to wholeness.

King believed that the Spirit of God known in Christ anointed him to stand against the war and for peace. In his view, the war was wrong not because it was bad politics, but because it deeply contradicted the cruciform love that he believed the Spirit of God in Christ called him to preach and enact. Speaking out might not be popular, according to King, but it was faithful to a God who made all individuals—American and Vietnamese—sisters and brothers. The preacher King found his point to be self-evident: "To me the relationship of this ministry to the making of peace is so obvious that I sometimes marvel at those who ask me why I am speaking against the war."[85]

His Riverside speech generated intense opposition, but King believed the authority of his pacifism flowed from the authority of God. At another staff retreat in 1967, King addressed the issue of political authority in the case of Vietnam by stating: "We must have the passion for peace born out of wretchedness and misery of war, giving our ultimate allegiance to the empire of eternity."[86] The SCLC, in his view, must become a colony of dissenters who would give ultimate allegiance to

---

[84] King, Jr., "To Charter Our Course," MLKJP, GAMK, 23.

[85] King, Jr., "A Time to Break Silence," in *A Testament of Hope*, 234.

[86] King, Jr., "The State of the Movement," MLKJP, GAMK, 9.

the God of peace and call upon the state to exercise the same type of allegiance.

Throughout the rest of his life, King continued to preach his belief that God did not call the United States to enter into a war in Vietnam. He offered this point most explicitly when he preached "The Drum Major Instinct" in February 1968: "God didn't call America to engage in a senseless, unjust war, as the war in Vietnam." And so the God of justice had cast judgment on the United States. Reflecting back to his first public speech in Montgomery, King declared that God "has a way of putting even nations in their place" and that, if the United States failed to change its Vietnam policy, God might "rise up and break the backbone" of American power.[87]

One month later, and less than a week before he was assassinated, King again delivered a threat of divine judgment to the United States for its role in the Vietnam War, and spoke of his conviction that the war was "one of the most unjust wars that has ever been fought in the history of the world."[88] King noted, once again, that the war destroyed the War on Poverty, set the United States against the self-determination of the majority of Vietnamese, propped up corrupt dictators, and threatened the existence of the entire world with nuclear annihilation. But he added some other reasons for his intense reaction: the Vietnam War wrongly strengthened the military-industrial complex as well as the reactionary forces of the United States. King did not expound on these additions, but simply implied that the complex supporting the War on Poverty, not the military-industrial complex, should have been strengthened.

More than all that, King claimed that the Vietnam War made the United States appear to the world as an arrogant superpower. In King's estimation, the United States has no authority to assume the role of world police officer. As he put it months earlier, "In short, God did not appoint America to be the policeman of the whole world. And America must recognize that she has not the capacity nor the power nor has she earned the moral right to be an American power, an Asian power, an Atlantic

---

[87] Martin Luther King, Jr., "The Drum Major Instinct," in *A Testament of Hope*, 265.

[88] Martin Luther King, Jr., "Remaining Awake through a Great Revolution," in *A Testament of Hope*, 275.

power and a South American power."[89] With these words, King suggested that the United States committed idolatry by arrogantly assuming the role of world police officer, and so deserved harsh divine judgment. The United States, in his view, is not God's military agent on earth.

Although he spoke of the Vietnam War in particular, King also spoke more generally of war itself, just as he had done in previous years. In his 1967 book, King again described war as obsolete, stating that the destructive power of nuclear weapons eliminates the possibility that war may serve a good. Once again, he also claimed that humanity has a God-given right to survive and that war threatens that basic human right. This time, however, King stated that war is obsolete for another reason as well. War is obsolete not only because it can no longer serve a good, but also because science and technology have taken away reasons for war. "In this day of man's highest technical achievement...there is no excuse for the kind of blind craving for power and resources that provoked the wars of previous generations. There is no need to fight for food and land."[90] Science and technology have made it possible for all to enjoy adequate means of survival. King thus believed that all wars, even limited wars, are obsolete. "A so-called limited war will leave little more than a calamitous legacy of human suffering, political turmoil, and spiritual disillusionment."[91]

Because war is obsolete, King wrote, the time has come for states to grant attention to the practice of nonviolence in international relations. In the last part of his career, King reiterated his belief, first stated in Oslo, that the practice of nonviolence should not remain in the hands of activists with grievances against local, state, or federal governments, but that it should become a serious subject for states to study and practice. "It is, after all, nation-states which make war, which have produced the weapons that threaten the survival of mankind and which are both genocidal and suicidal in character." Genocidal and suicidal, states could not be better candidates for the practice of nonviolence.

Unfortunately, once again, King did not explicate on ways in which states might practice nonviolence. He did, however, point to the United Nations as a place to begin the study. "The United Nations is a gesture in

---

[89] King, Jr., "To Charter Our Course," MLKJP, GAMK, 26.
[90] King, Jr., *Where Do We Go from Here?*, 181.
[91] Ibid., 184.

the direction of nonviolence on a world scale."[92] Behind this statement, too, are the comments King offered in the second part of his career, when he suggested that the United Nations could play a significant role in bringing about universal disarmament and in setting up a world police force—two goals that would help bring peace to the world.

King believed that specific behavioral changes, such as the practice of nonviolence in international relations, would help establish peace, but he also felt that peace would never really emerge until states begin to hold a completely different perspective on the underlying issues of war and peace. In a 1967 Christmas sermon on peace, King outlined a perspective that he believed states must begin to adopt if peace were to become a reality within history.

Peace would come, King preached, when individuals and states begin to understand that loyalties must transcend races, tribes, classes, and nations. Calling for the emergence of a world perspective, he declared: "No individual can live alone; no nation can live alone; and as long as we try, the more we are going to have war in this world."[93] The time has come for individuals and states to acknowledge the divine truth that all life is interrelated. "This is the way our universe is structured. This is its interrelated quality."[94] Peace on earth would not arrive, then, until states embrace the natural law of the interrelated structure of all existence. (King did not mention the word "love" at this point, but love is exactly what he had in mind. Indeed, on another occasion in the last part of his life, he stated: "This call for a worldwide fellowship that lifts neighborly concern beyond one's tribe, race, class, and nation is in reality a call for an all-embracing and unconditional love for all men."[95])

Peace would also come when states begin to understand that all human life is sacred, created in the image of God, and united in the cruciform love of Jesus Christ. "Every man is somebody because he is a child of God. And so when we say 'Thou shalt not kill,' we're really saying that human life is too sacred to be taken on the battlefields of the world.... Man is a child of God, made in His image, and therefore must be respected as such. Until men see this everywhere, until nations see this

---

[92] Ibid.

[93] King, Jr., *A Trumpet of Conscience*, 68.

[94] Ibid., 70.

[95] King, Jr., *Where Do We Go from Here?*, 190.

everywhere, we will be fighting wars."[96] A deep and abiding belief in the sacredness of the human personality would lead states to stop their exploitation and killing and to start loving their neighbors.

Further, peace would emerge when states begin to believe in the ultimate morality of the universe. King maintained that God in Christ has shown that wrong will not stand forever and that deception will not stand forever. When Christ was crucified and resurrected, God demonstrated that what is true, right, and good will always emerge in the end. When states begin to understand the endurance of the divine good, they will at long last seek the peace that God intends for humanity.[97]

Going beyond the matter of perspective, King also suggested, in an article published posthumously, that world peace would never arrive until the United States integrate its foreign policy field. King saw the issue of integration as more than just national in its implications. Racist decision-making by white men in the United States, he argued, led to disasters not only within the United States but also in such places as Vietnam and the Dominican Republic. "[These white men] don't really respect anyone who is not white." Thus, world peace would not arrive until blacks become decision-makers in the field of foreign policy.[98]

Like the constructive suggestions for peace that King offered in the second part of his career, the behavioral and perspectival changes that he set forth in his last years reveal his belief that the state is sinfully flawed and limited. The sinful state is genocidal and suicidal, bent on achieving power through military force at all costs. Parochial, the sinful state believes that it deserves ultimate loyalty and that it can exist unto itself. Deeply profane, the sinful state sees no sacredness in life beyond itself and completely ignores the enduring significance of God's good work in Christ. And deeply racist, the state makes decisions based only on the limited perspectives that whites offer.

Still, King's constructive suggestions also reveal his belief that the state can repent of its sinful ways and can develop behaviors and

---

[96] King, Jr., *A Trumpet of Conscience*, 72.

[97] Ibid., 75. Contrary to Lischer, *The Preacher King*, 252, this sermon, one of King's last, provides substantial evidence that King did not eliminate or replace his calls for love of enemy during the last part of his career. King's deepening realism, I believe, led him to a deeper sense of the need for love of enemy.

[98] Martin Luther King, Jr., "A Testament of Hope," in *A Testament of Hope*, 317–18.

perspectives that leave behind immoral militarism and embrace moral peace. King actually believed that the state could practice nonviolence in its international relations and change its parochial perspective into the world perspective that God intends for states to hold. By offering constructive suggestions, King suggested that the state is capable of redemption and revolution.

It is exactly a revolution in military values that King sought. In this last part of his career, King hoped to move the state away from militarism and towards a universalism that embraced the Christian virtues of love and peace. Nevertheless, in spite of the emphasis on peace throughout the last part of his career, King continued to rely on the state for its power and coercion when confronting opponents of his civil rights marches. Consider the Meredith March. At one point during the march, civil rights activists, King and Carmichael among them, attempted to spend the night on the grounds of an all-black school in Canton. City and school officials thought otherwise, and backing them was a group of highway patrol officers. Eventually, the standoff resulted in the firing of tear gas and the use of billy clubs by the patrol officers—an attack that King described as a great example of "a police state." Interestingly, Garrow reports that a day earlier King had wired President Johnson with a request for federal protection, by which King meant armed troops. A presidential emissary, Garrow reports, had promised the presence of the state patrol, the ones who eventually beat the civil rights activists.[99] Consider, too, the Chicago Campaign. On one march during the campaign, more than one thousand Chicago police officers, armed and willing, were enlisted to keep at bay groups of angry whites. To make it through the march, King had to rely on armed police officers surrounding him and his followers.

These two examples demonstrate that, during the last part of his career, King continued to rely heavily upon the power and coercion of the state in order to carry out his nonviolent protests. King's reliance was not passive, either. As he carefully planned his nonviolent marches, he also carefully engineered the presence of armed troops that would allow his nonviolent marches to move forward. Thus, King continued to emphasize the importance of the political value of justice as armed protection.

---

[99] Garrow, *Bearing the Cross*, 486.

Executing the Revolution:
The Role of the Poor and the Church

In the last part of his career, King also continued to believe that salvation does not lie within the political institutions themselves: the state, in and of itself, would never effect the revolution of values that King sought. In his view, which extended back to the Montgomery boycott, the real power for revolutionizing the state—for leading the state to provide the conditions required by the beloved community—lies with the power of the people.

At this point, "the people" came to mean not only the traditional civil rights workers, including the white liberal, but especially the poor—black and white. As noted above, King came to see the poor as the real revolutionaries who could effect a transformation in the values institutionalized in state economic policy. But King also envisioned a greater role for the poor, primarily because he saw the interrelations between economics and war and peace. In King's vision, then, the poor activists in the Poor People's Campaign would seek a revolution not only in economic policies but also in policies on war and peace. By demanding what is due them—basic economic goods—the poor would also be calling upon the state to move its resources from the Vietnam War to the War on Poverty. By fighting for economic justice, the poor would also be fighting for an ethic of peace. King believed that, with nothing to lose, the poor could stage a massive, aggressive, nonviolent protest that would force a revolution of values in state policy: economic justice would replace economic colonialism, and peace would replace militarism.

But King never meant to exclude others who would be willing to fight for economic justice and peace, primarily because he knew that confronting the belligerent state would require the use of all available resources, including personnel. With this belief in mind, King continued to call upon the church to fulfill its proper role in church-state relations, even though he devoted most of his time and energy to organizing the "real revolutionaries."

In a 1966 interview, King again emphasized, as he had done throughout his adult career, that the role of the church in its relations with the state is to be the conscience of the state. Further, he stressed that there is no area in the life of the state that is beyond the purview of the church. When asked how far the responsibility of the church extends in the domestic and international affairs of the state, King replied: "I see the church as a conscience of the community, the conscience of the nation, the conscience of the state, and consequently, the church must be involved in all of the vital issues of the day, whether it's in the area of civil rights, whether it's dealing with the question of war and peace."[100] The church's proper role is to explore issues of economics, race, war, and more, and to act as the state's omnipresent conscience on all these issues. In a rare moment, King briefly praised the church for its involvement in the civil rights struggle. Choosing not to expand on his simple declaration, King then quickly moved to criticize the church for its stance on the issue of war and peace. He was especially irritated by the church's inclination to baptize any war that might come along, including the Vietnam War.

In King's view, the church has a responsibility to take a stand against war in general by clarifying that war is the enemy of humanity. King did not use the interview as an occasion to make the theological case against war, but only to call upon the church to preach to the state about the evils of war. Further, he suggested that the church has a responsibility to take a stand against specific wars as well. Because of this responsibility, and in light of Vietnam, King spoke of how "happy" he was that the National Council of Churches, Pope Paul, and many rabbis had sharply criticized the Vietnam War and had called for a negotiated settlement.[101]

In the last period of his life, King continued to critique the church with the double attitude with which he criticized the state. On the one hand, he saw the church as sinful when it was silent, or actively obstructionist, on civil rights, or when it actively supported war in any form. On the other hand, he envisioned the church as a force for good when it became an active supporter of civil rights and the peace movement. King adjusted this attitude on a contextual basis, allowing it to shift back and forth in response to which part of the church, as well as the content of the issue, he was addressing.

Constant through his criticism was his belief that the church, though not the "real revolutionary," must become as revolutionary as ecclesiologically possible, not by overthrowing political institutions, but by seeking the institutionalization of an entirely new ethic—an ethic of economic justice and peace.

---

[100] Martin Luther King, Jr., interview by Hugh Downs, *Today Show*, NBC, 18 April 1966, MLKJP, GAMK, 2.
[101] Ibid., 3.

Summary

During the last part of his career, King offered, yet again, a theological interpretation of the state, but this time he found himself using familiar themes to address new issues. With the arrival of the Black Power movement, for example, King returned to his theological view of human nature to counter calls for a separate black state and black politics, as well as to his christology to oppose the use of any means necessary.

Influenced by Black Power, King understood his political ethic in this period as becoming revolutionary, and so he began to use the language of a revolutionary, though not the exact type spoken by SNCC and others, by declaring the immediate need for the state to institutionalize a revolution of values: economic justice must overthrow colonialism, he declared, and pacifism must replace militarism. Ultimately, however, it was King's christocentric vision of the beloved community, the interpretive key to his understanding of the state, which led him to call for a revolution of values. Peace with justice, in King's view, is a necessary ingredient of the beloved community.

The revolutionary King was not all that new. King had addressed economic justice ever since his high school speech on blacks and the Constitution. Nevertheless, this time he gave the topic sustained attention, especially in Chicago and Memphis and in planning for the Poor People's Campaign. Especially new was his emphasis on the guaranteed annual income, an idea he had mentioned only in passing in earlier years. In addition, as King pressed for guaranteed income, the language of entitlement, no stranger to Black Power, came to the foreground of his public rhetoric. People, King began to preach, are entitled to demand from the state, a trustee of the divine creation, what is already theirs—basic economic goods. Again, King's hope was for a massive welfare state, and, following many of his earlier teachers, he again expressed his preference for Sweden's democratic socialism, this time identifying it with the reign of God on earth.

Also new in this last period was King's belief, encouraged by Black Power, that justice means not only the elimination of poverty but also the direct participation of all, especially the poor, in decision-making about their economic life. Economic power came to mean not only the possession of economic goods but also the power to decide, with the state, about their distribution and redistribution. In his mature view, then, the proper internal work of the state is to establish economic justice and to grant the poor a direct role in decision-making on matters related to their economic lives.

In addition, King continued to claim that the proper internal work of the state is to enforce compliance with its just laws by prosecuting and punishing the disobedient and by providing physical protection, even through the use of force, for citizens unjustly brutalized. Facing mobs during the Meredith March and the Chicago Campaign, King continued to value a just order more than peace alone.[102]

During this last period, King also allowed the theme of economic justice to dominate his account of the external functions of the state. Emphasizing a theme he had touched upon in earlier years, King proposed a Marshall Plan for developing economies, making the case by appealing to natural law and to the image of God. Moreover, in accord with his earlier acknowledgment of the interrelations between war and poverty, he drew from his emphasis on economic justice to argue against the Vietnam War, claiming that the war diverted resources from the War on Poverty. His argument against Vietnam, then, did not reflect a simplistic pacifism based on Jesus' sayings. King also continued to argue against war in general; his revolt against militarism in this period was but a continuation of the pacifist inclinations he had been expressing for years. Still, this time King added that science and technology have eliminated the need to fight for food and land in any war.

The last part of his career also witnessed King's listing of specific ways in which states might reconcile with one another. He continued to suggest behavioral changes, including the practice of nonviolence in international relations, but his argument for peace moved to another level when he called upon states, not just individuals, to develop a new perspective that would affirm the interrelated structure of reality, the sacredness of human life, and the ultimate morality of the universe. Echoing Boston personalists, King stressed that the state must actually love other states.

---

[102] I agree with Adam Fairclough, "Martin Luther King, Jr. and the War in Vietnam," *Phylon*, 45 (March 1984), who argues that "King was not a strict pacifist" (21); and with Adam Roberts, "Martin Luther King and Nonviolent Resistance," *The World Today* 24 (June 1968), who observes that King's "was not an absolute ethical rejection of violence in all circumstances" (231). Because King actively sought support from the forcible means of the state, which sometimes resulted in injuries and death, King was far from a strict pacifist, if by strict pacifism we mean the refusal of all forcible means that use or threaten violence.

King's last years also saw a continuation of his double attitude towards the state. On the one hand, King continued to envision the state as a force for evil. Following Williams, Rauschenbusch, and the early Niebuhr, King focused on the classism of the state, though he never ignored the state's racist dimension. The intensity of his rhetoric on classism increased especially when he declared, from the slums of Chicago, that the state is an internal colonial power. Following Black Power, as well as the pacifists from his past, King also criticized the militarism of his own government, referring to it as "the greatest purveyor of violence on earth." With his ever-deepening realism, forged in the furnace of peace protests and the civil rights movement, King continued to refuse an unqualified Pauline ethic of subordination, preferring instead even greater levels of civil disobedience than he had ever experienced.

Even with his language of revolution, however, King never called for the overthrow of the state. Continuing to embrace the optimism he saw in his father and read about in Boston personalism, King hoped against hope that the state would assume its proper role in creating the conditions required by the beloved community, and that it would do so by embracing economic justice and pacifism, both of which, he believed, would break down artificial barriers between the people of God. Trusting that the day would come when the state would do so, and believing that no state is wholly demonic, King also continued to refuse an unqualified ethic of resistance, choosing instead to resist or affirm the state on a contextual basis.

In previous years, King had spoken of his increased optimism, but that theme did not come to prominence in the last period of his life. Rather, prompted by Black Power, King emphasized his ongoing belief that the state is not especially interested in changing its economic colonialism and militarism. King thus began to stress the importance of a personal ethic of self-esteem, the best antidote to a sinful state. In accord with Chivers, he also called upon especially the poor to join a massive campaign that would force the state to carry out its proper function of establishing the conditions of the beloved community, where every one would be free and, at long last, reconciled.

The state, King continued to preach, is for the flourishing of the human personality within the beloved community that God in Christ intends.

Conclusion

Summary and Response

A Theological Understanding of the State

I have argued throughout this book that King embraced a theologically-based dialectical attitude towards the state. On the one hand, he understood the state to be reflective of and necessarily involved in the creating, preserving, and reconciling work of God. On the other hand, he described the state as deeply sinful.

King believed that the state arose out of human sociality, and so is part of God's creative design for humanity. The state is for humanity; humanity is not for the state. For humanity, the state carries out its proper functions by mirroring divine justice and love through the work of preservation and reconciliation. The proper work of the state, in King's thought, is to protect citizens, especially as they fight for equality, and to create and preserve the physical conditions required by the beloved community that God in Christ intends for all of humanity—a community of reconciliation marked by integration, economic justice, and a just order. King's vision of the beloved community is the interpretive key to unlocking his understanding of the purpose of the state.

King turned to his vision of the beloved community when assessing the life of the state. The state is good, he argued, when its policies help establish integration, economic justice, and a just order—the historical manifestations of divine love and justice. Conversely, the state is evil when it formulates and implements policies based on racism, classism, and militarism. King's experiential theology, formed on the underside of political history, informed him that the state, like all people, is a force for not only good but also evil. His theological evaluation of the state was thoroughly contextual, shifting back and forth according to the particular context of the day. Consistent throughout the shifts, though, was his refusal to understand the state as having either supreme authority or no authority. King adopted a contextual understanding of political authority, as well as a contextual ethic of civil obedience and disobedience, thereby refusing an unqualified ethic of either subordination or resistance. Deeply related to this contextual stance was King's theological insistence that the state should never be the object of people's ultimate loyalty. Supreme authority resides in God alone.

In his pursuit of the beloved community, King granted more validity to democratic forms of state than to others, primarily because he believed that democracies outperformed other forms in respecting and supporting God-given human rights and human equality. Moreover, King embraced social democracies because he believed they best reflected and served the "network of mutuality" that God created among people. In King's theological vision, Sweden's welfare state was the good state.

Nevertheless, King's theology also led him to deny portraying the state as the savior of humanity. The state is but a tool—a limited one—in God's plans for ultimate salvation.

King as Bricoleur

My study has also shown that King's deeply theological understanding of the state emerged from a wide variety of sources. King was a *bricoleur* whose political ethics drew from the African-American religious tradition and from the European-American religious and republic traditions. As a young boy, King learned about the state from A.D. Williams, Daddy King, and Williams Holmes Borders, all of whom were black preachers and political activists with dialectical attitudes towards the state. Their understanding of the state as a force for good and evil found its way into King's political ethics and remained there throughout his life. As a college student, King learned about the state from black preachers and professors at Morehouse, especially the scholar-preacher Benjamin Mays, whose social gospel set forth a vision of social democracy that King readily adapted. In seminary and graduate school, King became exposed in greater detail to European-American political thought, especially Rein-hold Niebuhr's Christian realism and Boston personalism's theological liberalism, two schools of thought that intertwined, in varying degree, with the political ethics that King had learned from the black preachers and professors in his earlier years. Throughout his lifetime, King also relied heavily on the American republic tradition, including the founding documents of the United States, as a critical tool in his political ethics.

Though King as *bricoleur* drew from a wide variety of sources, the ultimate root of his political ethics is not in civic republicanism, Boston personalism, Niebuhrian realism, or in any other theoretical school, but in the black tradition he experienced through the black preachers and scholars in his life. King was a black *bricoleur*.

Constancy and Development in King's Thought

I have also demonstrated in this study that the fundamental elements of King's interpretation of the state remained relatively constant but deve-loped in substantive content and expression during his life. Throughout his public life, King consistently portrayed the state as a mixture of good and evil, made for the beloved community, limited in authority, and properly democratic. These basic political convictions remained con-sistent along with the underlying basic theological convictions noted above. From the time he delivered "The Negro and the Constitution," King consistently invoked the person and work of Jesus Christ when setting forth his understanding of the state. From the time he delivered his first speech in Montgomery, King regularly cited the just God he experienced through the prophets of the Hebrew Scripture. King always insisted on using theological language and categories to describe and assess the state, and this insistence itself contributed to constancy in the fundamental elements of his political thought.

Though constant in its fundamental elements, King's understanding of the state developed in substantive content and expression throughout his life.[1] King's thoughts on the character of the state experienced significant development. In the first part of his career, he continued to set forth the realistic interpretation of the state he had expressed in "The

---

[1] Both this section and the preceding one exclude any comments on the origin of the state. There is not enough relevant information to track the constancy and development of this base element.

Negro and the Constitution," as well as during his years of higher education, but he did so with a deepening sense of the sinfulness of the state. Faced with an increasingly recalcitrant and intransigent state in the early part of the civil rights movement, King began to refer to the character of the state as "evil," a new adjective in his political thought. More, King's public rhetoric in this period even went beyond Niebuhrian ambiguity when he claimed that he could see nothing but evil in collective life. The second period of his public career also witnessed intensification of his public rhetoric against the state. During his trip to Oslo, for example, King referred to states as "genocidal and suicidal in character," and, at home, he described the governing authorities of Alabama as a "racist oligarchy," reflecting his deepening frustration with the belligerence of Governor Wallace and his supporters in public office. In the last part of his career, King, prompted by the Black Power movement, intensified his rhetoric all the more when he referred to the United States as an internal colonial power, as well as "the greatest purveyor of violence on earth."

On a related note, King's ever-deepening realism had different foci throughout the various parts of his career. At different points in his life, King's realism targeted the state sins of racism, classism, and militarism. King recognized the interrelations between these sins, but allowed particular themes to rise in prominence in response to what he perceived to be the moral mandates of his particular context.

Interestingly, King claimed that, as his realism deepened, so too did his optimism in the ability of the state to assume its proper place and role in the creating, preserving, and reconciling work of God. This claim became most explicit in the second part of his career, during his trip to Scandinavia, when he claimed that the Nobel Peace Prize had given him faith that humanity "will indeed soon rise to the occasion and give new direction" to warmongering. This optimism, grounded partly in his theological belief that no person or institution is beyond the power of redemption, continued even in the last part of his career, when he encouraged states to develop a theological understanding of the individual and the world—an understanding that would allow for world peace. Nevertheless, it is important to note that, though King claimed earlier to have experienced a deepening optimism, the last part of his career expressed no such claims. In fact, the deepening realism, highlighted above, assumed a prominent role in his mature understanding of the state.

King's thought on the purpose of the state developed, too. As a high school student, King called upon the state to allow for "fair play" among all people. For King, this meant that the state should reverse policies that deny education, food, health care, space, respect, and market access to the black community. King added substantive theological depth to this early vision by suggesting that the state should provide the physical conditions required by the beloved community intended by God in Christ. He buttressed this general appeal in the second part of his career by embracing Sweden's social-democratic state in particular. In the last part of his life, King expressed his early vision in a new way by demanding that the state institutionalize nothing less than a revolution of values that would bring about the beloved community.

King's vision of the role of the state in establishing the beloved community assumed different foci throughout his life. The early King focused on the need for the state to eliminate segregation and discrimination. In mid-career, he focused on the need for the state to enfranchise the disfranchised and to establish economic justice. The mature King focused even more on the state's role in establishing economic justice, and began to emphasize, as he had not done before, the state's role in creating world peace. But these different foci came together in, and were part of, King's broad vision of the relationship between the state and the beloved community.

There is one noteworthy transformation in King's vision of the purpose of the state—one that occurred in the first part of his public career. With a sharpened focus on the mandates of cruciform love, and with a sense that the emergence of nuclear weapons would lead to total nuclear war, he moved away from his early acceptance of war and began to call upon the state to assume a pacifist stance in its international relations. These pacifist inclinations continued throughout the second and third parts of his career, when King sketched his hope for world government, universal disarmament, greater international aid, and the practice of nonviolence within the field of international relations. But King tempered a purely nonviolent approach when he expressed his hopes that a world police force might come into existence some day.

The first part of his career, however, did not witness a repudiation of forcible means that use or threaten violence in the field of domestic relations. With a need to protect civil rights workers from violent racists, King felt compelled, throughout his career, to affirm the role of the state in preserving and protecting those who do right and seek the common good. King's ongoing calls for the state to use its forcible means to protect his supporters waxed and waned according to the dictates of his immediate situation, and he never once suggested that the primary role of the state is to keep order, either at home or abroad.

Regarding the penultimate authority of the state, King never explicitly joined the Apostle Paul in claiming that God confers authority upon the governing authorities. Nor, for that matter, did he directly argue that the authority of the state derives from Christ or the people, or explicitly discuss Revelation's contention that the authority of the beast derives from Satan. Nevertheless, this study has drawn implications to suggest that, for King, political authority is a contextual issue.

As a student at Boston University, King preached a doctrine of God which held that only God rightly commands and demands our ultimate allegiances. After Boston and especially during his time in Montgomery and Birmingham, King refined his understanding of divine authority by stating that humanity has an obligation to obey God rather than human authority when the two conflict. In Birmingham, King also clarified his understanding of potential conflict between God and human authority by describing the difference between just laws and unjust laws. Unlike unjust laws, just laws are in accord with natural law and eternal law, both of which are reflected in the US Constitution. With all this in mind, King developed a contextual approach to political authority. For King, the state has authority when it expresses its goodness by formulating and implementing just laws. Conversely, the state has no authority when it expresses its sinfulness by formulating or implementing unjust laws.

Because of the interconnectedness between character, role, and authority in King's thought, his understanding of political authority developed in the same manner that his vision of the state's character and role developed. For example, when King's realism began to understand militarism to be a state sin in discord with natural and eternal law, and when he began to exclude the practice of war from his vision of the proper work of the state, King's view of political authority changed, too. Now, in his developing interpretation, the state that pursues war loses authority.

On a related note, King adopted a contextual approach to civil obedience and disobedience. Again, he clarified this view at Birmingham. On the one hand, refusing an unqualified ethic of resistance, he argued that a state which supports natural law and eternal law should be obeyed. On the other hand, refusing an unqualified ethic of subordination, he claimed that a state which ignores or undermines natural and eternal law should be disobeyed. But this is to put King's argument too simply, primarily because his approach to civil obedience and disobedience revolved around particular issues. Thus, King recognized the possibility that citizens would find themselves at once both supporting and resisting a particular state. Further, his actions throughout his life suggest that, unless the state clearly violated the limits of its authority, King simply assumed that the state had authority to command obedience from its citizens. The burden of proof, then, is on those who would deny the state its authority.

Like his view of political authority, the content of King's contextual approach to civil obedience and disobedience developed alongside the substantive changes in his vision of the character and role of the state. What is more, however, King's ethic of civil obedience and disobedience changed in expression and tactics as his realism deepened throughout his life. As King increasingly faced intransigence and recalcitrance from the state, he changed the ways that he and his followers disobeyed the state. For example, in Selma, King intensified the pressure on the state by increasing the number of alliances he formed for marches. By the end of his life, King had planned to increase the pressure all the more by turning to the poor and by organizing them in a massive protest that would bring the everyday functions of Washington to a halt. A transformation also appeared in King's thought when he conceded, in this last period, that a temporary formation of separate black institutions might best aid the cause of blacks in developing the material and emotional resources they needed to ensure full integration into power.

Finally, King's vision of democracy as the best form of state also developed in substantive content and expression throughout his life. In "The Negro and the Constitution," King denounced the gap between the promise and fulfillment of democracy, and embraced a social democracy that would provide for "fair play." Later, in the first part of his career, King added theological depth to this early understanding by claiming that democracy, unlike totalitarianism, acknowledges that each individual has

God-given rights and that all individuals are ends, not merely means, and are tied together in a web of mutuality. During this period, King also unpacked his embrace of democracy by extolling the virtues of Jeffersonian democracy—one with a federal government that respects both states' rights and God-given human rights, allowing the latter to trump the former when the two conflict. In the second part of his career, King also added to his early understanding by focusing his efforts on guaranteeing "the sacred right" of democracy—the right to vote. Democracy, in his view, was about representative government—of the people, by the people, and for the people—and the enfranchisement that supported it. King also began in this period to point to Sweden's social democracy as the form of state that best provides the material conditions required by the beloved community. In the last part of his life, King even identified Sweden's social democracy as the reign of God on earth.

For and Against: A Brief Critical Response

One element in this study is especially clear about King's understanding of the state: its theological character. Thus, any critical analysis of his political thought must engage his theology. With this in mind, I offer below additional summary statements as well as a brief critical response that engages theological issues. I intend, for the most part, to offer an internal criticism of King's thought, thereby sharply limiting the extent and depth of my critical responses.

THE ORIGIN OF THE STATE

Preston Williams was right to argue that King located the state's origin in the divinely created social dimension of the human personality. According to King, people simply needed to be together in order to realize their potential, and thus they formed the state so that it would lead to a more perfect community, a place where no person would be solely responsible for every dimension of her or his existence and where every human personality could flourish. Grounding the state in human sociality, King separated himself from his namesake, Martin Luther, who located the origin in the fall of humanity from a life of perfect grace and in divine need to rectify that fall. Choosing not to follow Luther, King avoided Luther's predictable emphasis on the coercive role of the state.

In my view, King rightly avoided such an emphasis, primarily because a stress on the coercive role of the state would have rendered him virtually defenseless in those times when the state's concern for justice, understood primarily as "law and order," led the state to repress, jail, and physically harm civil rights workers who were fighting for a new order.[2] Had he emphasized, with Luther, that the primary role of the state is to act as God's jailers, King would not have easily grasped the conceptual tools required to call the state away from its unjust repression of the cause of civil rights. King, of course, knew as much. As part of a family subjected to political repression, as one who was repeatedly jailed for disobeying unjust laws, and as a leader of those who suffered state-sanctioned brutalities, King was well aware of the tendency of the state to transform itself into a repressive police state, and so carefully chose not to provide any ontological grounding that might sanction an understanding of the state as primarily a coercive power. Thus, King grounded the state in human sociality, a move that easily enabled him to call upon the state to be more than a jailer.

Nevertheless, I contend that, given his desire for the state to be more than a jailer, more particularly, to provide the conditions in which human personalities might flourish within the beloved community, it would have been more theologically fitting for King to have offered a christocentric interpretation of the origin of the state. Had he explicitly located the origin of the state in the reconciling work of God in Christ, King could have provided a full ontological grounding for a state whose purpose is to serve the beloved community—the place of reconciliation that God in Christ intends for all of humanity. To be sure, locating the origin of the state in created sociality, as the Boston personalists did, allowed King to understand the primary function of the state to be the provision of conditions that empower people to relate together as interconnected personalities. But locating the state in creation did not fully support King's additional argument that the primary purpose of the

---

2 As Weber notes, Luther's view of the origin of the state has made it "difficult—although certainly not impossible—to expand the notion of justice into a dynamic concept, challenging established orders of privilege and power and requiring the state to take on broader responsibilities for the welfare of all the people." Theodore R. Weber, "State," in *Dictionary of the Ecumenical Movement*, ed. Nicholas Lassky, Jose Miguez Bonino, John Pobee, Tom Stransky, Geoffrey Wainwright, and Pauline Webb (Geneva: WCC Publications; Grand Rapids: William B. Eerdmans Publishing Company, 1991) 953.

state is to serve the cause of loving reconciliation known through God in Christ. In this sense, there is a fracture in King's interpretation of the state. King offers a christocentric view of the state's end but not of its beginning: he sets the end in relation to Christ, but the beginning only in relation to creation. In my view, had he refused personalism's view of the state's origin in favor of a christocentric grounding, King might have presented a much more coherent interpretation of the state.

I am suggesting that King would have done well to adopt the coherency visible in Dietrich Bonhoeffer's christocentric understanding of the state.[3] There are significant differences between Bonhoeffer's and King's understandings. For example, King presented a much more comprehensive role for the state than Bonhoeffer had. Whereas Bonhoeffer focused on the role of the state in establishing an order that would create space and time for the church to preach the gospel of justification, King focused on the role of the state in creating liberty and justice for all. Still, Bonhoeffer's method of relating the origin, character, and purpose of the state to Christ would have served King well in the development of a coherent understanding of the state.

THE CHARACTER OF THE STATE

King's dialectical attitude towards the state, forged in the crucible of his life experiences, is one of the greatest strengths of his political thought.

Partly because of his experiences on the underside of political society, including those with segregated buses in Montgomery, "naked state power" in Alabama, and bureaucratic resistance in Chicago, King understood the state to embody deeply sinful qualities. Yet King's approach to the state from the underside of political history also made him keenly—and personally—aware of the state's goodness. He found the state to be good partly because of his encounters with a Supreme Court that criminalized segregation, a federal government that provided troops to protect him and his followers, and a social-democratic state that promised to eliminate poverty. Further, moving from ghettos to corridors of power enabled King to recognize that it was the state that gave whites access, through the provision of jobs and contracts and tax

---

[3] Dietrich Bonhoeffer, *Ethics*, ed. Eberhard Bethge (New York: The Macmillan Company, 1962) 298–303.

incentives, to the so-called free market; that offered quality public education for children and youth in all-white schools; and that ensured law and order for suburbanites surrounded by lush lawns. With these experiences, King came to acknowledge that the state, unlike other social institutions, has the power to provide the material conditions for the beloved community.

King's dialectical attitude is exemplary. On the one hand, we know that the state embodies sinful qualities. One need only think of South's Africa's apartheid, Germany's fascism, Soviet Union's Stalinism, or US-sanctioned segregation, all of which King commented on, to recognize the sinfulness of the state. Thus, it is absurd to portray the state merely as God's minister for the good, or merely as the result of divine providence. An unqualified view of the state as good is experientially and theologically faulty: there are no pure saints in a fallen world.

On the other hand, however, we know that the state can embody goodness. With King, we need only think of the US Supreme Court's activism in the 1960s, or Sweden's attempts to eliminate poverty, or India's response to the caste system, to recognize that the state can be God's minister for good. Thus, it is absurd to portray the state as merely sinful. An unqualified degradation of the character of the state is just as experientially and theologically faulty as is an unqualified view of the goodness of the state: there are no pure demons in a world permeated by the grace of God.

The unsatisfying part of King's dialectic is not its content, or the way he presented it contextually, but its missing elements. Though he briefly addressed Romans 13, King chose not to expound on his response to Paul's high view of the governing authorities. Nor did King directly comment on Revelation 13:6-7, which depicts the state as wholly demonic in character. I cannot adequately explain why King, who used one biblical text after another in public speeches, chose not to offer substantial comments on either Romans 13 or Revelation 13 when explicating his thought—if, in fact, he chose not to do so. In my view, substantial commentary on either or both of these biblical texts would have added immeasurable substance to his interpretation of the character of the state. Given his use of the Bible, though, I remain hopeful that such significant statements will become public.

THE PURPOSE OF THE STATE

King's particular embrace of Sweden's welfare state, I aver, is in some discord with his realistic acknowledgement that the state is deeply and inescapably sinful. I argue this only because King did not suggest any reservations he might have had about the type of social-democratic state he experienced in Sweden. Although he was sharply critical of communist and capitalist states, and although he was deeply schooled in realism's warnings about the tendency of states "to discard the limits of power, put themselves in the place of God, destroy or absorb all other institutions and thereby make themselves the source and center of meaning and existence,"[4] King seemed so enamored of Sweden's social-democratic state that he failed to apply to Sweden any of his usual realistic inclinations. With an unbalanced optimism, King offered a glowing, uncritical review of Sweden's ability to eliminate poverty and transform political society into the beloved community. Recent history, of course, has proven King to be wrong: Sweden's social-democratic state, for various reasons, has waxed and waned, and so has yet to accomplish everything that King envisioned for it. I believe, then, that King's constructive suggestions on the internal functions of the state would have been stronger had he applied to his vision of the social-democratic state the type of realistic analysis to which he subjected capitalist and communist states.

Had he done so, King might have particularly spotted the potential problem for human freedom in a massive welfare state—a problem that briefly caught his attention in the last period of his life. While in Chicago, King noted, albeit in passing, the serious problem of welfare dependency—the diminishment of human freedom as a result of state aid. Given King's emphasis on human freedom, it was fitting for him to have identified the problem of welfare dependency as a threat to human freedom, and it would have been equally fitting for him to have transferred this concern to his assessment of Sweden's social-democratic state. But an overly optimistic King simply failed to note this danger when extolling the virtues of Sweden's democratic socialism.

---

[4] See Weber, "State," in *Dictionary of Ecumenical Movement*, 955. With these words, Weber identifies the lesson of totalitarian states—a lesson that the realist Kenneth Smith had taught King.

King certainly did not hold back his realism when discussing another internal function of the state—using forcible means to ensure the protection and preservation of citizens seeking justice. When confronting violent opponents, King was more than willing to elevate the political value of order and to call upon federal troops to use their force and power to quell unjust order, to preserve the civil rights workers, and to enforce just laws. For King, the state's use of forcible means in domestic relations was an issue of justice: the state that fights unjust disorder, he believed, mirrors the God of justice who threatens states with death and hell.

The theological issue that arises at this point concerns the place of cruciform love, that is, nonviolent love. The language of cruciform love so pervasive throughout King's speeches and sermons is glaringly absent in his statements about the state's domestic use of forcible means. King spoke of those means as "necessary" and "justifiable" under certain circumstances, but nowhere did he describe them as loving. I am only suggesting here that King did not offer a sufficient explanation of the relationship between his embrace of cruciform love and his deep reliance on the state's forcible means. Many Christian pacifists have long called for the use of police power on the domestic front while condemning the practice of resorting to and conducting war. It is apparent that King did the same, but his theological justification for doing so remains unclear. The lack of clarity becomes more pronounced when we remember that King held that the end of the state (cruciform love) must preexist in the means.

Perhaps the point to make here is that, in his political thought about domestic order, King simply did not hold a narrowly construed conception of cruciform love. We need not ask why. It simply would have been suicidal for King to have refused state force when marching among rabid and violent defenders of a racist system.

Unlike the young King, whose expanded notion of Christian love had led him to justify certain wars, the mature King embraced a cruciform love whose hallmark was nonviolence. Believing that humanity has a God-given right to survive, and embracing Jesus' example of nonviolence on the cross, the mature King viewed all wars as sinful.

Some of King's thought on war and peace, I believe, reveals an unbalanced optimism that is not present in other parts of his political thought. During his stay in Oslo, King suggested that states, not merely individuals, should study and experiment with the philosophy and practice of nonviolence. And in his 1967 Christmas sermon on peace, King called upon states, not just individuals, to develop a new perspective that would affirm the interrelated structure of reality, the sacredness of human life, and the ultimate morality of the universe. Echoing Boston personalists, King stressed that the state must actually love other states. These appeals to love, which he intended for political officials to take quite seriously, are deeply grounded in King's belief in the goodness of the state. But the basic problem with the proposals is their insufficiency in light of King's own belief about the character of the state: they appeal to the state's goodness while ignoring its ever-present selfishness. If states are not only good but also "evil," "genocidal," and "suicidal," then it is insufficient to appeal only to their goodness. More comprehensively, it is insufficient to ask a selfish (and good) state to be loving, just as it is insufficient to ask a good (and selfish) state to develop policies based only on national interest.

Given the insufficiency, I believe that King should have supplemented his calls for love with realistic policy proposals that seek to limit the inevitable genocidal and suicidal character of states in matters of war and peace. More particularly, I suggest that King would have done well to return to the tactic he used when dealing with Black Power's demands for racial separatism. Ever realistic, King recognized that because separatism would happen in some degree, he would do well to limit it. Thus, King announced that he favored temporary separatism over permanent, or unqualified, separatism. I contend that King could have strengthened his arguments on war and pacifism by adopting the same tactic. King began to do this when he expressed his hopes for a world police force, but he would have done better to attempt to limit the practice of war itself. With a realistic recognition of the ongoing possibility of wars, King should have not only preached love, but also defined criteria, *ad bellum* and *in bello*, to limit the resort to and execution of war. The adoption of just-war criteria, even while preaching that cruciform love requires the state to be nonviolent, would have been a sufficient response to King's dialectical attitude towards the state.

King did not always allow either his realism or his optimism to subside in matters of war and peace. When encouraging the state to become nonviolent, for example, King appealed to both the goodness and the sinfulness of the state by claiming that nonviolence is morally right in light of the mandates of love and that it is particularly smart in light of the state's interest in survival. Consider, as well, the tactic he used to support an increase in international aid. In the last part of his career, King recommended the formation of a Marshall Plan of sorts to eliminate poverty throughout the world, particularly in Asia, Africa, and South America. He justified this by pointing to the first natural law—the preservation of others. But King then added that "the real reason that we must use our resources to outlaw poverty goes beyond material concerns to the quality of our mind and spirit." Given his dialectical attitude towards the state, I argue, King's double appeal to the selfish and altruistic dimension of the state is especially fitting. Because the state is selfish, King rightly appealed to its self-interest, and because the state is also good, he rightly appealed to spiritual mandates.

Nevertheless, in matters of war and peace, King tended to downplay his realistic assessments of the state. One more example will suffice for my purposes. The mature King argued that war is obsolete because science and technology have made it "possible for all to enjoy adequate means of survival," thereby removing any "excuse for the kind of blind craving for power and resources that provoked the wars of previous generations." The obvious problem with this viewpoint is its sheer failure to recognize the historical truth that satisfaction with land, food, and other resources does not necessarily make the state less selfish, or less desirous of the accumulation of power, or less insistent on gaining recognition for itself. Totalitarian states have consistently taught us that states, however substantial their material resources may be, tend to be desirous of as much power and recognition as is possible for them to secure, even through violent means.

In summary, then, King's views on the issue of war and peace often downplayed, if not ignored, his realistic descriptions of the character of the state.

It would be tempting to suggest the same problem—the absence of a realistic perspective—in King's affirmation of world government, but such an internal criticism would be largely unfair, primarily because he did not offer enough substance on the issue of world government to warrant such a response. In an interview in which he was asked what he would do if he were to possess omnipotent powers, King simply stated that he "would consider some form of world government." Unfortunately, he did not provide any explanation of what he meant by world government, but he did suggest a theological rationale for his position—the interconnectedness of humanity, the inescapable fact that what affects one state affects all states.

At this point, I simply flag the issues of sovereignty and authority that arise in his acceptance of the legitimacy of world government. King's affirmation of world government reveals his belief that sovereign authority is neither constituent of nor essential to states and that states can transfer their authority to a world government. What King did not reveal, though, is his understanding of the derivation of sovereign authority as well as the way in which a transference of authority might happen. Does political authority derive from the people? Are the people the ones who should decide on transferring their authority? And how do they so decide? King left these questions unresolved, demonstrating his disinclination to offer an explicit analysis of authority in relationship to particular states, let alone world governments.

THE FORM OF THE STATE

Given his democratic inclinations, it seems safe to suggest that King would have favored a democratic transference of authority, however that may take shape, to a democratic world government. Following the theological path of his liberal Protestant professors, King closely identified democracy with Christianity. His enthusiasm for democracy was especially visible when he claimed in Montgomery that democracy is "the greatest form of government on earth."

I contend that King's enthusiasm for democracy in general, as expressed through America's founding documents, does not tightly cohere with, once again, his theological realism. As King failed to subject Sweden's democratic socialism to criticism, so too did he fail to criticize democracy in general. But, given King's own realism, it is never appropriate to fail to subject any political system, no matter how pure it may be, or any democratic creed, however Christian it may appear, to theological principles. All forms of the state, just because they are human forms, are appropriately subject to theological criticism. Nevertheless, this study has shown that, although King did not criticize democracy in general, he certainly criticized democracy as it appeared in the United States, labeling it as, among other things, "anemic." In this sense, King was the perfect counter example to Stanley Hauerwas's unqualified argument that "Christian fascination with democracy as 'our' form of government has rendered [Christians] defenseless when, for example, the state goes to war."[5] As an uncritical supporter of democracy, King used the democratic creed, as stated in America's founding documents, to subject US democracy in particular to relentless criticism even in times of war. King, then, was especially adept at offering an internal criticism that used the democratic creed to critique the practices of historical democracies.

What is more, King's use of the republican and social gospel traditions led him to support a particular structure of democracy—a mixture of Jefferson's and Mays's democracies. King's adoption of this structure, I argue, faithfully reflects his dialectical attitude towards the state. On the one hand, King was ever wary of the sinfulness of state power. Thus, he found refuge in Jefferson's arguments against centralized power, especially executive power. (Of course, King insisted that decentralization must never justify states' rights when the policies of the states are wrong. In this sense, he favored an activist federal government.) On the other hand, King saw the state as a force for good that can grasp and achieve the public good. Thus, he appropriately refused the notion of a democratic state that would be merely a neutral arbiter among competing interests, especially those of selfish individuals, groups, and institutions. For King, the best form of state is a social democracy that actively strives to institutionalize the morally substantive public good envisioned in his beloved community.

THE AUTHORITY OF THE STATE

Given his dialectical attitude towards the state, King's contextual approach to political authority is also theologically fitting. On the one hand, his refusal to offer an unqualified view of political authority fits his belief that the state is sometimes sinful. On the other hand, his refusal of an unqualified position which holds that the state has no authority fits his belief that the state is sometimes God's minister for good.

Nevertheless, in my view, King could have strengthened his argument by explicitly offering a christocentric view of political authority. King's understanding of the state would have been more coherent had he explicitly argued that God in Christ confers authority upon the state

---

[5] Stanley Hauerwas, "The Democratic Policing of Christianity," *Pro Ecclesia* 3 (Spring 1994): 230.

community of reconciliation, and, conversely, that God in Christ denies authority to states that undermine reconciliation. I do not mean to suggest that King did not imply such a view of political authority, but only that he could have deeply connected his views of political authority and the purpose of the state by offering an explicit christocentric interpretation of political authority. A similar critique, I believe, also holds for King's understanding of the related issues of civil obedience and disobedience.

King's contextual ethic of civil obedience and disobedience fits his theological interpretation of the character and authority of the state: his call for situational disobedience fits his recognition that a sinful state lacks authority, and his call for situational obedience fits his belief that a good state possesses authority. But I contend that King could have made his political thought more coherent by explicitly grounding his ethic of civil obedience and disobedience in his christocentric view of the end of the state, rather than in the mandates of natural or eternal law. In my view, King's contextual ethic of obedience and resistance would have cohered more deeply with his view of the end of the state had he explicitly argued that a citizen's obedience or disobedience to the state should depend upon whether the state serves or undermines the reconciliation known through God in Christ.

The problem with vague appeals to natural or divine law, as he defined them in his Birmingham ethic of obedience and disobedience, is that they are insufficient sources for King's project of encouraging the state to serve the beloved community, a hallmark characteristic of which is reconciliation known through God in Christ. Encouraging the state to build the beloved community requires not only an appeal to natural and divine law, as King briefly highlighted them, but also a direct appeal to the reconciling work of God in Christ. A christocentric project requires christocentric sources and tools.

Coda:
The Omnipresence of the State

The above criticism, limited in part by its internal nature, has highlighted just a few of the strengths and weaknesses of the various elements of King's understanding the state. In no way do I intend for my critical comments to be anything less than those of a friendly reviewer. Even though I have criticized King for occasional imbalances in his thought, I contend that, on the whole, his understanding of the state—its origin, character, purpose, authority, and form—is remarkably balanced and comprehensive. Informed by his theology and his experiences on the underside of political society, King avoided the tendency to deify or demonize the state, and challenged truncated theologies of the state by describing the state as part of the creating, preserving, and reconciling work of God in Christ.

More fundamentally, I contend that yet another great strength of King's interpretation of the state, as manifested through his words and deeds, is its consistent recognition of the omnipresence of the state. King rightly acknowledged that, from cradle to grave, the state plays an active role in our lives—registering who we are, regulating the air we breathe and the water we drink, defining the way in which we are educated, establishing the credentials for our various careers, and even limiting the ways for us to dispose of our bodies at the time of our death. Knowing that we live in, with, and under the presence and power of the state, King devoted his entire public life, not to preaching a sectarianism that futilely tries to separate itself from the state, but to understanding the state in all its various elements and to shaping the state even as it shapes us. With his dialectical attitude, King made himself omnipresent in the life of the state, praising and criticizing it, in the public square, with both the hope of shaping it in light of the demands of the beloved community and the realism of one who knows just how difficult it is to shape the state.

King knew all too well that his highly-publicized double attitude towards the omnipresent state could lead to his political and physical death, but he continued anyway to praise and criticize, believing that the beloved community—the communal embodiment of the sacrificial love of Christ—was worth the sacrifice of his own life as well as the lives of his followers. Thus, in response to threats to his life, some of them sanctioned by the state, the preacher King enacted, until the very end of his life, the religious word shouted out by so many of his followers when they heard him praise and criticize the state—Amen.

BIBLIOGRAPHY

Primary Sources

Carson, Clayborne, ed. *The Autobiography of Martin Luther King, Jr.* New York: Warner Books, 1998.

————, and Peter Holloran, eds. *A Knock at Midnight: Inspiration from the Great Sermons of Reverend Martin Luther King, Jr.* New York: Warner Books, 1998.

————, Ralph E. Luker, and Penny A. Russell, eds. *Called to Serve, January 1929–June 1951*. Volume 1 of *The Papers of Martin Luther King, Jr.* Berkeley: University of California Press, 1992.

————, Ralph E. Luker, Penny A. Russell, and Peter Holloran, eds. *Rediscovering Precious Values, July 1951–November 1955*. Volume 2 of *The Papers of Martin Luther King, Jr.* Berkeley: University of California Press, 1994.

————, Stewart Burns, Susan Carson, Peter Holloran, and Dana L. H. Powell, eds. *Birth of a New Age, December 1955–December 1956.* Volume 3 of *The Papers of Martin Luther King, Jr.* Berkeley: University of California Press, 1997.

————, Susan Carson, Adrienne Clay, Virginia Shadron, and Kieran Taylor, eds. *Symbol of the Movement, January 1957-December 1958.* Volume 4 of *The Papers of Martin Luther King, Jr.* Berkeley: University of California Press, 2000.

King, Martin Luther, Jr. Address at Conference of Religious Leaders under the Sponsorship of the President's Committee on Government Contracts. 11 May 1959. MLKJP, GAMK.

————. Address at the Conference on Religion and Race. Chicago. 17 January 1963. MLKJP, GAMK.

———. Address of Dr. Martin Luther King, Jr., to the South Africa Benefit of the American Committee on Africa. New York City. 10 December 1965. MLKJP, GAMK.

———. Address of Reverend Doctor Martin Luther King, Jr. Delivered to a Joint Convocation of the Two Houses of the General Court of Massachusetts. Boston. 22 April 1965. MLKJP, GAMK.

———. Address to the United Neighborhood Houses of New York. New York City. 6 December 1966. MLKJP, GAMK.

———. Annual Report of Martin Luther King, Jr. Savannah, Georgia. 2 October 1964. MLKJP, GAMK.

———. "An Appeal to the Honorable John F. Kennedy, President of the United States, for National Rededication to the Principles of the Emancipation Proclamation and for an Executive Order Prohibiting Segregation in the United States." 17 May 1962. MLKJP, GAMK.

———. *The Autobiography of Martin Luther King, Jr.* Edited by Clayborne Carson. New York: Warner Books, 1998.

———. "Brighter Day." Copy of Article for *Ebony*. March 1965. MLKJP, GAMK.

———. "A Christian Movement in a Revolutionary Age." Fall 1965. MLKJP, GAMK.

———. Class Notes on Christianity and Society. 4 May 1951. MLKP, MBU.

———. Comments on John F. Kennedy. Berlin, Germany. 13 September 1964. MLKJP, GAMK.

———. "The Dimensions of a Complete Life." *The Measure of Man.* Philadelphia: Fortress Press, 1988.

———. Draft of Speech on Passage of 1965 Voting Rights Act. August 1965. MLKJP, GAMK.

———. Draft of Statement Regarding Passage of the 1954 Civil Rights Act. June 1964. MLKJP, GAMK.

———. "East or West—God's Children." Berlin, Germany. 13 September 1964. MLKJP, GAMK.

———. "Gandhi and the World Crisis." January 1962. MLKJP, GAMK.

———. Interview by Hugh Downs. *Today Show*, NBC, 18 April 1966. MLKJP, GAMK.

———. "The Movement: Prospects for '65." Manuscript for *IUD Agenda*. MLKJP, GAMK.

———. "New Year Hopes." 5 January 1963. MLKJP, GAMK.

———. Nobel Prize Acceptance Speech. Oslo, Norway. 10 December 1964. MLKJP, GAMK.

———. Press Conference and Statement on Nobel Peace Prize. Forneby, Norway. 9 December 1964. MLKJP, GAMK.

————. Press Statement on Arrival in Sweden. Stockholm. 12 December 1964. MLKJP, GAMK.

————. "The Quest for Peace and Justice." Oslo, Norway. 11 December 1964. MLKJP, GAMK.

————. *Redbook*. Transcript of Interview with Martin Luther King, Jr. 5 November 1964. MLKJP, GAMK.

————. Remarks by King at the Convocation on Equal Justice under Law of the NAACP Legal Defense Fund. 28 May 1964. MLKJP, GAMK.

————. Remarks to the NAACP Sponsored Mass Rally for Civil Rights. Los Angeles. 10 July 1960. MLKJP, GAMK.

————. Report to the Administrative Committee Re: Voter Registration Since the 1965 Voting Rights Act. November 1965. MLKJP, GAMK.

————. "Revolution and Redemption." Amsterdam. 16 August 1964. MLKJP, GAMK.

————. SCLC Press Release: Address by Dr. Martin Luther King, Jr., at the State Capital, Atlanta. 14 January 1966. MLKJP, GAMK.

————. Section of Speech Given by Dr. Martin Luther King, Jr., President of Southern Christian Leadership Conference, at a Meeting Launching the Crusade for Citizenship. Miami. 12 February 1958. MLKJP, GAMK.

————. "Selma—the Shame and the Promise." *IUD Agenda* 1/2 (March 1965): 18–21.

————. Speech to Staff Retreat at Frogmore. Frogmore SC. 14 November 1966. MLKJP, GAMK.

————. Speech upon Acceptance of NYC Medallion Award. New York City. 17 December 1964. MLKJP, GAMK.

————. "The State of the Movement." Frogmore SC. 28 November 1967. MLKJP, GAMK.

————. Statement before the Credentials Committee of the Democratic National Convention. Atlantic City. 22 August 1964. MLKJP, GAMK.

————. Statement before the Platform Committee of the Democratic National Convention. Atlantic City. August, 1964. MLKJP, GAMK.

————. Statement before the Platform Committee of the Republican National Convention. San Francisco. 7 July 1964. MLKJP, GAMK.

————. Statement by Dr. Martin Luther King, Jr., Before the Senate Committee on Urban Reorganization. Washington, DC. 15 December 1966. MLKJP, GAMK.

————. Statement during Night Vigil. Selma. 13 March 1965. MLKJP, GAMK.

————. Statement of Dr. Martin Luther King, President, Southern Christian Leadership Conference, at the American Negro Leadership Conference on Africa. Arden House, Harriman, New York. 24 November 1962. MLKJP, GAMK.

———. Statement on Goldwater. St. Augustine. 16 July 1964. MLKJP, GAMK.

———. Statement to SCLC Board re Alabama Movement. 2 April 1965. MLKJP, GAMK.

———. *Strength to Love.* Philadelphia: Fortress Press, 1981.

———. *Stride Toward Freedom: The Montgomery Story.* New York: Harper & Row, 1958.

———. "To Charter Our Course." Frogmore. May 1967. MLKJP, GAMK.

———. Transcript of "March on Washington," Metropolitan Broadcast Television. 28 August 1963. MLKJP, GAMK.

———. *The Trumpet of Conscience.* San Francisco: Harper and Row, 1967.

———. Untitled Speech on 1965 and the Civil Rights Movement. MLKJP, GAMK.

———. "Virginia's Black Belt." *Amsterdam News.* 14 April 1962. MLKJP, GAMK.

———. "What Is Man?" 12 January 1958. MLKJP, GAMK.

———. "What Killed These Four Little Girls?" Virginia. 27 September 1963. MLKJP, GAMK.

———. *Where Do We Go from Here: Chaos or Community?* Boston: Beacon Press, 1968.

———. "Who Is Their God?" *The Nation* 195/11 (13 October 1963): 209–10.

———. "Why a Movement?" 11 November 1967. MLKJP, GAMK.

———. *Why We Can't Wait.* New York: Harper, 1963.

———. "Why We Must Go to Washington." Atlanta. 15 January 1968. MLKJP, GAMK.

Washington, James M. ed. *A Testament of Hope.* San Francisco: Harper & Row, 1986.

Secondary Sources

Alexander, Robert J. "Negro Business in Atlanta." *Southern Economic Business Journal* 17 (1951): 454–55.

Ansbro, John J. *Martin Luther King, Jr.: The Making of a Mind.* Maryknoll: Orbis Books, 1982.

Bacote, Clarence. "The Negro in Atlanta Politics." *Phylon* 16 (1955): 333–50.

Baker-Fletcher, Garth Anthony. *Somebodyness: Martin Luther King, Jr. and the Theory of Dignity.* Minneapolis: Fortress Press, 1993.

Baldwin, Lewis V. *There Is a Balm in Gilead: The Cultural Roots of Martin Luther King, Jr.* Minneapolis: Fortress Press, 1991.

———. *To Make the Wounded Whole: The Cultural Legacy of Martin Luther King, Jr.* Minneapolis: Fortress Press, 1992.

Barth, Karl. *Community, State, and Church.* Garden City: Doubleday, 1960.

Bass, S. Jonathan, *Blessed Are the Peacemakers: Martin Luther King Jr., Eight White Religious Leaders, and the "Letter from Birmingham Jail."* Baton Rouge: Louisiana State University Press, 2001.

Beckley, Harlan. *Passion for Justice: Retrieving the Legacies of Walter Rauschenbusch, John A. Ryan, and Reinhold Niebuhr.* Louisville: Westminster/John Knox Press, 1992.

Bellah, Robert N., Richard Madsen, William M. Sullivan, Ann Swidler, and Steven M. Tipton. *Habits of the Heart: Individualism and Commitment in American Life.* Berkeley: University of California Press, 1985.

Boozer, Jack. "The Place of Reason in Paul Tillich's Conception of God." Ph.D. diss., Boston University, 1952.

Bowne, Borden Parker. *The Principles of Ethics.* New York: Harper & Brothers, 1892.

Branch, Taylor. *Parting the Waters: America in the King Years, 1954–63.* New York: Simon & Schuster, 1988.

————. *Pillar of Fire: America in the King Years, 1963–65.* New York: Simon & Schuster, 1998.

Brightman, Edgar Sheffield. *Is Democracy Right?* Pamphlet reprinted from *World Affairs Interpreter* 9/3 (October 1938): 265–74.

————. *Moral Laws.* New York: Abingdon Press, 1933.

————. *Religious Values.* New York: Abingdon Press, 1925.

Carmichael, Stokely, and Charles V. Hamilton. *Black Power: The Politics of Liberation in America.* New York: Random House, 1967.

Carson, Clayborne. *In Struggle: SNCC and the Black Awakening of the 1960s.* Cambridge: Harvard University Press, 1981.

————. "Martin Luther King, Jr., and the African-American Gospel." In *African-American Religion: Interpretive Essays in History and Culture.* Edited by Timothy Fulop and Albert Raboteau. New York: Routledge, 1997.

Cartwright, John H., ed. *Essays in Honor of Martin Luther King, Jr.* Evanston: Garrett Evangelical Theological Seminary, 1977.

————. "The Social Eschatology of Martin Luther King, Jr." In *Essays in Honor of Martin Luther King, Jr.,* ed. John H. Cartwright, 1–13. Evanston: Garrett Evangelical Theological Seminary, 1977.

Chivers, Walter. "Northern Migration and the Health of the Negroes." *Journal of Negro Education* 8/1 (January 1939): 34–43.

————. "Current Trends and Events of National Importance in Negro Education: Trends of Race Relations in the South During War Times." *Journal of Negro Education* 13/1 (Winter 1944): 104–11.

Colaiaco, James A. *Martin Luther King, Jr.: Apostle of Militant Nonviolence.* New York: St. Martin's Press, 1988.

Cone, James H. *Martin & Malcolm & America*. Maryknoll: Orbis Books, 1991.

———. "Martin Luther King, Jr., Black Theology—Black Church." *Theology Today* 41 (January 1984): 409–20.

———. "The Theology of Martin Luther King, Jr." *Union Seminary Quarterly Review* 40 (January 1986): 21–39.

Cook, Anthony E. *The Least of These: Race, Law, and Religion in American Culture*. New York: Routledge, 1997.

Cullman, Oscar. *The State in the New Testament*. New York: Charles Scribner's Sons, 1956.

Culpepper, R. Alan. "1, 2, 3 John." In *Harper's Bible Commentary*, ed. James L. Mays, 1290–96. San Francisco: Harper & Row, 1988.

Darby, Henry E., and Margaret N. Rowley. "King on Vietnam and Beyond." *Phylon* 47 (Spring 1986): 43–50.

Davis, George W. "God and History." *Crozer Quarterly* 20 (January 1943): 18–36.

———. "In Praise of Liberalism." *Theology Today* 4/4 (January 1948): 485–92.

———. "Liberalism and a Theology of Depth." *Crozer Quarterly* 28/3 (July 1951): 193–211.

———. "Some Theological Continuities in the Crisis Theology." *Crozer Quarterly* 27/3 (July 1950): 208–19.

Deats, Paul, and Carol Robb, eds. *The Boston Personalist Tradition in Philosophy, Social Ethics, and Theology*. Macon: Mercer University Press, 1986.

DeWolf, L. Harold. "Martin Luther King, Jr., as Theologian." *Journal of the Interdenominational Theological Center* 4 (Spring 1977): 1–11.

———. *Responsible Freedom: Guidelines to Christian Action*. New York: Harper & Row, 1971.

Ditmer, John. *Black Georgia in the Progressive Era*. Urbana: University of Illinois Press, 1977.

Douglass, R. Bruce. "Liberalism." In *Encyclopaedia of Government and Politics*, ed. Mary Hawkesworth and Maurice Kogan, 129–38. London: Routledge, 1992.

Downing, Frederick L. "Martin Luther King, Jr. as Public Theologian." *Theology Today* 44 (April 1987): 15–31.

———. *To See the Promised Land: The Faith Pilgrimage of Martin Luther King, Jr*. Macon: Mercer University Press, 1986.

Erskine, Noel. *King Among the Theologians*. Cleveland: Pilgrim Press, 1994.

Fairclough, Adam. "Martin Luther King, Jr. and the War in Vietnam." *Phylon* 45 (March 1984): 19–39.

———. *Martin Luther King, Jr*. Athens: University of Georgia Press, 1990.

————. *To Redeem the Soul of America: The Southern Christian Leadership Conference and Martin Luther King, Jr.* Athens: University of Georgia Press, 1987.

————. "Was Martin Luther King a Marxist?" *History Workshop* 15 (Spring 1983): 117–25.

Fosdick, Harry Emerson. *Hope of the World.* New York: Harper, 1933.

————. *On Being Fit to Live With.* New York: Harper, 1946.

Fox, Richard. *Reinhold Niebuhr: A Biography.* New York: Pantheon, 1985.

Franklin, Robert Michael. "An Ethic of Hope: The Moral Thought of Martin Luther King, Jr." *Union Seminary Quarterly Review* 40 (January 1986): 41–51.

————. "In Pursuit of a Just Society." *Journal of Religious Ethics* 18 (Fall 1990): 57–77.

————. *Liberating Visions: Human Fulfillment and Social Justice in African-American Thought.* Minneapolis: Fortress Press, 1990.

Gandhi, Mahatma K. *The Moral and Political Writings of Mahatma Gandhi.* Edited by Raghaven Iyer. 3 volumes. Oxford: Clarendon Press, 1987.

Garber, Paul R. "Black Theology: The Latter Day Legacy of Martin Luther King, Jr." *Journal of the Interdenominational Theological Center* 2 (Spring 1975): 100–13.

————. "King Was a Black Theologian." *Journal of Religious Thought* 31 (Fall–Winter 1974–1975): 16–32.

Garfield, David. *Black, White, and Southern: Race Relations and Southern Culture, 1940 to the Present.* Baton Rouge: Louisiana State University Press, 1990.

Garrow, David J. *Bearing the Cross: Martin Luther King, Jr., and the Southern Christian Leadership Conference.* New York: Vintage Books, 1986.

————. "The Intellectual Development of Martin Luther King, Jr.: Influences and Commentaries." *Union Seminary Quarterly Review* 40 (January 1986): 5–20.

Garrow, David J., ed. *Martin Luther King, Jr.: Civil Rights Leader, Theologian, Orator.* 3 volumes. Brooklyn: Carlson Publishing, 1989.

Goldberg, Robert Alan. *Barry Goldwater.* New Haven: Yale University Press, 1995.

Goldwater, Barry. *The Conscience of a Conservative.* Shepherdsvile: Victor Publishing, 1960.

————. *Where I Stand.* New York: McGraw-Hill Book Company, 1964.

————. *Why Not Victory? A Fresh Look at American Foreign Policy.* New York: McGraw Hill Book Company, 1962.

Gordon, T. Crouther. *The Rebel Prophet: Studies in the Personality of Jeremiah.* New York: Harper & Brothers, 1932.

Gougeon, Len. "Thoreau and Reform." In *The Cambridge Companion to Henry David Thoreau*, edited by Joel Myerson, 194–214. Cambridge: Cambridge University Press.

Hall, John A. "Liberalism." In *The Oxford Companion to Politics of the World*, edited by Joel Krieger, 538–42. New York: Oxford University Press, 1993.

———. "State." In *The Oxford Companion to Politics of the World*, edited by Joel Krieger, 878–83. New York: Oxford University Press, 1993.

Hall, John A., and G. John Ikenberry. *The State*. Minneapolis: University of Minnesota Press, 1989.

Hamilton, J. Wallace. *Horns and Halos in Human Nature*. Westwood: Revell, 1954.

Harding, Vincent. *Martin Luther King: The Inconvenient Hero*. Maryknoll: Orbis Books, 1996.

Harvey, Paul. *Redeeming the South: Religious Cultures and Racial Identities among Southern Baptists, 1865–1925*. Chapel Hill: University of North Carolina Press, 1997.

Hauerwas, Stanley. "The Democratic Policing of Christianity." *Pro Ecclesia* 3 (Spring 1994): 215–31.

———. "Remembering Martin Luther King, Jr., Remembering." *Journal of Religious Ethics* 23/1 (Spring 1995): 135–48.

Held, David. *Political Theory and the Modern State: Essays on State, Power, and Democracy*. Stanford: Stanford University Press, 1989.

Horton, William Marshall. *Contemporary Continental Theology: An Interpretation for Anglo-Saxons*. New York: Harper & Brothers, 1938.

Hunter, Floyd. *Community Power Structure: A Study of Decision Makers*. Chapel Hill: University of North Carolina Press, 1953.

Ivory, Luther. *Toward a Theology of Radical Involvement: The Theological Legacy of Martin Luther King, Jr.* Nashville: Abingdon, 1997.

Kelsey, George. "The Christian Way in Race Relations." In *The Christian Way in Race Relations*, edited by William Nelson, 29–50. New York: Harper, 1948.

———. "The Churches and Freedom." *The Journal of Religious Thought* 9 (1956–1957): 17–26.

———. "Protestantism and Democratic Intergroup Living." *Phylon* 8/1 (1947): 77–82.

———. *Racism and the Christian Understanding of Man*. New York: Charles Scribner's Sons, 1965.

King, Martin Luther, Sr., with Clayton Riley. *Daddy King: An Autobiography*. New York: William Morrow, 1980.

Knudson, Albert. *The Principles of Christian Ethics*. Nashville: Abingdon Press, 1943.

Lebacqz, Karen. *Six Theories of Justice: Perspectives from Philosophical and Theological Ethics*. Minneapolis: Augsburg, 1986.

Lincoln, C. Eric, and Lawrence H. Mamiya. *The Black Church in the African American Experiment*. Durham: Duke University Press, 1990.

Lischer, Richard. *The Preacher King: Martin Luther King, Jr. and the Word That Moved America*. New York: Oxford University Press, 1995.

Lovin, Robin. *Reinhold Niebuhr and Christian Realism*. Cambridge: Cambridge University Press, 1995.

Luther, Martin. "Secular Authority." In *Luther and Calvin on Secular Authority*, translated and edited by Harro Hopfl, 13–43. Cambridge: Cambridge University Press, 1991.

McCartney, John T. *Black Power Ideologies: An Essay in African-American Political Thought*. Philadelphia: Temple University Press, 1992.

McCracken, Robert. *Questions People Ask*. New York: Harper & Brothers, 1951.

Majumdar, Biman Bihari, ed. *Gandhian Concept of State*. Calcutta: M. C. Sarkar & Sons, 1957.

Manis, Andrew Michael. *Southern Civil Religions in Conflict: Black and White Baptists and Civil Rights, 1947–1957*. Athens: University of Georgia Press, 1987.

Maritain, Jacques. *Christianity and Democracy*. London: Centenary Press, 1945.

———. *Man and the State*. Chicago: University of Chicago Press, 1951.

———. *Scholasticism and Politics*. London: Centenary Press, 1940.

Marx, Karl. *The Eighteenth Brumaire of Louis Bonaparte*. New York: International Publishers, 1963.

———. "The German Ideology." In *The Marx-Engels Reader*, ed. Robert C. Tucker, 146–200. New York: W. W. Norton, 1972.

Mayer, David N. *The Constitutional Thought of Thomas Jefferson*. Charlottesville: University Press of Virginia, 1994.

Mays, Benjamin E. "The American Negro and the Christian Religion." *Journal of Negro Education* 8 (July 1939): 530–38.

———. *Born to Rebel*. New York: Charles Scribner's Sons, 1971.

———. "Democratizing and Christianizing America in this Generation." *Journal of Negro Education* 14/4 (Fall 1945): 527–34.

———. "The Religious Life and Needs of Negro Students." *Journal of Negro Education* 9 (July 1940): 332–43.

———. *Seeking to Be Christian in Race Relations*. New York: Friendship Press, 1957.

———. "Veterans: It Need Not Happen Again." *Phylon* 6/3 (1945): 205–11.

Meier, August. "On the Role of Martin Luther King." *New Politics* 4 (Winter 1965): 52–59.

Mikelson, Thomas. "The Negro's God in the Theology of Martin Luther, King, Jr." Th.D. dissertation, Harvard University, 1988.

Miller, Keith D. *Voice of Deliverance: The Language of Martin Luther King, Jr. and Its Sources*. New York: The Free Press, 1992.

Moses, Greg. *Revolution of Conscience: Martin Luther King, Jr. and the Philosophy of Nonviolence*. New York: The Guilford Press, 1997.

Muelder, Walter G. *Foundations of the Responsible Society*. Nashville: Abingdon Press, 1959.

———. *Moral Law in Christian Social Ethics*. Richmond: John Knox Press, 1966.

———. "Philosophical and Theological Influences in the Thought and Action of Martin Luther King, Jr." *Debate & Understanding* 1 (1977): 179–89.

———. *Religion and Economic Responsibility*. New York: Charles Scribner's Sons, 1953.

Myerson, Joel, ed. *The Cambridge Companion to Henry David Thoreau*. Cambridge: Cambridge University Press, 1995.

Nalty, Bernard. *Strength for the Fight: A History of Black Americans in the Military*. New York: The Free Press, 1986.

Nelson, William Stuart. "Satyagraha: Gandhian Principles of Nonviolent Noncooperation." *Journal of Religious Thought* (Autumn–Winter 1957–1958): 15–24.

Niebuhr, Reinhold. *The Children of Light and the Children of Darkness*. New York: Charles Scribner's Sons, 1944.

———. *Human Nature*. Volume 1 of *The Nature and Destiny of Man: A Christian Interpretation*. New York: Charles Scribner's Sons, 1941.

———. *Human Destiny*. Volume 2 of *The Nature and Destiny of Man: A Christian Interpretation*. New York: Charles Scribner's Sons, 1943.

———. *An Interpretation of Christian Ethics*. New York: Meridian Books, 1956.

———. *Moral Man and Immoral Society*. New York: Charles Scribner's Sons, 1932.

Nieman, Donald G. *Promises to Keep: African-Americans and the Constitutional Order, 1776 to the Present*. New York: Oxford University Press, 1991.

Nygren, Anders. *Agape and Eros*. Translated by Philip Watson. Philadelphia: Westminster, 1953.

Oglesby, Enoch. "Martin Luther King, Jr.: Liberation Ethics in a Christian Context." *Journal of the Interdenominational Theological Center* 4 (Spring 1977): 33–41.

Paris, Peter J. *Black Leaders in Conflict: Joseph H. Jackson, Martin Luther King, Jr., Malcolm X, Adam Clayton Powell, Jr.* New York: Pilgrim Press, 1978.

————. *The Social Teachings of the Black Churches*. Philadelphia: Fortress Press, 1985.

Pilgrim, Walter. *Uneasy Neighbors: Church and State in the New Testament*. Minneapolis: Fortress Press, 1999.

Plant, Raymond. "Social Democracy." In *The Blackwell Encyclopedia of Political Thought*. Edited by David Miller, 481–85. Oxford: Basil Blackwell, 1987.

Ramsey, Paul. *Basic Christian Ethics*. New York: Charles Scribner's Sons, 1950. Chicago: University of Chicago Press, 1980.

Rathbun, John W. "Martin Luther King: The Theology of Social Action." *American Quarterly* 20 (Spring 1968): 38–53.

Rauschenbusch, Walter. *Christianity and the Social Crisis*. New York: Macmillan, 1907.

————. *A Theology for the Social Gospel*. New York: Macmillan, 1917.

————. *Christianizing the Social Order*. New York: Macmillan, 1912.

Roberts, Adam. "Martin Luther King and Nonviolent Resistance." *The World Today* 24 (June 1968): 226–36.

Ruether, Rosemary Radford. "The Relevance of Martin Luther King for Today." In *Essays in Honor of Martin Luther King, Jr.*, edited by John H. Cartwright, 1–10. Evanston: Garrett Evangelical Theological Seminary, 1977.

Silver, Christopher, and John V. Moeser. *The Separate City: Black Communities in the Urban South, 1940–1968*. Lexington: University Press of Kentucky, 1995.

Smith, Kenneth L. "The Radicalization of Martin Luther King, Jr.: The Last Three Years." *Journal of Ecumenical Studies* 26 (Spring 1989): 270–88.

————. "Syllabus for Christianity and Society." MLK, MABU.

Smith, Kenneth L. and Ira G. Zepp, Jr. *Search for the Beloved Community: The Thinking of Martin Luther King, Jr.* Valley Forge: Judson Press, 1974.

Smylie, James H. "On Jesus, Pharaohs, and the Chosen People: Martin Luther King as Biblical Interpreter and Humanist." *Interpretation* 24 (January 1970): 74–91.

Stout, Jeffrey. *Ethics after Babel: The Languages of Morals and their Discontents*. Boston: Beacon Press, 1988.

Sturm, Douglas. "Crisis in the American Republic: The Legal and Political Significance of Martin Luther King's *Letter from a Birmingham Jail*." *Journal of Law and Religion* 2 (1984): 309–24.

————. "Martin Luther King, Jr., as Democratic Socialist." *Journal of Religious Ethics* 18 (Fall 1990): 79–105.

Sullivan, William. *Reconstructing Public Philosophy*. Berkeley: University of California Press, 1982.

Tate, Katherine. *From Protest to Politics: The New Black Voters in American Elections.* Cambridge: Harvard University Press, 1993.

Thoreau, Henry David. "Resistance to Civil Government." In *Henry David Thoreau: Reform Papers,* edited by Wendell Glick, 63–90. Princeton: Princeton University Press, 1973.

———. "Whether the Government Ought to Educate." In *Henry David Thoreau: Early Essays and Miscellanies,* edited by Joseph J. Moldenhauer, Edwin Moser, and Alexander Kern, 60–61. Princeton: Princeton University Press, 1975.

Tilton, Tim. *The Political Theory of Swedish Social Democracy: Through the Welfare State to Socialism.* Oxford: Clarendon Press, 1990.

Walton, Hanes. *The Political Philosophy of Martin Luther King, Jr.* Westport: Greenwood Publishing Co., 1971.

Watley, William. *Roots of Resistance: The Nonviolent Ethic of Martin Luther King, Jr.* Valley Forge: Judson Press, 1985.

Weber, Theodore R. "State." In *Dictionary of the Ecumenical Movement,* edited by Nicholas Lassky, Jose Miguez Bonino, John Pobee, Tom Stransky, Geoffrey Wainwright, and Pauline Webb, 953–56. Geneva: WCC Publications; Grand Rapids: William B. Eerdmans Publishing Company, 1991.

Williams, Preston. "An Analysis of the Conception of Love and Its Influence on Justice in the Thought of Martin Luther King, Jr." *Journal of Religious Ethics* 18 (Fall 1990): 15–31.

Williams, Samuel. "Communism: A Christian Critique." *Journal of Religious Thought* 6/2 (1949): 120–35.

———. "The People's Progressive Party of Georgia." *Phylon* 10/3 (1949): 226–30.

Williamson, Joel. *The Crucible of Race: Black-White Relations in the American South Since Emancipation.* New York: Oxford University Press, 1984.

Woodward, C. Vann. *The Strange Career of Jim Crow.* New York: Oxford University Press, 1955.

X, Malcolm. *By Any Means Necessary: Speeches, Interviews and a Letter by Malcolm X.* Edited by George Breitman. New York: Pathfinder Press, 1970.

———. *Malcolm X Speaks: Selected Speeches and Statements.* Edited by George Breitman. New York: Merit Publishers, 1965.

———. *Malcolm X: Speeches at Harvard.* Edited by Archie Epps. New York: Paragon House, 1991.

Zepp, Ira. *The Social Vision of Martin Luther King, Jr.* Brooklyn: Carlson Publishing, 1989.

INDEX

CPSIA information can be obtained
at www.ICGtesting.com
Printed in the USA
LVHW011807100820
662831LV00011B/143